CW00324446

# Bridging the Services Chasm

# Bridging the Services Chasm

Aligning Services Strategy to Maximize Product Success

Thomas E. Lah

© 2009 Thomas E. Lah

All rights reserved. No part of this book may be reproduced, in any form or by any means, without permission in writing from the publisher.

Copies of this book may be purchased directly from thomaslah.com

Company and product names mentioned herein are the trademarks or registered trademarks of their respective owners.

Printed in the United States of America.

First Printing.

ISBN 978-0-692-00493-7

*To JB Wood, who helped me see the problem.*

*To Geoffrey Moore, who helped me frame the problem.*

*To Tom Rich and Bo DiMuccio, who helped me solve the problem.*

*To Dr. David Greenberger, who makes me believe I can solve any problem.*

*And to my wife Carole, son Michael, and daughter McKenna—*
*who put all the problems into perspective*

**Thomas E. Lah**

**July, 2009**

# Chapter 1

# Pattern of Failure

## Why It Needs Fixing Now

## CATALYST

Let me be very clear regarding a fundamental bias I currently have:

> *Effectively aligning a company's services strategy to the overall company strategy will become* **the defining discipline** *in any product company's success.*

Product companies that do not successfully align services strategy to drive company strategy find themselves following a predictable failure. The abstract for this pattern is shown in Figure 1-1. Later in this chapter, I will describe the details behind this fatal pattern.

I predict you are doing one of two things right now. Either you are nodding your head up and down in violent agreement and uttering "Amen brother!" Or, you are shrugging your shoulders and thinking "I'm not sure that is really true."[1] In this chapter, I will defend this bias.

Figure 1-1  The Failure Pattern

---

[1] Or you are violently shaking your head left to right and shouting "What the $%## is he talking about? Services might be important but they certainly don't make or break our overall company success."

I am not claiming products no longer matter to the success of product companies. Product innovation, product capabilities, and product success will remain at the heart of a technology company's success. However, **the approach of optimizing product economics in a vacuum, devoid of any services strategy, is outdated. The only economics that matter are the economics of the entire system: the products and the services sold to the customer**. Product companies need to understand what services secure product success. Also, product companies need to accurately model the impact of services offerings on total account profitability. Based on my work in the Technology Professional Services Association (TPSA) since 2005, I can report from the field that the technology industry is woefully underprepared for this new reality.

In 2001, my focus was documenting how professional services organizations are structured for success within product companies. The catalyst for this work was my personal experience as part of a management team that was attempting to build a profitable professional services organization within a large product company, Silicon Graphics (now SGI). Way back in 1996, SGI decided to build out a professional services (PS) capability for all the reasons your company may have the capability. Customers were asking for help implementing complex technologies. Executives believed easy revenue opportunities existed if SGI could attach services to hardware sales. Also, some executives believed a service presence could increase account control. What that experience taught me is that building service capabilities within product companies is fundamentally different than building a pure service company. The culmination of this work was captured in *Building Professional Services: The Sirens' Song*.

In 2004, my focus was creating a framework professional services management teams could use to align their PS strategy to executive expectations. My consulting experiences from 2001 to 2004 showed me two fundamental truths regarding PS strategy within product companies. First, the friction points surrounding the PS strategy were almost identical from product company to product company. It didn't matter if the company was selling hardware, software, scales, or industrial air conditioners. The disconnects between executive expectations and PS execution were very similar. Do we have PS to improve customer satisfaction or secure new sources of service profit? Does PS focus on the installed base or new emerging markets? Should the company simply be pushing all PS activities to service partners? And so on. The second truth was that PS leaders were having a very tough time articulating these strategy disconnects to their CEOs, COOs, CFOs, and sales executives. They needed a framework to anchor and accelerate the conversations. The culmination of this work was captured in *Mastering Professional Services*.

Five years have passed. Since publishing my last book, I helped incubate a new industry association focused on technology professional services organizations (www.tpsaonline.com). More importantly, that association is part of a family of associations that serves multiple service lines within technology companies. First, the Service and Support Professionals Association, or SSPA (www.thesspa.com), was founded over 20 years ago and focuses on support services. SSPA helped incubate TPSA in 2005. Then, SSPA and TPSA acquired the Association for Services Management International, or AFMSI (www.afsmi.com), which has a long heritage in technical field services. This family of associations and its CEO, J.B. Wood, exposed me to the broader issues facing product companies and their services businesses.

**Through our discussions and data collection with the over 200 technology companies in these associations, it became clear that the role of service was changing dramatically regarding the economic success of product companies.** It also became clear that a majority of product companies were not sure how to align their business strategies to these new economic realities. This reality dragged me and the other association executives into conversations that went way beyond the typical domain of an industry association. We were well prepared to answer questions surrounding common practices and results for service lines. "How much margin do companies achieve on professional service engagements?" "What percentage of support calls is handled by offshore resources?" "Should we implement a separate sales force to sell our service offerings?" These were the types of questions securely in our wheelhouse.

Starting in 2006, new questions arose that companies were attempting to resolve that did not map to our benchmarking data and operational frameworks. "How big should service revenues be in a product company?" "What is the most profitable mix of products and services for a product company?" "Why are my product revenues continuing to become a smaller portion of my overall revenues?" "What is the true economic impact of service activities on overall company success?" Companies were questioning the very basis of what it means to be a product company. It felt like service leaders were standing at the sea shore and noticing a significant drop in the water level. They could sense a large, strong, disruptive wave was coming. But how big? A real tsunami or just a sand castle crasher? These questions led me and my association colleagues on a new quest. How can we help product companies accelerate their services strategy decisions? How can we help them effectively gain the attention of product-centric executives and convince these executives that indeed a shift in the market tides took place? **This book represents one of the frameworks we developed to help executive teams survive the potentially treacherous wave surging over their historical business models.**

*Consequences*

This pending shift in market tides is not the imagination of a few nervous service executives. Several very real-world examples exist of the consequences faced by product companies when they do not successfully align their services strategy to market realities. We will spend more time on the gap between services strategy and market requirements later in the book. For now, let's focus on the pattern of failure that is very recognizable in established product companies:

1. **Disruption:** Product market matures or disruptive technology enters the market, making current product less competitive. This phenomenon is well documented and discussed in texts such as *The Innovator's Dilemma* by Clayton Christensen.

2. **Denial:** Company focuses on old technology and old consumption models for too long. The important observation here is that often it is not only what the customer is buying that changes, but also how the customer buys. For example, the shift from closed mainframe systems to open systems in the early 1990s was not just a shift from closed mainframes to open Unix servers, but also a shift from buying hardware, software, and support from one provider to buying best-of-breed components from separate providers.

3. **Decline:** Top-line revenues stagnate or shrink, and operating income begins to shrivel.

Once again, these first three steps in the failure pattern are well documented and discussed in the literature focused on product company success. It is the next four steps that are less well understood:

4. **Services Focus:** In an attempt to shore up top-line revenues and profits, the executive management team belatedly announces a focus on service opportunities. There are significant changes in service leadership announced by the company. Often, executives from pure service firms are brought into the product company executive suite. Press releases are sent out detailing a new focus on service revenue opportunities and capabilities.

5. **Services False Positive:** Service revenues do become a larger portion of total company revenues, but this is largely due to continued maintenance streams on top of a shrinking installed-product base. Very few product companies report the mix of their service revenues. However, the industry associations I work with, AFMSI, SSPA, and TPSA, do collect this mix information in industry benchmarks. Throughout

this book, I will refer to this group of executives and analysts at these industry associations that I work with as the collective "we." "We" can see the swell in maintenance revenues as a total percentage of company revenues.

6. **Services Failure:** Despite the belated focus on services, total company revenues continue to flatten or shrink. Operating income shrinks as a percentage of total revenues. Product revenues continue to evaporate. Advanced service offerings such as professional, consulting, or managed services gain little traction.

7. **Demise:** Finally, an abrupt change in corporate direction takes place. Services leadership or overall company leadership is suddenly changed. The company does one of three things: declares a renewed focus on product innovation, declares bankruptcy, or is acquired.

Company circumstances vary greatly as they go through this pattern of failure. Sometimes the disruptive technology was impossible to predict. Sometimes executive improprieties or missteps accelerate the company demise. Despite the variances in circumstances, an undeniable and clear pattern, as it relates to product and service synergies, can be seen. **The opportunity is to understand the pattern and identify the window of opportunity where services initiatives can create a buffer of both revenue and margin that can be used to fund new strategic directions.** We will explore this concept later in the text. First, let's review a few of the classic examples of product companies migrating through this failure pattern.

## Example: Baan and ERP

Enterprise Resource Planning (ERP) software is the easy poster child to start with. If you are in the world of business, you are well aware ERP implementations are challenging. The magnitude of the failure is staggering. According to *CIO Magazine*, "today's ERP rollout has only a 7 percent chance of coming in on time, will probably cost more than what you estimated, and will likely deliver very unsatisfying results."[2] This overpromising of business benefits and the emergence of new e-business platforms caught up with many ERP vendors in the late 1990s, and the number of vendors began to shrink. One of the causalities was the Baan Company out of the Netherlands.

---

[2] ERP Backlash Coming Soon to a Company Near You, Thomas Wailgum, blog http:// advice.cio.com/thomas_wailgum/erp_backlash_coming_soon_to_a_company_near_ you at, from Jan. 15, 2009.

The data in Figure 1-2 shows that by 1998, Baan had gone through the first three steps of the failure pattern. Disruptive technologies and consumption models crushed license sales. Also in 1998, Baan exhibited the services false positive, where services revenues were continuing to grow but the mix was very maintenance-centric. In 2000, Baan crossed over the final failure point by being acquired by Invensys. Interestingly, the Baan story does not stop there. The company was spun back out in 2002. In the process, the company stepped back to phase four (services focus) in the failure pattern. Read the excerpt from a press release titled "Baan touts new services strategy":

> *Baan is making plans to expand its services business, following confirmation that it will not be sold off by parent company Invensys. Announcing the enterprise software supplier's new strategy, President Laurens van der Tang said that the company's current offerings had been too limited. "We mostly provide basic services," he admitted. "We don't do all the services our customers typically require. We don't do well today in project management and taking responsibility for projects. We typically don't integrate our solutions with customers' legacy systems."*

> *As part of the service strategy, Baan will offer project management and take greater responsibility for projects. Over the next 12 months, it will focus on recruiting new staff to meet these needs. "We will offer stronger project management. We will help integrate and customize Baan solutions," said van der Tang. "We will take responsibility for hosting solutions for customers if that is what they require," he added. "We may use partners to do this because we may not want to establish the infrastructure for that, but we will be the primary partner and take responsibility for the hosted solution."*

> *But analysts were cautious in their reactions. Graham Fisher, senior analyst at Bloor Research, said: "Most vendors want to become more service oriented, but we haven't seen anyone deliver the goods so far. Everyone is trying to move themselves up the food chain, but Baan is going into services very late. Services is a different business model from products, and Baan's success will depend on whether it can get to grips with that model. Services is about selling people. It's about building a long-term relationship with the customer."[3]*

---

[3] "Baan touts new services strategy, Analysts react with caution" by Abigail Waraker, *Information World Review*, Feb. 20, 2002.

Figure 1-2  Baan Financial Results

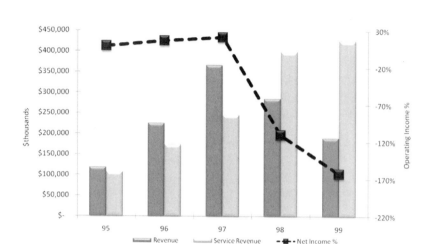

The question is why did Baan not consider this new services strategy back in 1997 or 1998 when it was clear customers were seeking more service assistance? Why did the company need to lose so much money before realizing services strategy needed to dramatically change? This is the pattern of failure we want to break.

## *Example: Novell and Networking*

In 2001, struggling software provider Novell had entered phase three of the failure pattern. Revenues were flat and profits were shrinking. The company decided to enter phase four (focus on services) with a big bang by purchasing systems integrator Cambridge Technology Partners. The objective was simple:

> *The acquisition significantly expands Novell's ability to deliver consulting support to customers and other IT services companies. The two companies are both addressing the deployment of business processes and IT resources across the Internet through new, secure, yet simplified, Web-based access. Cambridge accelerates Novell's adoption of a solutions-selling model that supports customers and partners transforming their businesses.[4]*

---

[4] Novell to acquire Cambridge Technology Partners; IT consulting and systems integration capabilities to accelerate Novell's move to solutions-selling model for net services. Novell Press Release, March 21, 2001.

However, the merger did not create the synergies hoped for. Figure 1-3 documents Novell's financials. As can be seen, the merger with Cambridge Technology Partners helped drive company profitability deep into negative territory. Analysts were predicting that many of Cambridge consultants would leave.[5] Indeed, this did occur and the hoped-for consulting capability became a rounding error in Novell's revenues. In essence, despite the merger with a systems integrator, Novell still plowed through phases five (services false positive) and six (services failure) and finds itself looped back to phase 3 (decline). The services strategy move did not create revenue and profit margin runway—quite the contrary. Now, Novell still faces the challenge of determining how to improve both top-line growth and bottom-line profitability.

## Example: SGI and Servers

While Novell was navigating the maturity of their software markets, Silicon Graphics was navigating the maturation of the high-end Unix server market. One of the disruptive technologies impacting SGI was cheap, open-source Linux arrays running relatively inexpensive Intel processors. In 1996, SGI had started to build its capability to provide professional services. In fact, the company had wisely started the endeavor before top-line revenues and bottom-line profitability were significantly impacted by the commoditization of their core

Figure 1-3 Novell Financials

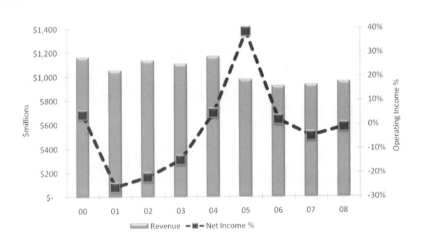

---

[5] Consulting Alert: Cambridge Staff Won't Warm to Novell. Business Wire, April 2, 2001.

markets. From 1996 to 1999 services revenue grew. More importantly, PS revenues were becoming a greater portion of total services. However, the company slammed into phase three (decline) by 2001, with top-line revenues shrinking 40 percent compared to 1998. Instead of relying on revenues and margins from the growing services capabilities to subsidize rapidly shrinking product revenues, the company jumped to the last phase of the failure cycle (demise) by making an abrupt change in strategy and executive leadership that refocused the company on products. The emerging PS capabilities were scaled down as documented in the annual report (10-K) published September of 2002:

> *Global Services revenue is comprised of hardware and software support and maintenance and professional services. Fiscal 2002 Global Services revenue decreased $141 million, or 24 percent, compared with fiscal 2001. This decrease is primarily attributable to declines in our professional services revenue as a result of the restructuring of our service organization and in our traditional customer support revenue, which is being affected by a lower volume of system sales.*

The company limped along with declining revenues and profits until it finally declared bankruptcy in 2006. Emerging from bankruptcy, the company announced a services aggressive strategy that offers both professional services and multi-vendor support programs. Like Novell, SGI finds itself looping back in the failure pattern, this time landing on phase 4 (services focus). The financial struggles of SGI are documented in Figure 1-4.

Figure 1-4  Silicon Graphics Financials

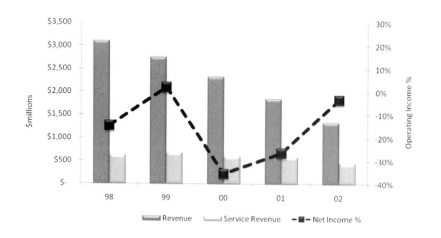

## *Example: Lucent and Telecom*

The post-dot-com bust threw telecom manufacturer Lucent Technologies into phase three of the failure pattern (decline) as shown in the Figure 1-5. Revenues declined sharply. Operating income was under pressure. New product opportunities evaporated overnight.

In 2003, Lucent migrated to phase 4 (services focus) by hiring John Meyer, a former Electronic Data Systems (EDS) executive, to head up global services. "Lucent is increasing its focus on its services business, and John's success and years of experience in leading a large professional services organization will help Lucent leverage and expand its already considerable pool of talent and expertise in this area," said Lucent CEO Pat Russo.[6] Multiple articles and press releases followed, emphasizing Lucent's new-found focus on service revenue opportunities. From 2003 to 2006, revenues from services grew. However, by 2006, they represented only 26 percent of total company revenues and those revenues were most likely very support oriented. The company experienced phase 5 (services false positive). Despite the commitment by CEO Russo to focus the company on service opportunities, Lucent remained a fundamentally product-centric company. Before experiencing phase 6 (services failure), the company moved to phase 7 (demise) by merging with Alcatel late in 2006.

Figure 1-5  Lucent Financials

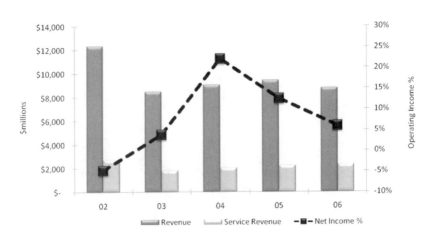

[6] "Former EDS executive joins Lucent," by Ed Frauenheim, staff Writer, CNET News. March 17, 2003.

## Example: Siebel and CRM

Siebel was a provider of customer relationship management (CRM) software and a poster child for rapid product growth. However, the company became schizophrenic in its final days regarding its services strategy. Figure 1-6 documents Siebel's total revenues, services revenues, and operating income from 1996 until 2004. By 2002, Siebel was clearly in phase 3 (decline).

In May, 2004 new CEO Mike Lawrie was hired away from IBM where he was a sales executive and the company moved to phase 4 (services focus). His vision for Siebel's return to glory was outlined in an *InformationWeek* article published in October, 2004:

> New to the job, Siebel Systems Inc. CEO Mike Lawrie is recasting the struggling customer-relationship-management software vendor as more of a partner in its customers' success, a strategy customers applauded during its user conference last week.
>
> "By more effectively mapping CRM deployments to companies' specific business processes, the vendor hopes to address the 41 percent of customers who say they haven't gotten the desired results from their Siebel deployments," Lawrie said in an interview. "CRM is not a product," Lawrie told an audience of 3,000 in Los Angeles. "It's a business strategy to drive companies closer to their customers."[7]

Figure 1-6  Siebel Financials

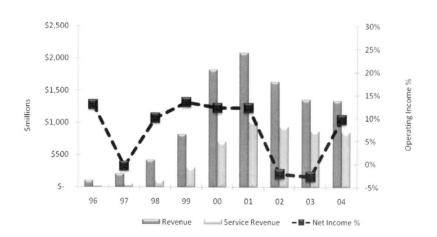

[7] "Siebel's new CEO focuses on customers" by Tony Kontzer, *InformationWeek*, October 2004.

Lawrie hired Eileen McPartland from Accenture to serve as SVP of the services area. Multiple articles and interviews emphasized how critical services were to the future success and growth of Siebel. This focus on services seemed to make sense because 64 percent of 2004 revenues were based on services, not new license sales. However, less than one year later, the company rapidly moved to phase 6 (services failure) when it unexpectedly let Mr. Lawrie go and emphasized a renewed commitment to on-demand offerings that would compete with upstart salesforce.com and other new front office software applications. This thrashing motion surrounding the services strategy was not the only chink in Siebel's armor, but the confusion clearly accelerated the demise. The company ended up in phase 7 when it was purchased by competitor Oracle in 2005. The benefit of 20/20 hindsight shows Siebel should have been earnestly reconsidering product and services strategy shifts back in 2002, not 2004. What if Siebel could have improved customer intimacy starting in 2002 with a strong emphasis on value-added services that actually drove the usage of all the software they had previously sold?

## SUMMARIZING THE FAILURE PATTERN

We have reviewed multiple companies that have experienced this predictable pattern of failure. Building off of the abstract introduced at the beginning of the chapter in Figure 1-1, Figure 1-7 provides a more detailed version of the pattern. The general trends for both product and services revenues are shown as a product company experiences the seven phases. Of course, it doesn't have to be this way. Clearly not all product companies fall down this fatal slope.

Figure 1-7  The Failure Pattern

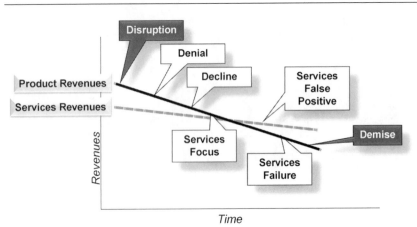

## The 25% Cushion

**There is a clear pattern of failure that occurs as product companies lose their product mojo. Currently, services strategy is often an albatross around the neck of the flailing product company that hastens the drowning.** Hopefully the above data makes that point very real for you. **In reality, services should be serving as a lifeboat that preserves revenue and margin dollars as the product company retools its product strategy.** How big is the services lifeboat in times of declining product margin dollars? We have modeled the answer to this question and will cover an example in a section titled "The Services Buffer" in Chapter 7. However, I wanted to get some of the math front and center in the discussion.

For example, let's model the growth of a software company as it grows to $200 million in revenue. We (my association colleagues and I) benchmark the margins generated from both support services and professional services within enterprise software companies. We also benchmark the revenue mix of software companies between these three categories. Using the data, we can map a typical growth scenario as shown in Table 1-1. Let's assume the time slices are years. The data shows that in the fourth year, the company has the most profitable revenue mix in terms of gross margin, generating 79 percent gross margin on $100 million in revenue. Sixty percent of that revenue comes from high-margin product licenses. However, by year 10, license revenues have slowed and maintenance revenues have become a significant portion of total revenues. Total revenues have doubled from year four, but the gross margin percentage has decreased to 69 percent. The shift from license-intensive to maintenance-intensive revenue streams is very common for mature enterprise software companies. The revenue mix shown in year 10 is exhibited by many software companies, where roughly only a third of revenues are coming from new license sales.

Table 1-1  Normal Growth of Software Company

| | 1 | 2 | 3 | 4 | 5 | 6 | 7 | 8 | 9 | 10 |
|---|---|---|---|---|---|---|---|---|---|---|
| License | $ 10 | $ 20 | $ 40 | $ 60 | $ 65 | $ 68 | $ 70 | $ 65 | $ 60 | $ 55 |
| Maintenance | $ 2 | $ 10 | $ 20 | $ 30 | $ 40 | $ 50 | $ 60 | $ 80 | $ 100 | $ 110 |
| PS | $ 10 | $ 10 | $ 10 | $ 10 | $ 12 | $ 15 | $ 20 | $ 23 | $ 28 | $ 30 |
| Managed Services | $ - | $ - | $ - | $ - | $ - | $ - | $ 3 | $ 5 | $ 10 | $ 15 |
| | | | | | | | | | | |
| Total Revenue | $ 22 | $ 40 | $ 70 | $ 100 | $ 117 | $ 133 | $ 153 | $ 173 | $ 198 | $ 210 |
| | | | | | | | | | | |
| Margin $ | $ 13.00 | $ 28.00 | $ 53.50 | $ 79.00 | $ 91.50 | $102.45 | $ 114.05 | $ 126.00 | $ 139.50 | $ 144.75 |
| Margin % | 59% | 70% | 76% | 79% | 78% | 77% | 75% | 73% | 70% | 69% |
| Servce Margin $ | $ 4.10 | $ 10.50 | $ 18.50 | $ 26.50 | $ 35.00 | $ 43.75 | $ 54.05 | $ 71.50 | $ 90.50 | $ 100.75 |
| Service Margin % | 19% | 26% | 26% | 27% | 30% | 33% | 35% | 41% | 46% | 48% |

Once again, we will spend more time on this modeling later in the book, but what if the management team decided in year four that services were really a secondary concern for the company. By using such a strategy, the executive team has made two decisions:

1. Invest more in product R&D than in services optimization.

2. Push almost all nonsupport service activities to services partners.

If we model the impact of these two decisions by reducing PS revenues and maintenance margins over the years, the resulting ten-year pro forma looks slightly different, as shown in Table 1-2. Even with license revenues remaining exactly the same, there are several key differences to observe:

- Total revenues do not reach $200 million in year 10.

- Maximum gross margin is reduced from 79 percent to 77 percent.

- **The company loses $68 million in top-line revenues and over $30 million in margin dollars that could have been used to fund new product development or other shifts in business strategy.**

Making relatively small changes in services strategy can have a significant impact on the overall economics of the company—specifically when product revenues are under pressure. Services strategy decisions and services execution can clearly buy time for a product company as it retools products or go-to-market strategies. Yes, poor services strategy can cripple product companies at critical junctures.

Table 1-2  Services Light Software Company

| | 1 | 2 | 3 | 4 | 5 | 6 | 7 | 8 | 9 | 10 |
|---|---|---|---|---|---|---|---|---|---|---|
| License | $ 10 | $ 20 | $ 40 | $ 60 | $ 65 | $ 68 | $ 70 | $ 65 | $ 60 | $ 55 |
| Maintenance | $ 2 | $ 10 | $ 20 | $ 30 | $ 40 | $ 50 | $ 60 | $ 80 | $ 100 | $ 110 |
| PS | $ 10 | $ 10 | $ 10 | $ 10 | $ 10 | $ 10 | $ 10 | $ 9 | $ 8 | $ 7 |
| Managed Services | $ - | $ - | $ - | $ - | $ - | $ - | $ - | $ - | $ - | $ - |
| | | | | | | | | | | |
| Total Revenue | $ 22 | $ 40 | $ 70 | $ 100 | $ 115 | $ 128 | $ 140 | $ 154 | $ 168 | $ 172 |
| | | | | | | | | | | |
| Margin $ | $ 12.40 | $ 27.00 | $ 52.00 | $ 77.00 | $ 88.50 | $ 98.20 | $ 107.00 | $ 116.30 | $ 125.60 | $127.90 |
| Margin % | 56% | 68% | 74% | 77% | 77% | 77% | 76% | 76% | 75% | 74% |
| Servce Margin $ | $ 4.10 | $ 10.50 | $ 18.50 | $ 26.50 | $ 34.50 | $ 42.50 | $ 50.50 | $ 66.25 | $ 82.00 | $ 89.75 |
| Service Margin % | 19% | 26% | 26% | 27% | 30% | 33% | 36% | 43% | 49% | 52% |

| | | |
|---|---|---|
| Lost Revenue $ | $ 30.00 | $ 38.00 |
| Lost Margin $ | $ 13.90 | $ 16.85 |
| Total Lost Revenue $ | $ 68.00 | |
| Total Lost Margin $ | $ 30.75 | |

I want to close this section by stating that, despite analyzing the failure patterns of many product companies and putting math behind the arguments, I don't believe I have uncovered much new insight regarding the importance of product success and services strategy. These correlations between service capabilities and product success have been talked about for years. In fact, on my bookshelf right now, there is a tome titled *Product Plus: How Product + Service = Competitive Advantage* by Christopher Lovelock. The book was published in 1994. The book jacket has the following text:

> *"If a firm is to survive and prosper into the twenty-first century, its top management must find ways to create a product plus organization. Whatever your product, service holds the key. Improving or reengineering service processes should lie at the heart of any strategy."*

The book contains chapters titled "Every Business Competes on Service" and "User-Friendly versus User-Hostile." Many of the premises are the same ones outlined in this chapter. Here we stand as a technology industry, 15 years later, having the same discussions regarding services strategy. But so little has changed. So few product companies have taken the discipline of services strategy seriously. **From our vantage point of gazing across the many companies engaged in our associations, we believe that lethargy surrounding services strategy is coming to an end. New pressures in the system force executives at product companies to take a very hard look at services strategy.**

## CRITICALITY

The stories of Dell, EMC, Microsoft, Sun Microsystems, and Unisys could easily be added to the stories of Baan, Novell, Siebel, Lucent, and SGI. They are all product companies that face various levels of pressure to realign services strategy to achieve new levels of company success. Yet, product companies are notorious for remaining exclusively focused on product success. Why will companies have to behave differently today? Why will they be forced to embrace the services strategy dialogue when historically they have buried it? Three attributes of today's technology market are forcing new levels of attention on services strategy:

1. The shift in product-service mix
2. The increasing cost of sales and services
3. The cloud

## PRODUCT–SERVICE REVENUE MIX

In the introduction to *Mastering Professional Services*, I documented a significant shift that was occurring in the product revenue mix of both enterprise hardware and enterprise software companies. In the 1990s, hardware companies averaged roughly 20 percent of their total company revenues from services. Those service revenues came predominantly from maintenance. In the 1990s, software companies averaged about 35 percent of their revenues from services. Also, predominantly from maintenance. By 2004, when *Mastering Professional Services* was published, hardware and software companies had doubled the amount of revenue coming from services. At the time of publication, some executives told me they believed the revenue mix would shift to be more product-centric as the technology industry rebounded. Well, the industry did rebound quite nicely from 2004 to 2008. Our industry associations track the financial performance of 50 of the largest providers of technology services in the industry.[8] The index includes companies such as Cisco, CA (formerly Computer Associates), Dell, HP, IBM, Oracle, and SAP. Despite strong increases in both top-line revenue growth and bottom-line profitability for these companies over the past four years, their revenue mixes did not shift back toward being more product-centric. In fact, both hardware and software companies continued to experience record levels of revenues from services. Figure 1-8 shows the updated revenue mix data.

Figure 1-8  Trends in Revenue Mix

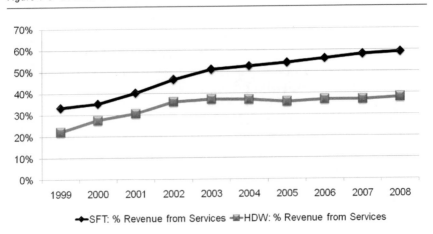

SFT: % Revenue from Services    HDW: % Revenue from Services

---

[8] For more information on this quarterly index, visit www.tpsaonline.com/the_service_50.asp.

While total services revenues steadily grew, product companies also expanded the types of services they offer. One set of data our associations benchmark is revenue mix not available in the public record. How much revenue is coming from products, support, professional services, managed services, and so on? The data shows that service capabilities, such as professional services and managed services, are on the rise. For mature software companies, professional services can easily represent 15 to 25 percent of total company revenues. **Now, enter the global downturn of 2008. In these times, available capital shrivels. Product companies become even more reliant on optimizing their service revenue streams. In other words, there is now too much money on the table for these product companies to ignore or suboptimize their services business strategy.** Even as I am writing this chapter, the earnings reports for technology titans EMC, IBM, and HP have just been released. In Q4 2008, EMC saw product revenues grow a measly 1 percent from the previous year while services revenues grew 14 percent. More importantly, services margin dollars represented 36 percent of total margin dollars for EMC that quarter. IBM saw product revenues drop almost 20 percent that same quarter while services revenues held flat. For their Q1 2009, HP reported that product revenues shrank 18 percent while services revenues grew 116 percent with the acquisition of EDS.

## COST OF SELLING, COST OF SERVING

The second force creating new pressure is the increased cost of marketing, selling, and servicing technology products. As highlighted previously, product companies had a nice financial run from 2004 through 2008. However, if you look under the covers at their business models, you'll find some interesting trends:

- General and administrative costs have been shrinking as a percentage of total company revenues.

- Research and development costs have been held flat.

- Sales and marketing costs are increasing for some companies.

- Cost of services as a percentage of total company revenues is increasing.

Technology companies have been doing an outstanding job of reducing general overhead and containing the costs required to develop new products. These moves have helped increase operating incomes. However, the cost to secure and serve new customers is not yet under control. This reality will put incredible pressure on operating incomes if not rectified. Figure 1-9 provides a simple example of what will happen to the financials of a product company if the percentage of revenue coming from services increases (which it has) and service margins have a slight reduction (which is currently occurring). **As can be seen, a greater portion of every dollar the company makes will be required to pay for the cost of servicing existing customers. This reality will force product companies to spend much more energy to align and optimize their services endeavors.**

## THE CLOUD

If you are not satisfied with a service, what do you do? You most likely change the provider. What if all providers deliver the same poor service? You remain frustrated until a new provider emerges. For enterprise technology companies, that new provider is arriving in the shape of a wispy cloud.

The historical model for consuming enterprise technology is very stovepiped. Product companies force three distinct consumption conversations with their customers. First, the product company convinces the customer the product has the feature functionality required to get the job done. The customer pays a price for that product. Next, the customer may need help integrating that technology into their company environment. That creates a second sales conversation surrounding the cost of project-based professional services, delivered by the product provider or a services partner. Finally, the customer needs to purchase the insurance policy for the massive technology investment they just made. This is the third sales transaction and it centers around a maintenance contract. These three distinct offerings (product, PS,

Figure 1-9  Impact of Poor Services Margins

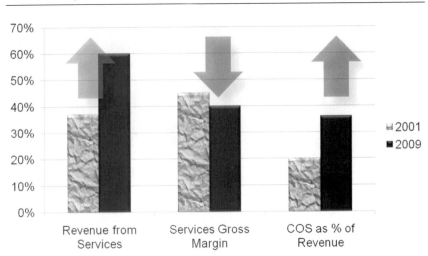

and support) are managed by three distinct organizations within the product provider, making the navigation of the overall transaction even more complex for the customer. These three distinct stovepipes are shown in Figure 1-10.

This three-pronged approach has served product providers well as they have delivered solutions into the customer's environment. This is known as providing a customer premise equipment (CPE) offering. This approach often requires a lot of customization and integration to occur. It also incurs a lot of expense. However, it may not result in delivering all of the business benefits the customer had hoped for (remember our poor ERP customers). JB Wood, the CEO of our family of industry associations, has been arguing for several years that the critical failure point in the current model is successful product adoption. He asks a simple question: "Which one of these three stovepipes is responsible for true customer success?" His argument: "The product sales force is focused on acquiring the initial product sale. The professional services group within the product company is chartered to complete initial implementation so the customer pays for the product. Support is chartered to keep the customer up and running. But who makes sure the customer is actually using and adopting the product?" The answer can be found in the data. Poor adoption of product features has become the legacy of IT providers. In 2003, research firm Gartner reported that 42 percent of all CRM licenses purchased had yet to be installed.[9] When a product company is not focused on driving adoption, customer renewal rates can lag. One case study TPSA analyzed

Figure 1-10  Consuming CPE Technology

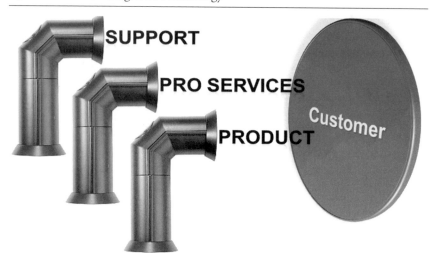

---

[9] Forty-two percent of CRM Software Goes Unused, Gartner survey, Feb 2003.

showed the renewal rate for a software product ranged from 52 percent when no adoption services were offered to the customer to 86 percent when adoption services were offered. **The main point is simple: The current stovepipe model, with little focus on long-term customer adoption, is creaking and groaning under customer frustration.**

If this three-pronged, CPE approach were the only consumption model available, customers would be forced to tough it out. But that is no longer true. These three separate stovepipes are being collapsed by customers into one pipe classified as a "subscription" or simply a "service." Customers subscribe to a technology solution that is hosted off site (or off premise). They pay one price for the service—much like paying to turn the lights on. No integration. No separate insurance policy. This approach is being employed in everything from customer relationship software (salesforce.com) to enterprise storage (Glasshouse) and presents itself in concepts such as software-as-a-service, utility computing, and cloud computing. The economics for customers are becoming compelling. In a paper titled Should Your Email Live in the Cloud?[10] technology market research firm Forrester analyzed the cost of having corporate email managed in a CPE model vs. in various cloud models. As shown in Table 1-3, the data was overwhelmingly favorable for a cloud model being offered by Google.

This new cloud model is changing the way customers consume and adopt technology. Instead of big bang approaches where companies must implement stepped functions of IT capability to support both current usage and future growth, customers can bite off just the amount of capacity they need.

Although this new model makes it easier on the customer, it upends the product providers. Now, product providers must collapse both offerings and internal organizations to migrate from a product + product services + support model to one service offering. Lots of historical walls need to be broken down. We will revisit the challenges of this migration in Chapter 13: Emerging

Table 1-3  Email Solutions

| Offering | Cost per user per month (15,000 employees or less) |
| --- | --- |
| On-premise email solution | $25.18 |
| Google applications | $8.47 |

---

[10] Should Your Email Live in the Cloud? An Infrastructure and Operations Analysis Rethinking Where Your Email Lives and Who's Managing It, by Christopher Voce, Jan 5, 2009.

Profiles. Is a centralized cloud approach the future of all technology consumption? How real is this trend? Mark Hurd, CEO of Hewlett Packard, the first $100 billion technology company, has been aligning capabilities to migrate HP from a CPE delivery model to one that supports consumption through the cloud. In July of 2008, HP announced a partnership with Intel and Yahoo! to create multiple cloud computing research centers. Some speculation exists that the purchase of EDS was a move to augment HP's ability to deliver their products through services offerings. And off the record, HP executives have commented that the company is convinced all enterprise products made by the company will eventually be primarily consumed in a utility, or services model.

Three critical trends exist: Revenue mixes are becoming services intensive, companies are under duress to reduce cost structures, and customers are changing the way they consume technology. All three trends are placing new pressures on product companies to truly align and optimize their services strategy. **For product company executives, this is not the time to ignore the realities. This is the time to embrace the conversation and identify new market opportunities being created by the inaction of competitors locked in dated go-to-market models.**

## CONCLUSION

I started this chapter by stating a fact I and my industry association colleagues believe to be true:

> *Effectively aligning a company's services strategy to the overall company strategy will become the defining discipline in any product company's success.*

The changing dynamics in technology markets are making this statement a cold reality. Product revenues are slowing in many mature technology markets. Consumption models for technology infrastructure are moving from customer premise equipment-based models to subscription- and services-based models. Customers are asking for more help realizing business value from their technology investments. Service activities are generating more and more of the revenues and profits for traditionally product-centric companies. The level of traditional product revenues and product margins is receding. These are facts in the world of technology solutions. These tides have caused the profits from traditional product business models to recede and expose a rocky shore of uncertainty. There is a wave coming. Product companies will either be crushed by the weight or they will latch onto new business models that allow them to surf the surge. There will be little room for companies that simply want to tread water.

# Chapter 2

# Services-Strategy Profiles

## By Thomas E. Lah and Geoffrey Moore

In the previous chapter, a pattern of failure experienced by maturing product companies was introduced. The sobering news is that the technology marketplace, overall, has been maturing. Over the past ten years, this maturation has caused profit pools to migrate from products to services. This in turn is driving urgent discussions among technology executives as to the current and future role of services in the overall company portfolio. To help technology companies with this critical services-strategy discussion, I partnered with author Geoffrey Moore to create a framework to focus the dialogue. This chapter introduces the key component of that framework: **services-strategy profiles**.

## FRAMEWORK IMAGE

As the enterprise IT marketplace over all has matured, product sales have slowed, and product margins have decreased in many mainstay technology segments, such as enterprise storage, computer processors, computing servers, resource planning software, and document-processing infrastructure. The previous chapter highlighted companies that ultimately failed in navigating a critical juncture in product and services strategy. However, not all product companies fail in their efforts to align services strategy with market realities. In fact, our research has revealed distinct, successful profiles in services strategy that have emerged from within technology companies. These profiles are best understood by visualizing the different economic engines product companies pursue. For example, Figure 2-1 models the revenue engine of Cisco vs. that of IBM. In this chapter, we will provide a framework and taxonomy for defining and understanding these very different economic engines. It will also become very clear that services play a very different role in these different engines. But first, a little commentary on the aging of an industry.

Figure 2-1  Economic Engines of Product Companies

## THE MATURING TECHNOLOGY MARKETPLACE

To illustrate how the general maturation of technology markets is accelerating the importance of services-strategy decisions, we will quickly examine the revenue and profit trends of several anchors in the IT industry. We will focus on the financial dynamics of EMC, Intel, Sun, Oracle, and Xerox from after the dot com bust (2001) to before the global economic downturn (2008).

### EMC: More Revenue, Less Hardware Profit

Let's start in the world of storage. Figure 2-2 documents EMC's revenues and profits from 1995 to 2008. As can be seen, since the deluge of 2001, EMC has recovered all of the lost ground regarding top-line revenue growth and avoided the pattern of failure that ends with decline or demise. Much of the new revenue growth has been driven by acquisition of software companies that complement the EMC hardware platform and new services offerings. The recovery of both the top line and bottom is not solely based on recovering hardware sales. Services revenues and profits have become integral to EMC's economic success. Services questions facing a company like EMC at this juncture would include:

- As software maintenance revenues increase, how large should the services revenue stream become for the company?

- With both hardware and software in the company portfolio, should EMC aggressively expand integration capabilities?

- How will existing services partners respond to EMC's evolving services strategy?

Figure 2-2  EMC Revenues and Profits

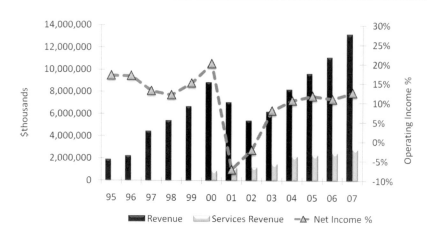

## Intel: More Revenue, Less Profit

Another company that maps into the same trend of recovering revenues is Intel. Figure 2-3 documents Intel revenues and profits from 1995 to 2007. Once again, here is a company that has recovered all of the lost ground regarding top-line revenues. However, operating profits have not regained their luster. Average operating income from 1995 to 2000 was 26 percent. The company's operating income for the past two years has been well below 20 percent. Intel does not break out services revenues, so it is unlikely they represent any significant revenue to the company. Services questions facing a company like Intel at this junction would include:

Figure 2-3  Intel Revenues and Profits

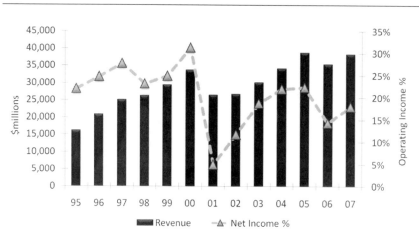

- Are new services capabilities a path to improved profitability?

- Are new services capabilities a weapon to fend off new competitors?

- What product-services mix should Intel aspire to as the processor market becomes less lucrative?

## Sun: Less Revenue, Less Profit

In this maturing landscape, some technology companies have not been able to recapture top-line revenues or bottom-line profitability. Drops in price and/or volume can be deadly. Figure 2-4 documents Sun Microsystems's revenues and profits from 2000 to 2007. Unfortunately for Sun, revenues and operating profits peaked in 2001. Services revenues clearly helped provide the cushion described in Chapter 1. However, the new plateau in operating income is currently negative. Services-strategy questions facing a company like Sun would include:

- If our products are truly commoditizing, will services be the only way to differentiate and return to profitability?

- How do we grow value-added services capabilities without alienating our channel partners that currently offer those services?

- Can services capabilities lead Sun into new, more lucrative product markets?

**Figure 2-4**  Sun Financial Trends

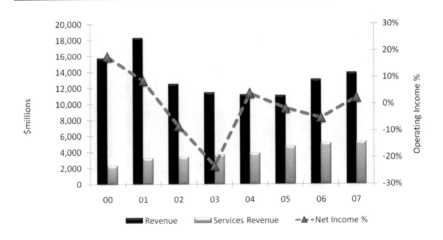

## Oracle: Slowing Revenue, More Profit

The next example we want to reference is Oracle. Clearly, since 2001, the top-line revenue growth for Oracle has matured. Top-line growth in recent years has been driven more by acquisition than by new database licenses. However, unlike EMC, Intel, and Sun, Oracle has not experienced a decrease in operating income since 2001. In fact, the services-intensive revenue streams of Oracle have been generating a higher operating income. Figure 2-5 documents this trend.

Where is this improvement in revenue coming from? In 2006, Oracle reported the following revenue mix on its $11.8 billion in revenues:

This margin mix validates the long-understood dictum of enterprise systems and software that it is more profitable to provide an existing customer maintenance than to acquire a new one for license fees. To be sure, part of the

Table 2-1  Oracle Financials, 2006

| Revenue Stream | $ Billions | Gross Margin % | % of Total Revenue |
|---|---|---|---|
| New License | $4,091 | 37% | 34% |
| Maintenance | $5,330 | 86% | 45% |
| Consulting | $1,810 | 14% | 15% |
| Advanced Services | $299 | 15% | 2.5% |
| Education Services | $269 | 16% | 2% |

Figure 2-5  Oracle Financial Trends

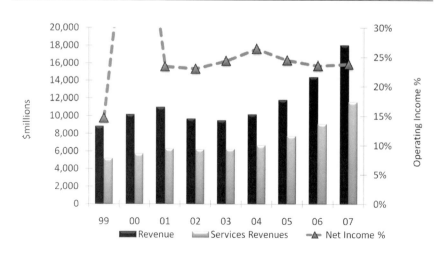

discount that license sales entail is in recognition of the net present value of future maintenance revenues. But as markets mature, it is more efficient to acquire new customers through buying the installed bases of existing companies rather than winning them one at a time in sales competitions. Since maintenance is treated as a service, this effectively shifts the revenue mix heavily to the services side.

Given the huge discrepancy on gross margins between maintenance and the other forms of services, a company in Oracle's position must grapple with the following services-strategy questions:

- How do we continue to maximize the profitability of maintenance contracts?

- How do we avoid pricing pressure on maintenance contracts?

- Despite their lower margins, what advanced services offerings, such as consulting and education services, help increase renewal rates?

### Xerox: Stagnant Revenue, Moderate Profits

The last example we want to reference is Xerox. Since 1998, top-line revenues for Xerox have been declining. However, since 2001, operating income has been improving. Figure 2-6 documents this trend. In this context it is important to note that in 2005, equipment revenues represented 29 percent of total revenues, whereas in 2000, when operating income was still negative, equipment sales represented 54 percent of total revenues. The company powered through decline by successfully spinning up a host of services including consulting, outsourcing, and managed services, and even leasing services. Now, a company like Xerox has to be asking the following questions:

- How can we optimize this new services-intensive revenue mix to improve operating income?

- How far will product margins compress as our legacy markets commoditize?

- Are we becoming too services intensive?

If your company is experiencing the same type of product-services revenue trends as one of the above companies, your management team is most likely debating the role of services in the overall economic health of the company. **In a landscape of maturing product markets, executives must decide how the business model for their company will adjust to these new economic realities. A critical component of that business model is the percentage of revenues the company will target from services.** As discussed in the Oracle,

Figure 2-6  Xerox Financial Trends

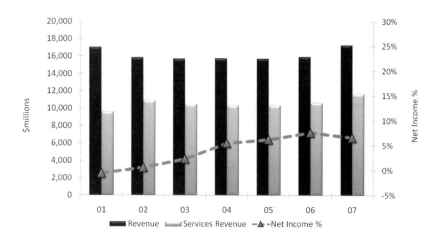

EMC, and Xerox examples, such service revenue streams can be a critical source of revenue, margin, and secured product renewal.

**To help answer the question "How much revenue should come from services?" we recommend companies understand their current services strategy in light of one or more of the four sustainable profiles that have already emerged in the technology industry and that we outline in the following pages.**

## INTRODUCTION TO SERVICES-STRATEGY PROFILES

To begin this discussion on services-strategy profiles, we must first clearly define three distinct revenue streams that occur when a product is being consumed by the technology marketplace:

1. **Product Revenue:** Lump-sum revenues received when a customer purchases a product such as hardware or software.

2. **Professional Services Revenue:** Accrual-based revenues received to design, install, integrate, and optimize a specific technology offering.

3. **Support Revenues:** Annuity-based revenues received to support the product investment the customer has made.

Historically, the common practice for product companies is to aggregate professional services and support revenues, reporting them simply as *services revenue*. This big bucket of services is what was shown in all the company examples used in the first pages of this chapter. However, not understanding the actual mix of services revenues that comes from support vs. professional services is misleading as the nature of the risk and return in the two areas is radically different.

In particular, such lumping masks the problematic role that professional services plays inside a product company. Although the adjectives "lucrative" and "high margin" have often been used to describe the professional services business, industry benchmarks validate it is often the lowest margin activity a product company can pursue. In other words, if measured simply for its contribution to margins and profits, professional services can be a *dilutive stock* in the company portfolio of offerings. This means company executives typically are very cautious before expanding professional services.

Despite the need for such caution, the list of product companies aggressively pursuing professional service revenues is ever increasing. The reason is simple. In a maturing category, as it becomes harder and harder to grow product revenues, the search for growth inevitably shifts to services. This reality played out in the Chapter 1 case examples of Novell and Siebel. Growing support services when product revenues are declining is difficult to do organically—hence the increased interest in merger and acquisition (M&A) activities. Growing professional services as an alternative, by contrast, is fraught with risk, exposing the company to staffing and utilization challenges during fluctuating business cycles and the risk of alienating service-providing partners who provide a key source of new customers.

There is no single correct answer to the challenge of how best to manage professional services as a part of the overall revenue mix. Instead, our research shows companies gravitating toward one of four strategies, each characterized by a distinctive product-service ratio. The four strategies are:

1. Solution Providers

2. Product Providers

3. Product Extenders

4. Systems Providers

Specifically, for each profile we uncovered, four attributes help define the differences between each profile:

- **Product Revenue Mix:** The amount of revenue the company receives from products, professional services, and support.

- **Sales Ignition Gear:** The manner in which the company typically initiates a sales cycle within its target marketplace.

- **PS Charter:** The charter of the embedded professional services organization.

- **Services Offerings:** The typical portfolio of professional services offerings.

To help us communicate the differences among strategies, we use a diagram of intermeshed gears to represent the economic engine at work. The size of each gear is proportional to the amount of total revenue the company receives from product, project, and support revenues. Each diagram also has a chevron to indicate the gear that starts the customer interaction and sets the economic engine in motion. And because we refer so frequently to professional services throughout, we will use the abbreviation PS frequently.

Finally, for each one of the profiles, we have assigned an animal as a representative icon. This calls attention to the distinctive attributes of each profile and makes it easier visually to map their sweet spot onto a market-maturity life cycle, which we will do at the end of this chapter.

## PROFILE #1: THE SOLUTION PROVIDER

As you can see, for the solution providers, we have assigned the icon of a giraffe. This acknowledges the fact that a successful solution provider must stretch down to graze on emerging technologies and reach all the way up to solve specific business problems being faced by target customers. And if that is a bit of a stretch, well, that's another reason to pick a giraffe.

### The Economic Engine of a Solution Provider

The overall economic engine for a solution provider is shown in Figure 2-7. Examples of public companies that have exhibited a solution-provider mix include Amdocs, Callidus Software, Compuware, and Blue Martini.

For solution providers, the largest gear in the economic engine is professional services. PS revenues typically represent over 35 percent of total company revenues. PS is also the catalyzing function that is used to start the conversation with the customer. Typically the company is leading with a consultative conversation because the product technology it provides is emerging, standards are fluid, partner ecosystems are nascent, and the customer therefore requires a customized implementation.

This pattern is highly characteristic of start-up product companies that have not yet grown a significant installed base. When such companies seek to "cross

Figure 2-7  Solution-Provider Revenue Mix

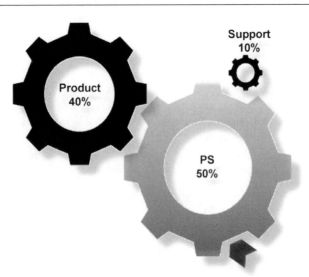

the chasm," they must provide a significant amount of project-oriented professional services to drive product adoption and reduce customer risk associated with implementing an unproven product.

The pattern is equally characteristic of divisions within large corporations seeking to introduce next-generation architectures or seeking to penetrate new vertical markets. Again, the area of professional services is filling in the gaps that over time will seal as the solution set matures.

## Chartering the PS Function

When PS organizations are embedded within companies that sell products, they are commonly chartered to achieve one (or more) of the following objectives:

1. Drive the adoption of products (increase product market share)

2. Improve or maintain customer satisfaction with company products

3. Grow PS revenues

4. Maintain or improve PS profits

When a company has adopted a solution provider profile, the priority objectives for the PS organization become service revenue (3) and product share (1).

Figure 2-8  The PS Charter for a Solution Provider

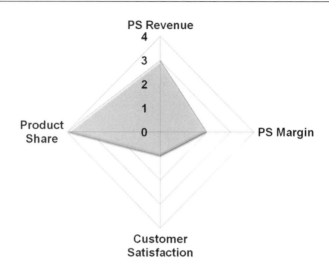

That is, PS must secure incoming revenues to help pay the bills and demonstrate company growth. At the same time, however, it must help meet the ultimate objective of accelerating customer adoption of the emerging technology so that future revenues from product and support will grow. Such adoption may come with a few heartaches, so maximizing customer satisfaction is not yet the goal. Additionally, this strategy decreases the focus on PS profits as services are often sold at a discount to ensure speedy product adoption.

To visualize this charter, we take the four primary objectives of an embedded PS organization, rate their importance, and plot them on a simple graph. The scale is one to four. A rating of 1 implies this factor has little importance to the PS organization relative to the other factors. A rating of 2 or 3 implies some importance. A rating of 4 means this is the primary objective of the PS organization.

As the Figure 2-8 shows, the PS organization in this profile is forced to walk a fine line between securing service revenue and investing in customer success.

## The Service Offerings of a Solution Provider

What types of PS offerings are typical for a solution provider? Table 2-2 documents the common types of services offered in the technology industry. It was generated with the help of the advisory board of the Technology Professional Services Association (TPSA).

Table 2-2  Services Offerings

| Services Type | Tagline | Description |
|---|---|---|
| **Support Services** | *Paid to support your product* | Services designed to keep product environment running and available for the customer. |
| **Education Services** | *Paid to teach about your product* | Services designed to enable the customer to use product features. |
| **Implementation Services** | *Paid for what you do with your product* | Services to accelerate the implementation of a product into the customer's environment. |
| **Integration Services** | *Paid for what you do with other people's products* | Services to integrate the company's product with other well-known industry products that exist in the customer's environment. |
| **Technology Consulting** | *Paid for what you know about the technology* | Services that provide recommended technical architectures or designs for the customer. |
| **Business Domain Consulting** | *Paid for what you know about the business impact of the technology* | Services that provide assistance in modifying business processes to fully leverage product capabilities. |
| **Managed Services** | *Paid to operate* | Services designed to help a customer manage their technology environment on an ongoing basis. |
| **Outsourcing Services** | *Paid to own* | Services designed to take full responsibility for the customer's technology environment—including both technology and the human resources required to manage the environment. |
| **Third-Party Support** | *Paid to support other people's products* | Services designed to provide support coverage for products not made by the company but may interface with company products. |

In this context, Table 2-3 highlights the types of services the solution provider must offer customers to accelerate and secure product adoption.

In this model, the solution-provider enterprise as a whole provides all the services marked with a check, with the PS organization performing the functions highlighted.

Table 2-3  Solution-Provider Services Offerings

| Services Type | Tagline | Solution Provider |
|---|---|---|
| **Support Services** | *Paid to support your product* | ✓ |
| **Education Services** | *Paid to teach about your product* | ✓ |
| **Implementation Services** | *Paid for what you do with your product* | ✓ |
| **Integration Services** | *Paid for what you do with other people's products* | ✓ |
| **Technology Consulting** | *Paid for what you know about the technology* | ✓ |
| **Business Domain Consulting** | *Paid for what you know about the business impact of the technology* | ✓ |
| **Managed Services** | *Paid to operate* | ✓ |
| **Outsourcing Services** | *Paid to own* | |
| **Third-Party Support** | *Paid to support other people's products* | |

## PROFILE #2: THE PRODUCT PROVIDER

Companies with the product provider profile are focused on getting as much product into the market as they possibly can, and the animal we associate with these companies is a cheetah. Organizations inside these companies race frantically to rapidly scale product sales. Time-to-market is a critical success factor. So cheetahs are all about speed: Speed of the product. Speed to market. Speed to the next release.

### *The Economic Engine of a Product Provider*

To illustrate the product-provider profile in Figure 2-9, we are using the revenue mix of Cisco Systems for the fiscal year ending July 29, 2006. Cisco has a very diverse hardware product portfolio. The company does not publicly report the split between support and PS revenues. However, the public records tell us that total service revenues represent less than 20 percent of total company revenues. Other technology companies with a very similar revenue mix include Juniper Networks and Network Appliance.

Figure 2-9  Product-Provider Revenue Mix

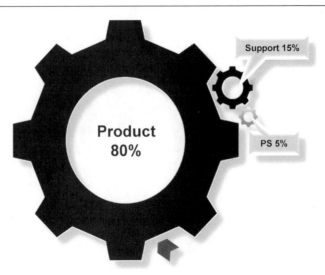

In the product-provider profile, the largest gear in the economic engine is product.  Product revenues will typically represent over 60 percent of total company revenues. This is also the economic gear that typically is used to start the conversation with the customer.  That is, unlike the solution provider, the product provider leads with the feature functionality of the product offerings and is typically selling to a product specialist in the customer organization.

### The PS Charter for Product Providers

With a product-provider profile, the priority objectives for the PS organization become product market share and customer satisfaction, the former in service to maximizing revenues, the latter in service to maximizing profit margins. The charter of the product provider is shown in Figure 2-10. Since PS revenues are less than 10 percent of total company revenues in this profile, the organization's own revenues and profits are not strategic in and of themselves.

### The Service Offerings of Product Providers

Table 2-4 documents the types of services a company with this profile will typically offer in comparison to the solution-provider profile previously discussed.

Figure 2-10  The PS Charter for Product Provider

Table 2-4  Product-Provider Service Offerings

| Services Type | Tagline | Solution Provider | Product Provider |
|---|---|---|---|
| **Support Services** | *Paid to support your product* | ✓ | ✓ |
| **Education Services** | *Paid to teach about your product* | ✓ | ✓ |
| **Implementation Services** | *Paid for what you do with your product* | ✓ | ✓ |
| **Integration Services** | *Paid for what you do with other people's products* | ✓ | |
| **Technology Consulting** | *Paid for what you know about the technology* | ✓ | ✓ |
| **Business Domain Consulting** | *Paid for what you know about the business impact of the technology* | ✓ | |
| **Managed Services** | *Paid to operate* | ✓ | |
| **Outsourcing Services** | *Paid to own* | | |
| **Third-Party Support** | *Paid to support other people's products* | | |

Product providers are laser focused on driving product sales and will typically offer a scaled-back PS portfolio focused on implementation and basic integration services. These companies are highly motivated to engage partners to deliver whatever higher-complexity, higher-margin services are further required because by their very nature they would slow their cheetah model down.

## PROFILE #3: THE PRODUCT EXTENDER

Companies with this profile are often leaders in their target markets, and so their icon is a lion. Having already achieved strong market share and secured a significant support revenue stream, they are less focused on acquiring new customers and more focused on maintaining their current status as king of the jungle. Despite this symbol of strength, they face some very real challenges. Everyday the lion fights to maintain his position on the Serengeti. Everyday, product extenders must decide how they will keep their economic engine running—especially once the water hole of product growth begins to dry up.

### *The Economic Engine of Product Extenders*

An example economic engine for a company with a product extender profile is shown in Figure 2-11.

In this example, we are using the revenue mix of Oracle Systems. Oracle is one of a few publicly traded software companies that reports the split of service revenues between support and other services. In this snapshot taken from Oracle's 10K published on 07/21/06, we can see that nonsupport service actually represents 20 percent of total company revenues. Other technology companies with a similar product-extender revenue mix include other enterprise software companies, such as SAP and Business Objects (before they were purchased by Oracle).

In the product-extender profile, the most profitable gear in the economic engine of the company has become support. Annuity revenues will typically represent between 25 and 50 percent of total company revenues, the more the better. Product revenues in this profile normally represent considerably less than half of total company revenues. Nonetheless, the customer conversation is still initiated with discussions about the product capabilities, whether it be a discussion about buying a new product or maintaining an existing investment.

Figure 2-11  Product-Extender Revenue Mix

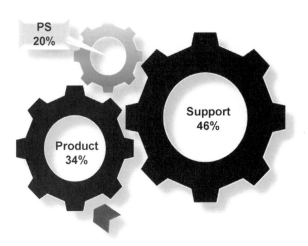

PS revenues have a resurgence to represent at least 15 percent of total company revenues for reasons we discuss in the following paragraphs.

## The PS Charter for Product Extenders

In the product-extender strategy, maintaining the support and product revenue streams from the installed base is the primary imperative. This is reflected in the PS charter documented in Figure 2-12. In this context, the PS organization focuses increasingly on integration projects that assimilate newer waves of product, both from the company and others, into the existing infrastructure. By so doing, the enterprise can keep other competitors at bay and grow profitable revenues from complex services. Because the opportunity to garner new customers is dwindling, there is little need to discount PS in the way a solution provider is often forced to.

## The Service Offerings of Product Extenders

A company with this PS strategy profile wants to leverage sticky customer relationships and market-leader status to reposition itself as a trusted advisor for high-margin, high-complexity projects that build off of its installed infrastructure.

Table 2-5 documents the expanded service portfolio of a company with this profile in comparison to the prior two.

Figure 2-12  The PS Charter for Product Extenders

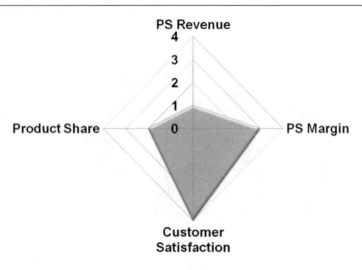

Table 2-5  Product-Extender Service Offerings

| Services Type | Tagline | Solution Provider | Product Provider | Product Extender |
|---|---|:---:|:---:|:---:|
| **Support Services** | *Paid to support your product* | ✓ | ✓ | ✓ |
| **Education Services** | *Paid to teach about your product* | ✓ | ✓ | ✓ |
| **Implementation Services** | *Paid for what you do with your product* | ✓ | ✓ | ✓ |
| **Integration Services** | *Paid for what you do with other people's products* | ✓ | | ✓ |
| **Technology Consulting** | *Paid for what you know about the technology* | ✓ | ✓ | ✓ |
| **Business Domain Consulting** | *Paid for what you know about the business impact of the technology* | ✓ | | ✓ |
| **Managed Services** | *Paid to operate* | ✓ | | ✓ |
| **Outsourcing Services** | *Paid to own* | | | |
| **Third-Party Support** | *Paid to support other people's products* | | | |

Note that the extensions into business domain consulting and managed services are intended primarily to cement the product extender's prime-vendor position in its installed base. Effectively the product extender seeks to convert its installed products into a platform for future extensions and is leveraging its own PS organization to do so, because no other company shares its motives.

## PROFILE #4: THE SYSTEMS PROVIDER

The fourth and final services-strategy profile in our taxonomy is the systems provider. Its profile exhibits the most complex economic engine of the four. In acknowledgement of IBM's long-standing status as a systems provider and in deference to Lou Gerstner's book *Who Says Elephants Can't Dance?* (Harper-Collins, 2002), we have associated an elephant with this profile. System providers must have substantial girth to offer the portfolio of comprehensive services required by this strategy. And while others may see them as slow and lumbering, customers value their deliberate pace as well as their very long life expectancy.

### *The Economic Engine of a Systems Provider*

A systems provider typically has over half of its revenues coming from services. However, unlike product extenders, support is no longer the dominant service revenue stream. Instead service revenues are distributed relatively equally among professional services, support services, and outsourcing. Given the complexity of this array of possibilities, the company uses professional services to initiate the customer conversation, often with a consulting or planning engagement.

An example economic engine for a company with a systems-provider profile is shown in Figure 2-13. In this case, we are mapping the 2005 fiscal year revenue mix of IBM, the definitive systems provider in the IT marketplace. Xerox is another stalwart of the technology industry that has migrated to systems-provider profile.

### *The PS Charter for Systems Providers*

With a systems-provider profile, service revenues have now become a critical source of both revenue and profit. The priority for professional services shifts to driving both top-line PS revenues and bottom-line PS profits. The visualization of this charter is shown in Figure 2-14.

Figure 2-13  Systems-Provider Revenue Mix

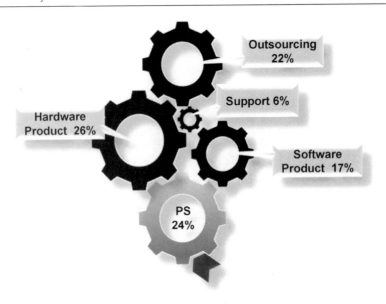

Figure 2-14  The PS Charter for Systems Provider

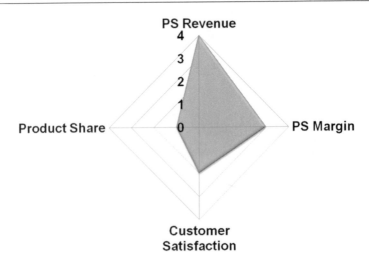

## THE SERVICE OFFERINGS OF PRODUCT ENABLEMENT

Table 2-6 documents the end-to-end scope of the systems provider's services portfolio.

Table 2-6  Systems Profile Service Offerings

| Services Type | Tagline | Solution Provider | Product Provider | Product Extender | Systems Provider |
|---|---|---|---|---|---|
| **Support Services** | *Paid to support your product* | ✓ | ✓ | ✓ | ✓ |
| **Education Services** | *Paid to teach about your product* | ✓ | ✓ | ✓ | ✓ |
| **Implementation Services** | *Paid for what you do with your product* | ✓ | ✓ | ✓ | ✓ |
| **Integration Services** | *Paid for what you do with other people's products* | ✓ | | ✓ | ✓ |
| **Technology Consulting** | *Paid for what you know about the technology* | ✓ | ✓ | ✓ | ✓ |
| **Business Domain Consulting** | *Paid for what you know about the business impact of the technology* | ✓ | | ✓ | ✓ |
| **Managed Services** | *Paid to operate* | ✓ | | ✓ | ✓ |
| **Outsourcing Services** | *Paid to own* | | | | ✓ |
| **Third-Party Support** | *Paid to support other people's products* | | | | ✓ |

A company with this services-strategy profile is aggressively pursuing PS opportunities in the marketplace. The company also hopes to leverage a subset of these projects to secure managed and outsourcing service engagements. To further extend its service reach, the company will begin supporting products not even produced by the company.

## SOFTWARE AS A SERVICE: A POSTSCRIPT

As we were developing these services-strategy profiles, questions recurrently arose around the software-as-a-service (SaaS) business model that has emerged in the software industry. In essence, SaaS providers, such as salesforce.com, fuse what would traditionally have been product (license) revenue from new customer acquisition and what would traditionally have been maintenance

revenue from existing customers into one bucket titled "subscription revenues." PS revenues are typically reported separately by these companies. So,
how do these four services-strategy profiles relate to SaaS providers? In reality, SaaS providers can pursue a solution-provider, a product-provider, or a
product-extender strategy. Their approach to revenue reporting just makes it
harder to discern what strategy is being pursued. The key indicators, however,
are PS revenues and subscription growth.

For example, the revenue mix for salesforce.com as reported in their 10-K
for 2006 is shown in Figure 2-15.

As can be seen, the company had only 9 percent of total revenues coming
from professional services. Also, we know that salesforce.com had been rapidly growing top-line revenue through new customer acquisition. These two
facts combined tell us salesforce.com was really a classic product provider at
the time. Their professional service strategy would have a lot in common with
Cisco's.

Now, if Oracle converted their entire business to a subscription model, their
revenue mix, at first glance, would look somewhat similar to salesforce.com's
as shown in Figure 2-16.

Figure 2-15  Revenue Mix for salesforce.com

Figure 2-16  Oracle as SaaS

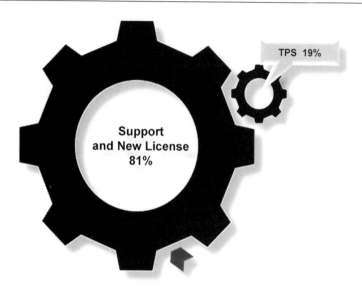

TPS 19%

Support
and New License
81%

However, there are two key differences between the salesforce.com and Oracle economic engines. First of all, Oracle has over 10 percent of total revenues coming from professional services. This is the first indication that Oracle is actually in a product extender mode, not a product provider mode. Secondly, we know that less than half of the subscription revenues shown in Figure 2-16 actually come from new subscribers. This is the second indication that Oracle does not have the same services-strategy profile as salesforce.com. To say the least, the veil of subscription revenues will become very attractive to older software firms that do not want to admit their high-growth product provider days are well behind them.

## PROFILES AND MARKET MATURITY

After identifying these four unique services-strategy profiles that product companies assimilate, the natural question becomes, why? Why do companies gravitate to one profile as opposed to another? **We believe the fundamental driver in determining what services-strategy profile a company adopts is the profile of the market the company is serving**. To illustrate this point, we refer to the product-adoption life cycle previously defined in *Crossing the Chasm* (HarperBusiness, 1991). This framework defines four distinct phases defined by the types of buyers that new product offerings encounter as they are adopted by a marketplace:

**Phase A:** *Innovators* experiment with a new product to create competitive differentiation. For a product company to be successful, it must take an early stage concept and acquire a critical mass of customers that are willing to invest in the new concept. Crossing this product adoption chasm is critical in the early life of a product offering.

**Phase B:** *Early Adopters* with less internal technical expertise but a strong belief in the potential of the technology, based largely on peer references, implement the product.

**Phase C:** *Early Majority* companies that implement the product because they can now see the proven success of innovators and adopters.

**Phase D:** *Late Majority* companies that must implement the product or face a competitive disadvantage.

In Figure 2-17, the animal icons we have associated with each services-strategy profile are mapped to the four phases of the product adoption life cycle. Table 2-7 provides more detail to this mapping. Each services-strategy profile helps the product company successfully navigate the dynamics of a specific market phase.

A solution-provider profile is most commonly found in the early phases of product adoption. The product company must offer extensive PS to assist in integration and reduce customer risk. A product-provider profile is dominant when a company has high-growth product sales. Product-extender profiles emerge when core product markets begin to slow, but the installed base has reached a significant size. Finally, a systems-provider profile becomes predominant when a product company is involved in maturing markets and has decided to pursue natural service opportunities.

Figure 2-17  Services-Strategy Profiles and Market Maturity

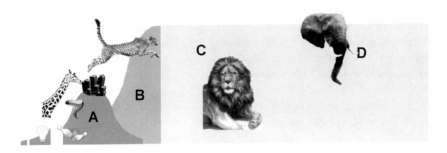

Table 2-7  Service-Strategy Profiles Details

| Product Adoption Phase | Service Strategy Type | PS Charter | Ignition Gear | Defining PS Service |
|---|---|---|---|---|
| A | **Solution Provider** | Revenue Share | PS | Bus Domain Consulting |
| B | **Product Enabler** | Sat Share | Product | Implementation Services |
| C | **Product Enhancer** | Share Profit | Product | Integration Services |
| D | **Systems Provider** | Revenue Profit | PS or Outsourcing | Outsourcing Services |

We have found this mapping runs a little counterintuitive to how product executives think about services strategy. Product companies always talk about delivering a business solution. However, it is the early stage product category that requires the product company to deliver a majority of that solution directly and assume the revenue mix of the solution-provider profile. As product markets grow, independent service providers enter to provide many of the services required by the marketplace. Only when product revenues wane does the product company again consider growing professional service revenues to become a service-led lion or a service-intensive elephant.

## SUMMARY THOUGHTS

Successful product companies have gravitated to one of four clearly recognizable services strategies. The easiest way to distinguish these services strategies is to model the economic engine of the product company. Figure 2-18 shows the revenue mix of product provider Cisco next to the revenue mix of systems provider IBM. Even without further elaboration, it is clear from this picture that services must be playing a very different role in the business model of these two companies.

With this overview of services-strategy profiles in place, we can now take a deeper dive into the specific objectives of each profile. The next four chapters will define, in greater detail, the key parameters and dynamics of each profile. With a clear understanding of each profile, we will then move into the challenge of the services chasm—when product companies have misaligned market maturity and their services-strategy profile.

Figure 2-18  Cisco and IBM Revenue Engines

# Chapter 3

# The Solution Provider

The second chapter introduces four common, successful services-strategy profiles that product companies adopt to meet both product adoption and market needs. Now, we will begin our journey through the four services-strategy profiles. Each of the next four chapters will allow management teams to answer these questions:

1. Is our company currently executing this services strategy?

2. Should our company consider executing this services-strategy profile?

3. How should our company set key services-strategy parameters to maximize the productivity of this profile?

4. What real-world companies have assumed this services-strategy profile?

By having a common understanding of a specific services strategy, management team discussions can be much more productive. Leaders can move beyond broad-based statements such as "we should increase our commitment to services" and move to very specific, practical statements surrounding specific services-strategy settings.

Let's begin the process to better understanding specific services strategies by better understanding the behaviors and habits of the solution provider. As a reminder, the revenue mix of a solution provider is very services intensive as shown in Figure 3-1. More specifically, the revenue mix is heavy on the professional services side with professional services driving 40 to 60 percent of total company revenues.

We assigned the icon of a giraffe to this profile. This lanky, yet speedy animal is the perfect symbol for a services-strategy profile that is awkward for most product companies to pursue (because it is so services intensive). However, solution providers can reach customer revenues that other product companies, executing different services strategies, cannot.

Figure 3-1 Solution-Provider Revenue Mix

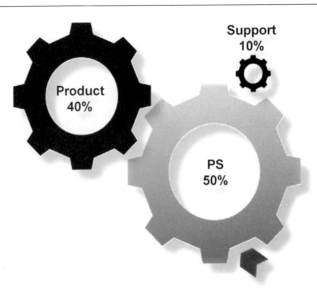

## SOLUTION-PROVIDER LITMUS TESTS

Many product-centric companies have been claiming they are no longer simply product providers but "solution providers." Nobody wants to simply dump off a product and say "best of luck." Everyone wants to provide a total solution that truly solves the customer's needs. The problem with this positioning is that to truly deliver a comprehensive business solution, a product company will need to provide services. Services are the glue that makes business solutions real. Unfortunately, companies that are making a lot of money selling successful products are not normally interested in building human-capital-intensive services lines.

A story was related to me by a colleague that underlines the typical sentiments of product executives toward services business. The colleague describes sitting with the executive of a large hardware company based in Silicon Valley. They were discussing services strategy. The executive then cut the conversation short with the following statement: "Services are for losers." That sentiment runs deep and wide in the corridors of product companies throughout the world. Who can blame product companies for focusing on product sales? If products are flying off the shelf, that means the product is so well engineered that services are not required to make the product a solution. Right? Or, much more likely, customers and service partners are taking care of any messy service work that might be required to deliver the business solution. **Having a product company focus on product growth is not a bad thing. But what happens if the product growth is not exponential? What if products are not flying off the shelf because customers do need help with the total solution and there are no services partners in place? This is the fertile ground where true solution providers are born.**

When product companies have an emerging product offering, they may be required to provide a fair amount of professional services to accelerate initial adoption of the product. Product companies with other established products in place may invest in services for an emerging product to drive initial product adoption. We call this "subsidized" solution offerings. For smaller companies or companies with one core product, offering subsidized service work to drive product adoption is not an economically viable option. For these companies, they must assume a solution-provider services-strategy profile to survive. As we have stated before, management teams serve the best interest of customers, employees, and investors by aligning the appropriate services strategy to the realities of the marketplace. What follows are tools to help management teams determine if they, do indeed, need to be a solution provider and not simply say they are providing a solution—the two statements are not the same.

## Some Simple Questions

**For each services-strategy profile, we expect the strategy variables for the professional services (PS) organization to be set a little differently. These nuances in PS strategy are the "marker genes" for services-strategy profiles.** As a starting point for the management dialogue regarding services-strategy profile, the team can individually answer the twelve questions outlined in Table 3-1 that are related to the role of professional services to company success.

**If a majority of the management team comfortably answered 9 to 12 of these questions with a resounding "yes," then the company most likely requires a solution-provider services strategy to thrive. The information provided in this chapter will provide guidance regarding the optimization of that services strategy.** If, however, the management team answered six or less of these questions with a "yes," there should be a pause. Also, if there was a large disparity in some of the answers from manager to manager, the team is not aligned around executing a solution provider strategy and this chapter should be used to better understand what it means to truly execute this profile. At this point, it is okay if debate exists regarding the optimal services strategy. This book is designed to tease out and frame that debate.

Table 3-1  Solution-Provider Alignment Questions

| Question for the Management Team | YES | NO |
|---|---|---|
| 1. Are professional service revenues more than 30% of total company revenues? | | |
| 2. Are professional service revenues more than 50% of the total deal when professional services and product are sold together? | | |
| 3. Are professional service revenues growing faster than product revenues? | | |
| 4. Are professional services involved from the very beginning of all sales cycles? | | |
| 5. Are professional services absolutely required to secure the product sale? | | |
| 6. Are professional services such a significant portion of our revenues that we can no longer afford to significantly discount them? | | |
| 7. Is our ability to scale professional services the deciding factor in product sales and new product adoption? | | |
| 8. Is the partner environment surrounding our product immature? | | |
| 9. Have customers expressed they would not purchase our product unless we provided direct PS capabilities? | | |
| 10. Do we provide professional services beyond basic implementation to enable our product in the customer environment? | | |
| 11. Do we get involved in our customers' business processes, not just their technical processes? | | |
| 12. Do we staff consultants that have intimate understanding of our customers industry? | | |

## Guiding Principles of Professional Services

A second tactic management teams can use to determine how closely they are aligned regarding services-strategy profile is to review the guiding principles of the PS organization. The following guiding principles would be very appropriate for PS organizations within a solution-provider strategy:

- Professional services owns the successful adoption of company products in new customers.

- Professional services must have both the technical and business expertise required to secure new product customers.

- PS project pricing must support both the top-line and bottom-line financial objectives of the company.

- Professional services owns the development of service methodologies for implementing company technology.

- The success of professional services will be evaluated by the number of new customer accounts, total customer spending with the company, and the profitability of PS engagements.

Note, it is the first two guiding principles that are most unique to solution providers. Not all product companies expect their internal PS organization to drive product adoption—that responsibility may be ceded to the partner ecosystem. In addition, PS project profitability may not be a requirement in companies where PS revenues are a rounding error. **If the management team cannot agree on the guiding principles of professional services, the services-strategy profile needs work. Product companies often think of professional services as a cost of sales. For solution providers, professional services as a cost of sales sinks the company.** One way this misalignment in expectations presents itself is disagreement on what guiding principles make sense for the PS organization.

## Product Maturity

A third tactic management teams can use to determine how closely they are aligned regarding services-strategy profile is to discuss the maturity of the product portfolio. Using Geoffrey Moore's product-adoption life cycle, product companies most likely to pursue a solution-provider profile have not yet achieved significant adoption of their product in the market. Product revenues are just beginning to take hold, or the product continues to require intense service activity for customers to realize the full value of the product. These market realities force the company to maintain a sizable PS capability relative to overall company resources. **For most product companies, it would be unthinkable to have more staff allocated to professional services than to product engineering. For a solution provider, this may indeed be the reality. For without these PS resources, the efforts of product engineering are wasted as customers will not successfully leverage the product without the assistance of services.** Figure 3-2 captures where the solution-provider profile is often applied during the product-adoption life cycle. Companies can continue to execute the solution-provider profile as the product gains traction, but they are more likely to reduce PS revenues and engage services partners. Now that these services partners are convinced the product will be successful and it is worth building a services practice around it.

Figure 3-2 Market Maturity and the Solution-Provider Profile

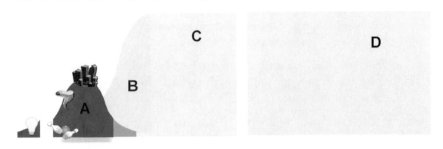

**Despite all the hoopla from product companies that they want to pro-
vide solutions, the solution-provider profile is rarely pursued with vigor.
Early stage product companies have visions of being product providers,
not PS firms.** This focus makes it difficult for executive teams to embrace the
ramping of PS capabilities. Yet market needs can trump executive concerns. As
always, the worst scenario is confusion within the management team regarding
the services-strategy profile the company is attempting to execute. If customers require service assistance and the company does not invest in professional
services, product adoption will suffer and the company may never be given the
chance to prove itself as a successful product vendor. This framework should
be used to help align the management team to current market realities and
current customer expectations regarding service capabilities to determine if a
solution-provider profile really should be employed at this time.

## Special Cases

All of the discussion so far has been focused on the overarching, or the aggregate, services-strategy profile of the company. We are trying to define the role
of services in a majority of the go-to-market scenarios for company products.
However, a product company may have existing, more mature product offerings that do not require intense services involvement to drive adoption. The
company may simply be struggling with the adoption of a new release or a new
product line. In this case, the answers to some of the previous questions may
be different:

- Professional services is much less than 30 percent of total company
  revenues.

- Many partners are enabled to delivered the more mature products
  offered by the company.

In these cases, the company must consider if the solution provider profile is really only required on a one-off basis. If this is true, it does not mean the company is changing its overall services-strategy profile. However, if the main source of future company revenues will be coming from a product that requires intense services activity, the company must consider that the solution-provider profile is truly the overarching profile required for the company to survive and thrive.

## SERVICES-STRATEGY VARIABLE SETTINGS FOR THE SOLUTION PROVIDER

### Overview of the Nine Strategy Variables

In the book *Mastering Professional Services*, three pillars of a mature PS strategy are introduced:

> **The Revenues Pillar**: Strategy variables in this pillar help define what the company hopes the PS business will achieve financially. How much money should professional services make?

> **The Services Pillar**: Strategy variables in this pillar help define what markets and specific services the PS group will support to help maximize product success. What services will professional services offer and to whom?

> **The Skills Pillar**: Strategy variables in this pillar define how the company will source the delivery of PS engagements. How will we pick the PS money up off the table?

Within the three pillars, a management team must discuss and then set nine critical variables. If these nine variables are not reviewed, the services strategy is not mature and potentially not viable. Figure 3-3 presents the nine variables that require attention.

As highlighted at the beginning of this chapter, for each services-strategy profile, we expect the strategy variables for the PS organization to be set a little differently. These nuances in PS strategy are the "marker genes" for services-strategy profiles. For example, the charter of a PS organization within a solution provider is very different from the charter of professional services within a product provider. The same can be observed for financial targets and the services-partner strategy. This section overviews how solution providers set these nine PS parameters to maximize the overall impact of their services strategy.

Figure 3-3  Nine Variables of a Services Strategy

| REVENUES | SERVICES | SKILLS |
|----------|----------|--------|
| CHARTER | MARKETS | CORE |
| BUSINESS MODEL | SERVICE OFFERINGS | PARTNERS |
| FINANCIAL TARGETS | CHANNELS | SCALABILITY MIX |

## *Charter, Business Model, and Financial Objectives*

The first services-strategy variable that a management team needs to review is the charter of the PS business. Every business function has a set of primary reasons for existing. For product companies, four primary reasons exist for having an embedded PS organization:

**Services Revenue**: The product company is looking for additional sources of top-line revenue growth.

**Services Margin**: The product company is looking for higher margin revenue sources in order to offset shrinking product margins.

**Customer Satisfaction**: The product company views services as a vehicle to improve customer satisfaction and protect account relationships.

**Product Market Share**: The product company would like to use value-added services to expand product sales. Services are used to accelerate the adoption of new products or to carry existing products into new vertical markets.

For solution providers, the PS charter is weighted toward securing new product customers and ongoing PS revenues. Solution providers must be very focused on the PS revenue stream. The solution provider does not yet have a substantial product revenue stream, so PS revenues are critical to financial viability. Ranking the four reasons professional services exists, where 4 is the most important factor and 1 is the least important factor, solution providers will have a charter that is weighted as shown in Figure 3-4.

Figure 3-4  Charter of Professional Services for the Solution Provider

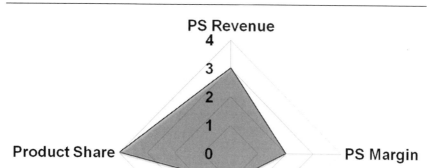

After setting the PS charter, the management team should review the target financial business model of the PS organization. Of course, the business model should be 100 percent aligned with the charter. TPSA benchmarks PS business models extensively, and actually segments that data by services-strategy profile to understand what differences exist between these profiles. Figure 3-5 contrasts the business model for solution providers to the business models for other services-strategy profiles we will be exploring in the book. The TPSA average is based on the average performance of embedded PS organizations

Figure 3-5  Solution-Provider Business Model

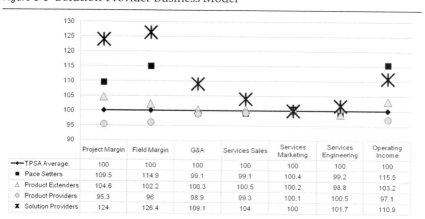

| | Project Margin | Field Margin | G&A | Services Sales | Services Marketing | Services Engineering | Operating Income |
|---|---|---|---|---|---|---|---|
| TPSA Average. | 100 | 100 | 100 | 100 | 100 | 100 | 100 |
| Pace Setters | 109.5 | 114.9 | 99.1 | 99.1 | 100.4 | 99.2 | 115.5 |
| Product Extenders | 104.6 | 102.2 | 100.3 | 100.5 | 100.2 | 98.8 | 103.2 |
| Product Providers | 95.3 | 96 | 98.9 | 99.3 | 100.1 | 100.5 | 97.1 |
| Solution Providers | 124 | 126.4 | 109.1 | 104 | 100 | 101.7 | 110.9 |

in both hardware and software companies. The graph also shows the performance of PS Pacesetters. These are the top 25 percent of PS organizations, in terms of financial performance, that have benchmarked with TPSA.

As can be seen, solution providers are driving superior PS project margins compared to the overall benchmark average. Solution providers are working hard to secure new product sales, but the PS activities are absolutely viewed as a profit-and-loss center that should generate reasonable profits. **If solution providers are not able to execute profitable PS projects, the financial viability of the company will eventually come under duress.** Some solution providers use early stage capital to subsidize PS activities with the anticipation that product sales will eventually accelerate and a services-strategy profile requiring less services revenues can be assumed. This strategy is high risk if product sales ramp at a slower pace than projected. The additional consequence of this subsidization strategy is the reality that customers have now been trained to expect expensive PS resources for free!

With the charter and target business model in place, the third strategy variable to review is financial objectives. What are the growth expectations for the PS business? For solution providers, PS growth rate vs. product growth rate can vary wildly. If the product is in a very early stage, PS revenues may be growing much faster than product revenues that are far and few between. For solution providers starting to successfully ramp product sales, PS growth may mirror product growth. In any case, professional services **will at least keep pace with product revenues**. When product revenue growth begins to significantly outpace PS growth, the company is migrating into a product-provider profile, which will be defined in the next chapter. Figure 3-6 maps an expected strike zone for PS growth within a solution-provider services strategy.

Figure 3-6   PS Growth Rates for Solution Provider

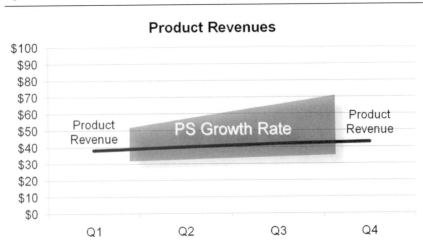

At this point, the management team has reviewed the charter of the PS organization, the financial business model, and the growth objectives. There is now clear definition surrounding the financial expectations of the PS business. But where, specifically, will PS revenues come from? That is the focus of the next three strategy variables.

### Target Markets, Offerings, and Sales Channels

With financial expectations set, the management team should now discuss where PS revenues will come from. This is the focus of the *services pillar*.

The first strategy variable in this pillar is target markets. What customers will the PS function serve? For solution providers, the focus is on developing and securing new customers. Figure 3-7 provides a classic mapping where markets are segmented into four categories:

Figure 3-7  Four Target Markets

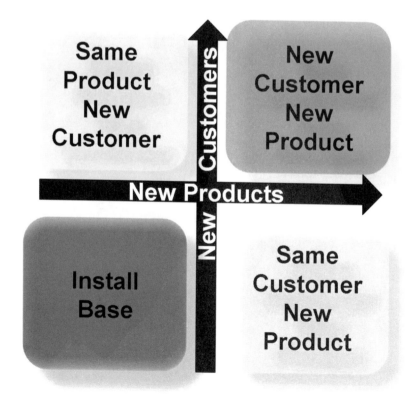

1. Existing customers

2. New customers for your existing products

3. New products for your existing customers

4. Brand new customers you have never sold to but you now have a new product that makes them a viable market for you pursue

As we know, it becomes more difficult to address the target markets as you move from your install base to new customers that you want to sell an emerging product. It is much easier to sell upgrades to existing customers than sell a brand new technology to a customer that has never heard of you. However, professional services in the solution-provider profile is focused on this most difficult market sector—securing new customers and accelerating the adoption

Figure 3-8  Market Focus of Professional Services in a Solution Provider

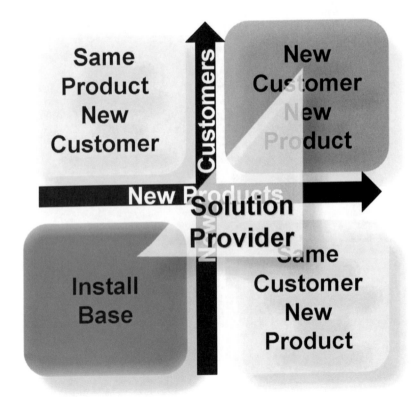

of a new product. Figure 3-8 documents where solution providers direct PS resources.

The second variable in the services pillar concerns target offerings. As introduced in the previous chapter, TPSA has documented a standard taxonomy for the spectrum of services offerings provided by product companies. As shown in Table 3-2, for solution providers, the entire PS spectrum is in play, based on customer needs. Solution providers must provide implementation, integration, and technology consulting services because no partner environment is in place to perform those services. In addition, the solution provider will also provide the business domain consulting required to secure product adoption. Unlike other services-strategy profiles we will document, solution providers must step up and provide the business expertise required for customers to benefit from the emerging technology solution.

The solution provider is delivering all of the services required to enable the product with perhaps the leverage of some partners during integration and ongoing system management. As the product install base grows, the solution provider can attract service-delivery partners. When the product install base is emerging, the solution provider must stay aggressively involved throughout the customer-engagement life cycle as shown in Figure 3-9. Figure 3-10 compares the involvement of solution providers to other services-strategy profiles. This contrast makes it clear why very few product companies truly want to be solution providers—the service responsibilities throughout the customer-engagement life cycle are simply too intense.

Table 3-2  Solution-Provider Services Offerings

| Services Type | Tagline | Solution Provider |
|---|---|---|
| **Support Services** | *Paid to support your product* | ✓ |
| **Education Services** | *Paid to teach about your product* | ✓ |
| **Implementation Services** | *Paid for what you do with your product* | ✓ |
| **Integration Services** | *Paid for what you do with other people's products* | ✓ |
| **Technology Consulting** | *Paid for what you know about the technology.* | ✓ |
| **Business Domain Consulting** | *Paid for what you know about the business impact of the technology* | ✓ |
| **Managed Services** | *Paid to operate* | ✓ |
| **Outsourcing Services** | *Paid to own* | |
| **Third-Party Support** | *Paid to support other people's products* | |

Figure 3-9  Solution-Provider Direct Customer Engagement

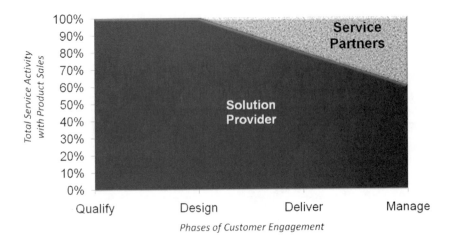

Figure 3-10  Solution-Provider Engagement vs. Other Profiles

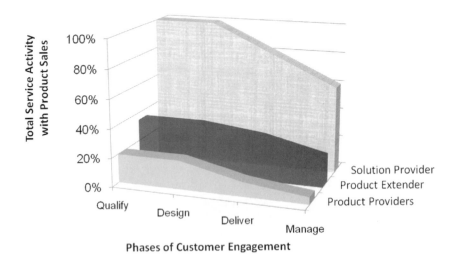

The final variable in the services pillar concerns sales channels. How are PS offerings sold by the solution provider? To sell their professional services, product companies can turn to several channels:

**Product Sales Force**: The current sales force that is responsible for selling the product.

**Overlay Services Sales Force**: A specialist hired to augment the product sales force and focus on selling the PS portfolio.

**Product Channel Partners**: Partners that are selling the product could be offered incentives to sell the PS offerings of the company as well.

**Services Partners**: System integrators could be encouraged to sell the PS capabilities of the product company as part of a large solution.

For solution providers, the preferred sales channel for direct professional service engagements is the specialized services sales reps that are comfortable selling service-intensive projects. Solution providers are not selling product transactions but consulting engagements. A traditional product-centric sales force is not the optimal channel at this point in time. Also, professional services play a significant role in the economic engine of the company. The company cannot afford for PS resources to be given away for free or PS deals to be poorly scoped. Figure 3-11 documents this sales channel preference.

The target markets, target offerings, and preferred sales channels have now been reviewed for the PS business strategy. This provides a solid baseline for where the company expects PS service revenues to come from. But we have not discussed how solution providers deliver their services portfolio.

Figure 3-11  Solution-Provider Sales Channel

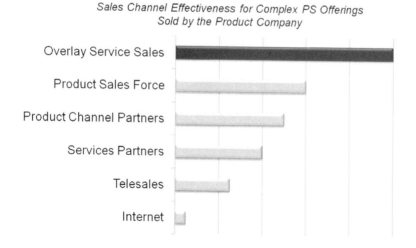

## *Core Skills, Partners, and Scalability*

The final pillar of a mature services strategy concerns skills. How will the company source the skills required to execute the PS business? To frame this conversation, we can use the PS hourglass model previously published in *Mastering Professional Services*. This model defines seven key skills sets involved in managing a PS business within a product company:

1.  **Product Account Reps**: The largest direct sales force employed by the product company. Critical resource regarding the identification of PS opportunities.

2.  **Services Sales Reps**: An overlay sales force specializing in selling the PS portfolio.

3.  **Practice Managers**: Senior managers responsible for the profit and loss management of the PS business.

4.  **Solution Architects**: The senior technical consultants that are able to review customer business requirements and translate them into a recommended technology solution.

5.  **Resource Managers**: The management layer responsible for sourcing sold PS engagements.

6.  **Project Managers, Technical Architects**: Senior delivery resources required to deliver PS engagements.

7.  **Technical Specialists**: Delivery resource required to deliver PS engagements.

For solution providers, the focus is on providing the complete hourglass of skills required to sell and deliver a complete business solution. At the beginning of the sales cycle, the solution provider must have services sales reps with specific industry and business expertise that can be leveraged to show prospective customers how the solution will change their business. The solution provider must then have a delivery force that is capable of implementing and integrating the solution from cradle to grave. More junior roles may be subcontracted if the appropriate technical expertise is available. Figure 3-12 highlights the positions that are core to the solution provider. About the only position skills the solution provider are able to subcontract are commodity technical skills that are required to deliver the solution but are readily found in the marketplace at reasonable prices.

After understanding what skills are core to the execution of the PS strategy, a management team must consider how it will leverage partners. For companies that make products, solution providers face the smallest amount of partner conflict regarding service activities. This lack of conflict exists only because the partner environment is not yet developed for the product offering.

Figure 3-12  Core PS Skills for the Solution Provider

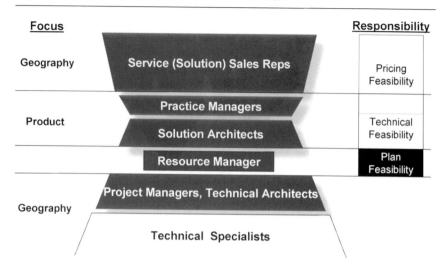

For solution providers, services partners may provide staff to augment service engagements booked by the product company, but there are likely no services partners in place to take prime responsibility for product implementation and integration.

Five natural pools of resources are used by a PS organization to deliver services offerings:

1. **Direct Local Resources**: These are PS consultants employed directly by the product company and residing locally, close to customer-engagement sites.

2. **Corporate Practice Resources**: These are PS consultants that have hard-to-find, specialized skills. They are leveraged across multiple geographies.

3. **Centralized Solution Center Resources**: These are delivery resources that can be leveraged to deliver portions of a PS engagement without being on the customer site. These resources are typically clustered where labor costs are lower.

4. **Local Delivery Partners**: These are services-delivery partners that are identified and engaged by an individual country or specific region.

5. **Global Delivery Partners**: These are services-delivery partners that are identified, selected, and enabled at a global level.

The management team must decide what combination of these direct and indirect resources will be employed to scale the delivery capabilities of professional services. In the solution-provider profile, the key to services scalability is the enablement of direct PS resources. An example target-delivery mix for a solution provider is represented in Figure 3-13. The delivery mix for the product provider is shown to contrast the resourcing mixes. As can be seen, the solution-provider sourcing strategy is weighted toward using internal resources (shown on the right side of the graph). In today's globalized services marketplace, solution providers should explore a combination of centralized solution centers, corporate practices and local employees to deliver a majority of all the PS activities that must occur to make the customer successful. Local or global partners should be used sparingly to provide commodity technical skills. Product providers, as we will explore in the next chapter, will look to external resources to deliver a majority of the PS requirements the customer may have.

Solution providers are always looking for ways to leverage hard-to-find technical skills. The solution provider should be more aggressive, with centralized solution centers providing technical skills to multiple geographies. By leveraging centralized resource pools, the solution provider can alleviate some of the hiring requirements that are local to the customer. We will discuss resourcing strategies in more detail in Chapter 10: Sourcing Services.

Figure 3-13  Resourcing Mix for all PS Activities

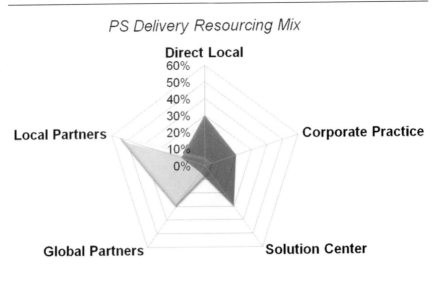

## ORGANIZATIONAL STRUCTURE OF THE SOLUTION PROVIDER

After reviewing the nine services-strategy variables and how we would expect them to be set for a solution provider, it would be worthwhile to spend a little time on organizational structure. For every embedded PS organization, four fundamental organizational design decisions must be optimized:

1. Where does global leadership for PS report?

2. Where does local, or geographic-specific, PS leadership report?

3. Who makes decisions on local PS hiring?

4. Where does the overlay PS sales organization report?

AFMSI, SSPA, and TPSA have conducted organizational structure surveys. At this point in time, it is difficult to state what the optimal organizational structure should be for a high-performing solution provider. However, we know that in a solution-provider profile, professional services must take the lead in the sales cycle. With this reality in mind, professional services must be an integral part of the sales organization. In fact, no separation may exist between professional services and sales as can exist in other services strategies. The solution provider should consider an organizational design where professional services and sales are part of one reporting chain as shown in Figure 3-14. Solution providers need to aggressively share technical resources across geographic boundaries. This means the dominate sales structure may not be geographic as it is in product-centric companies but may be industry or practice or solution oriented. In other words, go-to-market resources are organized around a specific offering not a specific geography. In this model the following parameters apply:

- Global PS leadership reports to the head of all global services, or a CXO executive.

- Local geographic PS management report hard line to global PS management and dotted line to local country management. Companies do this to drive consistency and scalability around the PS business.

- Local PS managers make the final decision on what PS staff are hired within the country. The PS managers have ultimate responsibility for the profit and loss of their region. Professional services has its own profit and loss.

This organizational structure offers more opportunities for sharing of practices and centralizing resources across geographies. However, it requires the product company to break the tight profit-and-loss ownership often held by the regional executives in a more product-centric organizational structure.

Figure 3-14  PS Organizational Structure in a Solution Provider

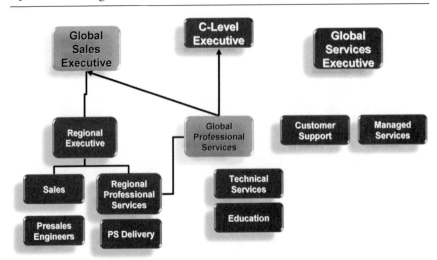

## THE ECONOMIC ENGINE OF THE SOLUTION PROVIDER

At this point, we have reviewed the solution-provider services strategy in detail. But how does this profile play out regarding company economics? Once again, companies with this profile are working to drive either emerging products or service-intensive products into the marketplace. Solution providers are all about delivering a complete business solution to the customer. The ramification is that solution providers have a significant amount of revenue coming from professional services. As presented at the beginning of the chapter, Figure 3-15 reminds us of the typical revenue mix for a solution provider.

Despite the significant reliance on PS revenues, product revenues are critical to overall health of the solution provider. They are an emerging revenue stream that represent the future of company success. Maintenance revenues are nascent because a substantial product install base is not yet in place. For the solution provider, the ignition gear of the engine is professional services and its consultative capabilities to deliver a unique solution to the customer.

### Example Solution Providers

So what product companies execute a solution-provider services strategy? This strategy is very common among emerging software companies. However, finding example companies with public data to reference is challenging. Most solution providers are still privately held companies, working to increase the product install base so they can eventually go public. Their revenue mix

Figure 3-15  Economic Engine of the Solution Provider

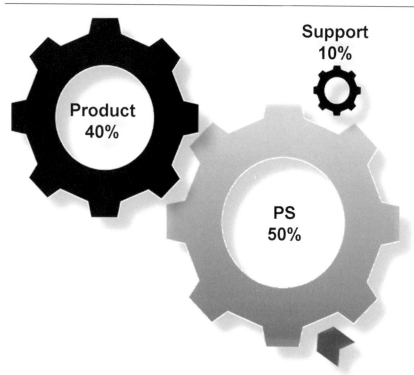

data cannot be referenced in this format. Despite this handicap in the public dataset, some examples can be referenced. Table 3-3 provides a snapshot of the revenue mix for three companies that have executed a solution-provider services strategy. This table references public data available from the companies and compares product revenues to all services revenues. Very few product companies break out the individual revenue streams for support services and PS revenues.

We start the list of example companies with a bit of an anomaly: a multi-billion dollar solution provider. Amdocs is a provider of software and services for communication service providers. They focus on primarily Tier 1 and Tier 2 communications companies, including leading wireline and wireless telecommunications, broadband, cable, and satellite service providers. They develop, implement, and manage software and services associated with the business support systems (BSS) and operational support systems (OSS). Their 2007 annual report makes it clear that Amdocs believes a solution services-strategy profile is required to meet the needs of the maturing and competitive marketplace of telecommunications:

Table 3-3  Example Solution Providers

| Company Name | Data Source | Total Annual Revenue | Net Income % | % Revenue from Products | % Revenue from ALL Services |
|---|---|---|---|---|---|
| Amdocs | 20-F, Dec. 3, 2007 | $2.8B | 12.9% | 6% | 94% |
| Blue Martini | 10-K, Dec. 31, 2004 | $28M | -43% | 26% | 74% |
| Compuware | 10-K, March 31, 2008 | $1.2B | 11% | 24% | 76% |

> *As many communications companies strive to become more customer oriented, they are concentrating efforts and internal resources on servicing their customers and expanding their services offerings. In order to implement efficient, flexible, cost-effective information systems on a timely basis, many providers are looking to buy customer experience systems from external vendors, rather than developing new systems with their own internal resources. We believe this creates significant opportunities for vendors of information technology software products and providers of managed services, such as Amdocs.*

In the 2007 annual report, Amdocs highlights the following aspects of its solution portfolio:

- Software Products.

- Consulting Services. Amdocs' consulting services include customization, implementation, integration, maintenance, ongoing support, and managed services.

- Solutions Combining Products, Services and Partner Technologies.

- Deep Industry Expertise and Highly Skilled Personnel.

Amdocs seems to be convinced the way for them to win with their product portfolio is to wrap it with a comprehensive services portfolio that secures customer intimacy.

Blue Martini provided software designed to help companies increase revenues, or optimize sales, by proactively guiding sales people, partners, and customers through sales interactions. In the last year of the company's existence, 41 percent of the revenues came from professional services. Clearly, the software they implemented required intense involvement from professional services. In many ways, Blue Martini is the poster child for a badly executed solution-provider profile. They also represent the reason many software companies avoid this profile—Blue Martini was not profitable. The company was unable to grow the product gear to a higher percentage of total company revenues.

Compuware provides software products, professional services, and application services that improve the performance of information technology (IT) organizations. Originally founded in 1973 as a PS company, the company began to offer mainframe productivity tools for fault diagnosis, file and data management, and application debugging in the late 1970s. Thirty-seven percent of Compuware's revenue is still attributed to professional services. Like many solution providers, the company started as a consulting company and migrated into a product portfolio.

## UNIQUE CHALLENGES AND KEY METRICS

Companies who desire to execute a solution-provider services strategy should be aware of the unique challenges that will present themselves within the PS business.

### Scaling PS Capabilities

Because solution providers are delivering technologies that require intensive PS capabilities, the ability to scale qualified delivery staff becomes a gating item to overall company growth. The PS organization in a solution provider must be extremely effective in hiring and training new staff.

### Productizing the Solution

A majority of solution providers have the desire to increase product revenues and reduce the need to have large, human-capital-intensive PS organizations. To achieve this reality, the PS organization must focus on capturing attributes of customer solutions and codifying them into the product. This behavior of productizing knowledge is not second nature to consultants. The PS organization will have to emphasize processes that assure this translation occurs. Otherwise, every customer engagement will remain consultative, custom, and PS intensive. That is the desired model for consulting firms like Accenture, but that is not the desired model for a product company trying to expand product revenues.

## *Satisfying the Investors*

The solution-provider profile is an appropriate approach for any product company that has an emerging technology or solution. The PS capabilities help accelerate early customer and market success. However, venture capitalist firms often frown on business models that are services intensive. Venture capitalists are focused on product development and product sales. After all, high products sales are what enable start-ups to go public. These investors may push back on the money required to staff required PS capabilities. This poor guidance needs to be countered with analysis that shows the impact of professional services on product success—which leads to the next section on measuring success.

## *Measuring Success*

With these common friction points in mind, companies executing this services-strategy profile should consider a set of success metrics that map to the strategic objectives of the PS function. Specifically, solution providers should gravitate to the following metrics when evaluating the success of professional services:

> **New Installs**: How many new product installations has the PS organization enabled?

> **Reference Rate**: How many customers where professional services has been involved have become solid references for the product?

> **Project Profitability**: Are PS project margins acceptable to the company? In this profile, professional services is a large portion of the company revenue stream. If project margins are weak or negative, the consequence could be the failure of the company.

## SUMMARY

The concept of the services-strategy profile provides a mechanism for executive teams to frame the overarching role and objectives of the PS organization. When a company is considering the adoption of a solution-provider services-strategy profile, the following points should be considered:

1. **Professional Services Drives Greater Product Sales**: A product company considering this profile should be facing the reality that the product cannot successfully be sold without the involvement of consultative capabilities.

2.  **Revenue Mix Implications**: A solution provider accepts the fact a large portion of revenues will be secured through PS engagements. Is this mix acceptable to executives and investors?

3.  **Skills Implications**: To successfully execute a solution-provider profile, a product company needs the right skills in service management in place. Otherwise, the PS gear could sink the company.

Now, you may have read the details of this profile and concluded this is not the right services strategy to meet your business objectives. Perhaps your products do not require such a services-intensive approach. Or perhaps services partners can deliver on the services requirements of your customers. Not to worry. Three other successful services-strategy profiles have emerged within technology product companies that your company can pursue.

# Chapter 4

# The Product Provider

In Chapter 3, we introduced four services-strategy profiles that are common within product companies. In the last chapter, we explored the services-strategy profile for product companies that must deliver a high degree of professional services to enable their product. These solution providers often exist in emerging markets where technologies are not yet mature and customers are just beginning the adoption process. However, markets do migrate from emerging to high growth where customer volume increases dramatically. Large product markets are fertile ground for the next services-strategy profile we will explore: the product provider. Indeed, this is perhaps one of the most desired services-strategy profiles—desired by product executives that have little interest in building services capabilities. This chapter takes a deep dive into when the product-provider profile applies and how key services-strategy parameters are typically set for this profile.

## PRODUCT-PROVIDER LITMUS TESTS

**This services-strategy profile is well suited for companies with fast-growing product sales and a robust service partner environment—the desired end game for almost every product company.** However, as previously emphasized, the appropriate services-strategy profile is driven not just by management team desire but also by the maturity of the product set and the requirements of the marketplace being served. Understanding what services-strategy profile is truly the best fit for a company is a complex management dialogue and decision process. As introduced in the previous chapter, there are three tools that can be used to start that management dialogue.

### Some Simple Questions

Perhaps the management team answered the questions for the solution-provider litmus test and quickly determined this is not the services strategy the company wants to pursue. If that is the case, the team can individually

Table 4-1  Product-Provider Alignment Questions

| Question for the Management Team | YES | NO |
|---|---|---|
| 1. Are PS revenues less than 10% of total company revenues? | | |
| 2. Are PS revenues less than 25% of the total deal when professional services and products are sold together? | | |
| 3. Are product revenues growing faster than PS revenues? | | |
| 4. Does the PS organization in your company exist primarily to make sure product sales are successful? | | |
| 5. Do sales reps, with the support of sales management, often discount professional services to ensure a product sale? | | |
| 6. Does executive management become concerned if professional service revenues are growing faster than product revenues? | | |
| 7. Is professional services encouraged to send service opportunities to service partners? | | |
| 8. Is there a dedicated sales force selling professional services? | | |
| 9. Does our company prefer to defer prime responsibility for large integration projects to service partners? | | |
| 10. Are PS hiring decisions made by the regional manager that is responsible for the overall profitability of the region (products + services)? | | |
| 11. Is a product dollar worth much more than a PS dollar to our company? | | |
| 12. Does professional services spend a great deal of time with customers that are not in a buying cycle? | | |

answer the 12 questions outlined in Table 4-1 related to the role of professional services and company success. As mentioned in the previous chapter, for each services-strategy profile, we expect the strategy variables for the PS organization to be set a little differently. The strategy surrounding professional services provides significant insight into the overarching services strategy of the company.

If a majority of the management team comfortably answered 9 to 12 of these questions with a resounding "yes," then the company is most likely executing a product-provider services strategy. The information provided in this chapter will provide strong guidance regarding the optimization of that services strategy. If there was a large disparity in some of the answers from manager to manager, the team is not aligned around executing a product-provider strategy and this chapter should be used to better understand what it means to truly execute this profile.

## Guiding Principles of Professional Services

A second tactic management teams can use to determine how closely they are aligned regarding services-strategy profile is to review the guiding principles of the PS organization. The following guiding principles would be very appropriate for PS organizations within a product-provider strategy:

- Professional services accelerates and deepens adoption of new company products into target industries.

- Professional services enables customer referencability.

- Professional services owns the development of service methodologies for implementing company technology.

- Professional services owns the enablement of partners to deliver these service methodologies.

- The success of professional services will be evaluated by customer reference rate, customer loyalty, and total customer spending with the company.

One of the guiding principles notably missing from this list is PS project profitability. A product provider may engage PS capabilities in many projects that experience poor services margins but result in large product sales. If the management team cannot agree on the guiding principles of professional services, the services-strategy profile needs work. If the management team agreed upon guiding principles for professional services, but they look nothing like the ones listed above, the product-provider profile is most likely not the profile in play.

## Product Maturity

A third tactic management teams can use to determine how closely they are aligned regarding services-strategy profile is to discuss the maturity of the product portfolio. Using Geoffrey Moore's product-adoption life cycle once again, companies most suited to execute a product-provider services strategy profile have a majority of revenues coming from new product sales, and product sales are growing at a healthy clip. These economic dynamics allow the company to fund discounted PS services with product-margin dollars.

Figure 4-1  Product-Provider Strike Zone

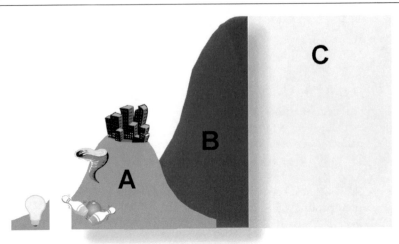

Figure 4-1 documents the natural strike zone during the product-adoption life cycle when a product-provider service strategy makes sense. Companies can execute the product-provider profile a little left or right of this strike zone, but it is hard to use this profile if the company product portfolio is extremely immature or extremely mature.

Perhaps the company is not a classic product provider after all. Perhaps the company was a product provider but markets have matured and customer expectations changed. The worst scenario is confusion within the management team regarding the services-strategy profile the company is attempting to execute. This framework should be used to provide clarity about where the management team is currently aligned or misaligned regarding key service strategy parameters and objectives.

## Special Cases

The litmus tests above are focused on the overarching, or aggregate, services-strategy profile of the company. We are trying to define what the role of professional services is in a majority of the go-to-market scenarios for company products. However, a product company may have a new product offering that requires intense PS involvement to drive adoption. In this case, the answers to some of the previous questions may be different:

- Professional services is much more than 25 percent of the total deal when this new product is sold.

- No partners exist yet who are enabled to deliver the required PS activities.

- PS revenues are actually growing faster than the product revenues for this offering.

These special cases will always exist. It does not mean the company is changing its aggregate services-strategy profile. **The clarifying question for the management team is simple: When this product matures, do we want to continue all of these PS activities, or do we want to enable partners and have professional services migrate back to its traditional product provider role? If the management team agrees the PS intensive role is temporary, the product-provider profile is still in play.**

## SERVICES-STRATEGY VARIABLE SETTINGS FOR THE PRODUCT PROVIDER

For each services strategy profile, we expect nine strategy variables related to the professional services business to be set a little differently. For example, the charter of a PS organization within a product provider is very different from the charter of PS within a solution provider. The same can be observed for financial targets and the services-partner strategy. This section overviews how product providers set these nine variables to maximize the impact of their PS business.

### *Charter, Business Model, and Financial Objectives*

The first service strategy variable that a management team needs to review is the charter of the PS business. Every business function has a set of primary reasons for existing. For product companies, four primary reasons exist for having an internal professional services organization:

**Service Revenues**: The product company is looking for additional sources of top-line revenue growth.

**Service Margins**: The product company is looking for higher margin revenue sources in order to offset shrinking product margins.

**Customer Satisfaction**: The product company views services as a vehicle to improve customer satisfaction and protect account relationships.

**Product Market Share**: The product company would like to use value-added services to expand product sales. Services are used to accelerate the adoption of new products or to carry existing products into new vertical markets.

Figure 4-2  PS Charter for Product Provider

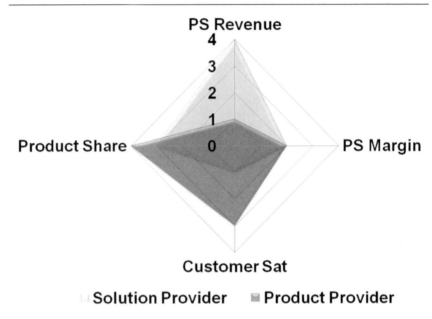

**Solution Provider**     **Product Provider**

**For product providers, the PS charter is weighted toward enabling product market share and improving customer satisfaction.** Ranking the four reasons PS exists, where 4 is the most important factor, and 1 is the least important factor, product providers will have a charter that is weighted as shown in Figure 4-2. The figure contrasts the PS charter for product providers to that of the solution providers documented in the previous chapter. As can be seen, the charter of PS is almost polar opposite for these two services strategies.

After setting the charter, the management team should review the target financial business model of the PS organization. Of course, the business model should be 100 percent aligned with the charter. The Technology Professional Services Organization (TPSA) benchmarks PS business models and segments that data by services-strategy profile to understand what differences exist between services-strategy profiles. Figure 4-3 shows the business model for product providers compared to industry averages for the PS businesses within hardware and software companies. The figure also shows the performance of PS Pacesetters. These are the top 25 percent of PS organizations, in terms of financial performance, that have benchmarked with TPSA.

As can be seen, product providers have a tendency to invest more in services engineering to develop service methodologies to drive product adoption through service partners. Product providers also have a tendency to exhibit

Figure 4-3 Product-Provider PS Business Model

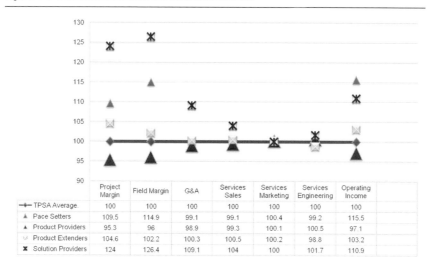

| | Project Margin | Field Margin | G&A | Services Sales | Services Marketing | Services Engineering | Operating Income |
|---|---|---|---|---|---|---|---|
| ◆ TPSA Average | 100 | 100 | 100 | 100 | 100 | 100 | 100 |
| ▲ Pace Setters | 109.5 | 114.9 | 99.1 | 99.1 | 100.4 | 99.2 | 115.5 |
| ▲ Product Providers | 95.3 | 96 | 98.9 | 99.3 | 100.1 | 100.5 | 97.1 |
| ◻ Product Extenders | 104.6 | 102.2 | 100.3 | 100.5 | 100.2 | 98.8 | 103.2 |
| ✖ Solution Providers | 124 | 126.4 | 109.1 | 104 | 100 | 101.7 | 110.9 |

lower net operating income for professional services compared to industry averages. **The key messages regarding the PS business model is that product providers are expected to invest in activities that enable service partners and keep large customers happy. These investments have financial consequences that manifest themselves in lower operating margins for the PS business.**

With the charter and target business model in place, the third strategy variable to review is financial objectives. What are the growth expectations for the PS business? For product providers, the expectation is that PS revenues never grow faster than the product revenues. PS revenues may even grow more slowly than product revenues if service partners are being enabled to deliver more of the services required by the product customers. Figure 4-4 maps an expected strike zone for PS growth within a product-provider service strategy.

At this point, the management team has reviewed the charter of the PS organization, the financial business model, and the growth objectives. Clear definition surrounding the financial expectations of the PS business is now available. But where, specifically, will PS revenues come from? That is the focus of the next three strategy variables.

## Target Markets, Offerings, and Sales Channels

With financial expectations set in the revenues pillar, the management team should now discuss where PS revenues will come from. This is the focus of the services pillar.

Figure 4-4  Target Growth Rate for PS in a Product Provider

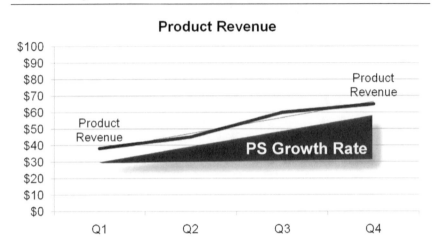

The first strategy variable in this pillar is target markets. What customers will the PS function serve? **For product providers, the market focus of professional services is two-fold: strategic install base customers and strategic prospective customers.**

Remember, professional services is a small gear in the product-provider profile. Resources are not infinite, so professional services must focus on a subset of accounts where ROI is high. As we know, it is much easier to sell upgrades to existing customers than to sell brand new technology to a customer that has never heard of you. How does the PS organization cover these four target markets? **Professional services in the product-provider profile plays a four-corner strategy. Professional services will focus on the edge of all four markets, driving product adoption in the most strategic opportunities.** However, product providers will focus PS capabilities on the most difficult customer engagements, where the supporting partner environment may not be in place. This means PS activities within a product provider will be weighted toward new customers attempting to adopt new company products. Figure 4-5 documents where product providers should prioritize direct PS engagement.

The second variable in the services pillar concerns target offerings. **For product providers, we expect the focus to be on implementation, light integration, and technology consulting. Intense customer integration projects will be pushed to system integrators as will extensive business domain consulting.** The contrast between the services offerings of solution providers and those of product providers is documented in Table 4-2.

Product providers will provide services that are applicable earlier in the customer-engagement life cycle, and then they will back off to allow service

Figure 4-5  Market Focus of PS in a Product Provider

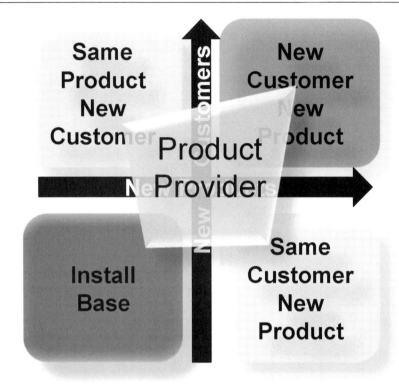

Table 4-2  Product-Provider Services Offerings

| Services Type | Tagline | Solution Provider | Product Provider |
|---|---|---|---|
| **Support Services** | *Paid to support your product* | ✓ | ✓ |
| **Education Services** | *Paid to teach about your product* | ✓ | ✓ |
| **Implementation Services** | *Paid for what you do with your product* | ✓ | ✓ |
| **Integration Services** | *Paid for what you do with other people's products* | ✓ | |
| **Technology Consulting** | *Paid for what you know about the technology.* | ✓ | ✓ |
| **Business Domain Consulting** | *Paid for what you know about the business impact of the technology* | ✓ | |
| **Managed Services** | *Paid to operate* | ✓ | |
| **Outsourcing Services** | *Paid to own* | | |
| **Third-Party Support** | *Paid to support other people's products* | | |

Figure 4-6  Product-Provider Direct Customer Engagement

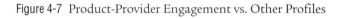

partners to execute the larger service activities. But keep in mind the product provider is never capturing a significant portion of the total service opportunity occurring around product sales. Figure 4-6 provides a logical view of where the product provider is engaging the customer with direct service offerings and what portion of the total service opportunity is being captured by the product provider vs. by services partners. Figure 4-7 provides the comparison in customer engagement between product providers and solution providers.

Figure 4-7  Product-Provider Engagement vs. Other Profiles

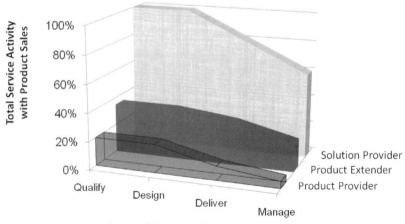

Figure 4-8  Product-Provider Service Sales Channels

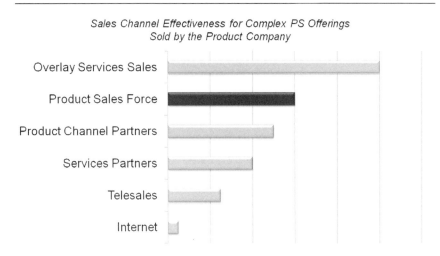

*Sales Channel Effectiveness for Complex PS Offerings*
*Sold by the Product Company*

The final variable in the services pillar concerns sales channels. How are PS offerings sold by a product provider? To sell their professional services, product companies can turn to several channels:

> **Product Sales Force**: The current sales force that is responsible for selling the product.
>
> **Overlay Service Sales Force**: Specialist hired to augment the product sales force and focus on selling the PS portfolio.
>
> **Product Channel Partners**: Partners that are selling the product could be offered incentives to sell the PS offerings of the company as well.
>
> **Service Partners**: System integrators could be encouraged to sell the PS capabilities of the product company as part of a large solution.

**For product providers, the preferred sales channel for direct PS engagements is the product sales force.** Since the company is not attempting to expand PS revenues, investing in enabling other sales channels makes little sense. The direct product sales force will be used to position direct PS capabilities in strategic account opportunities. Figure 4-8 documents this sales channel preference.

The target markets, target offerings, and preferred sales channels have now been reviewed for the PS business strategy. This provides a solid baseline for where the company expects PS service revenues to come from. But we have not discussed how product providers deliver their service portfolio.

## Core Skills, Partners, and Scalability

The final pillar of a mature services strategy concerns skills. How will the company source the skills required to execute the PS business? To frame this conversation, we use the PS hourglass model that defines seven key skills sets involved in managing a PS business within a product company:

1. **Product Account Reps**: The largest direct sales force employed by the product company.

2. **Service Sales Reps**: An overlay sales force specializing in selling the professional services portfolio.

3. **Practice Managers**: Senior managers responsible for the profit and loss management of the PS business.

4. **Solution Architects**: The senior technical consultants that are able to review customer business requirements and translate them into a recommended technology solution.

5. **Resource Managers**: The management layer responsible for sourcing sold PS engagements.

6. **Project Managers, Technical Architects**: Senior delivery resources required to deliver PS engagements.

7. **Technical Specialists**: Delivery resource required to deliver PS engagements.

For the product provider, the focus is on the solution architects and senior consultants that live in the middle of the PS hourglass. Figure 4-9 highlights the positions that are core to the product provider.

After understanding what skills are core to the execution of the PS strategy, a management team must consider how it will leverage partners. Product providers are expected to be extremely partner friendly. For product providers, service partners not only provide staff to augment service engagements booked by the product company, but these service partners are the primary vehicle for delivering the PS services required when products are sold. This leads to the final strategy variable of scalability and resourcing strategy.

Five natural pools of resources can be used to deliver a PS organization's service offerings:

1. **Direct Local Resources**: These are PS consultants employed directly by the product company and residing locally, close to customer engagement sites.

Figure 4-9  Core PS Skills for the Product Provider

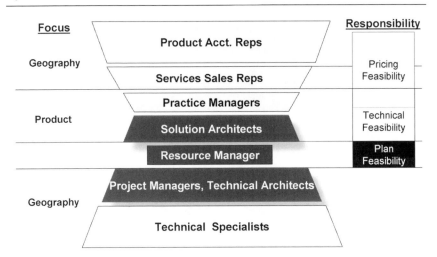

2.  **Corporate Practice Resources**: These are PS consultants that have hard-to-find, specialized skills. They are leveraged across multiple geographies.

3.  **Centralized Solution Center Resources**: These are delivery resources that can be leveraged to deliver portions of a PS engagement without being on the customer site. These resources are typically clustered where labor costs are lower.

4.  **Local Delivery Partners**: These are service-delivery partners that are identified and engaged by an individual country or specific region.

5.  **Global Delivery Partners**: These are service-delivery partners that are identified, selected, and enabled at a global level.

The management team must decide what combination of these direct and indirect resources will be employed to scale the delivery capabilities of professional services. **In the product-provider profile, the ultimate key to service scalability is partner enablement. The product provider wants to minimize the reliance on direct resources.** So, with product providers, a majority of all the PS activity required to integrate a company product will be delivered by the partner environment. This reality is reflected in the example target delivery mix for a product provider represented in Figure 4-10. This diagram reflects the fact that product providers will rely on external service partners to deliver a majority of the PS activity required to integrate company products.

Figure 4-10  Resource Mix for All PS Activity

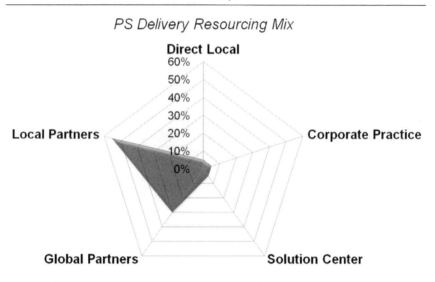

For the PS activity delivered directly, the product provider is always looking for ways to leverage hard-to-find technical skills by establishing both corporate practices and centralized solution centers. Figure 4-11 shows a recommended resource mix for the PS engagements delivered directly by the product provider. Table 4-3 provides the data for Figures 4-10 and 4-11.

Figure 4-11  Resource Mix for PS Engagements Delivered Directly

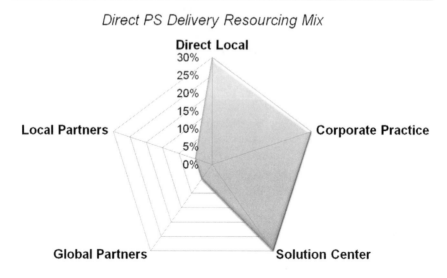

Table 4-3  Target Resourcing Mixes for the Product Provider

|  | % TOTAL PS Revenues Delivered by Resource Pool | % DIRECT PS Revenue Delivered by Resource Pool |
|---|---|---|
| **Direct Local** | 5% | 30% |
| **Corporate Practice** | 5% | 30% |
| **Solution Center** | 5% | 30% |
| **Global Partners** | 30% | 5% |
| **Local Partners** | 55% | 5% |
|  | 100% | 100% |

## ORGANIZATIONAL STRUCTURE OF THE PRODUCT PROVIDER

After reviewing the nine service strategy variables and how we would expect them to be set for a product provider, it would be worthwhile to spend a little time on organizational structure. For every embedded PS organization, four fundamental organizational design decisions must be optimized:

1. Where does global leadership PS report?

2. Where does local, or geographic-specific, PS leadership report?

3. Who makes decisions on local PS hiring?

4. Where does the overlay PS sales organization report?

TPSA has conducted organizational structure surveys. From these surveys, we can observe the common organizational structure for product providers and why these structures exist:

- Global PS leadership report to the head of global sales, the head of all global services, or a CXO executive. It is not recommended for PS management to report to the head of customer support, but that does occasionally occur.

- Local geographic PS management report hard line to the local country manager and dotted line to global PS management. Companies do this to maintain tight alignment within countries. Product-centric companies have a tendency to be geo-centric in their management structure and power base. It is difficult for the relatively small PS organization to buck this reality.

- Country managers make the final decision on what PS staff are hired within the country. The country managers have ultimate responsibility for the profit and loss of their region. Professional services is a shadow profit and loss statement against these geo-centric profit and loss statements.

- There is no PS-specific sales organization in play.

Putting this all together, professional services in a product provider is often structured as shown in Figure 4-12. We know that this organizational structure has limitations in scaling PS capabilities and supporting PS-intensive product offerings on a consistent, global basis. However, for product providers, these limitations are worth the benefits of keeping a closed loop between country managers and PS staff.

## THE ECONOMIC ENGINE OF THE PRODUCT PROVIDER

At this point, we have reviewed the product-provider service strategy in detail. But how does this profile play out regarding company economics? Once again, companies with the product-provider profile are focused on getting as much product into the market as they possibly can. Organizations inside these companies race frantically to rapidly scale product sales. The time it takes to bring a product-to-market is a critical success factor. **Product providers are all about speed: Speed of the product. Speed to market. Speed to the next release. This intense focus on product sales is justified due to the**

Figure 4-12  PS Organizational Structure in a Product Provider

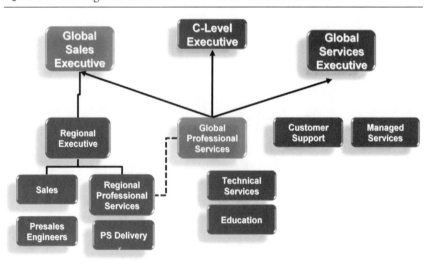

Figure 4-13  Economic Engine of the Product Provider

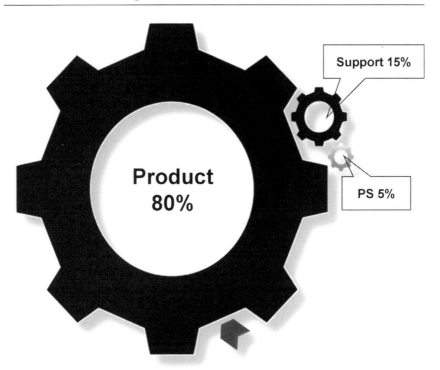

**immense portion of company revenues attributed to product sales.** The ramification is that product providers have very little total company revenue coming from professional services: anywhere from 1 to 10 percent. Figure 4-13 documents the typical revenue mix for a product provider.

As can be seen in the product-provider profile, the largest gear in the economic engine is always product. Product revenues will typically represent over 60 to 80 percent of total company revenues with the remaining revenue streams composed of mostly support services and a sprinkling of PS activity. The product is also the economic gear that typically is used to start the conversation with the customer, as indicated by the red arrow in the above graph. The product provider leads with the feature functionality of the product offerings and is typically selling to a product specialist in the customer organization.

## Example Product Providers

So what product companies execute a product-provider service strategy? This strategy is very common among companies that are selling hardware that is

Table 4-4  Example Product Providers

| Company Name | Data Source | Total Annual Revenues | Net Income % | % Revenue from Products | % Revenue from ALL Services |
|---|---|---|---|---|---|
| Apple | 10-K, Sept. 9, 2007 | $24B | 14.6% | >94% | <6% |
| Autodesk | 10-K, March 28, 2008 | $2.1B | 16% | 75% | 25% |
| Cisco | 10-K, Sept. 18, 2007 | $34.9B | 20.9% | 84.4% | 15.6% |
| HP | 10-K, Dec. 18, 2007 | $104B | 7% | 84% | 16% |
| salesforce.com | 10-K, Feb. 29, 2008 | $.749B | 2.4% | 91% | 8% |
| Sun Microsystems | 10-K, Sept. 27, 1999 | $11.7B | 13.7% | 86.1% | 13.9% |

flying off of the shelves. However, some software companies have adopted and maintained this strategy profile. Table 4-4 provides a snapshot of the revenue mix for six companies that have executed a product-provider services strategy. This table references public data available from the company and compares product revenues to all service revenues. Very few product companies break out the individual revenue streams for support services and PS revenues. However, it is a safe assumption that a majority of the service revenue being experienced by these companies in these snapshots is related to support services, not project-based professional services.

Apple is a well-documented company in the world of consumer technology with a minor footprint in enterprise technology. In the 2007 annual report, Apple lumps all service revenues with software sales so it impossible to determine exactly how much revenue Apple obtains from support and professional services. However, it is clear PS activities are minimal for the company. Growth in 2007 service revenues were attributed to an increase in the sales of customer care packages.

Autodesk is a company that provides autocad software used in designing products from cars to the bridges they cross. Service revenues from maintenance represent 25 percent of total company revenues. All other service revenues were lumped in with license sales. The report stated the sales of services, training, and support included in "License and other" are immaterial for all periods presented.

Cisco is the industry-dominant provider of networking gear for both enterprise and consumer customers. Cisco does not segment the amount of revenue coming from maintenance vs. from project-based professional services. However, with total service revenues less than 16 percent of total company revenues, it is clear professional services are not a large gear in the Cisco economic engine.

Hewlett Packard is a $100 billion technology behemoth that provides everything from PCs to high-end services. Categorizing HP as a product provider strikes many in the industry as odd. After all, HP offers outsourcing and extensive integration services. HP is managing a multi-billion dollar service business. Also, the company bought out systems integrator EDS in 2008. These points are true, yet we must pull back the lens and ascertain where HP makes its money. It is clear that a majority of HP's top-line revenue and bottom-line profits come from servers and storage and printers—not outsourcing or integration projects. This economic reality makes the product-provider profile much more applicable to HP's overall services strategy than any other profile we will document. Of course, HP has PS-intensive product offerings within its vast product portfolio. The reality that a company the size of HP must juggle several services-strategy profiles under the covers is a concept we will explore later in the book. Yet, to reiterate, HP has historically been a hard-core product provider.

Salesforce.com shook the software industry in 1999 by offering on-demand software that was centrally hosted and did not require on-site implementation. What is interesting is that software-as-a-service (SAS) companies like salesforce. com often assume a product-provider service strategy. Salesforce.com does not have a maintenance revenue stream; that is included in the product subscription revenues. The 8 percent in service revenues is entirely attributed to PS and education activities. With the subscription model, the goal is to keep customization and integration to a minimum. The good news is this approach makes it much easier for customers to turn on the platform within their business. The bad news for SAS providers is it makes it much easier for customers to turn off the platform as well. As the software-as-a-service model matures, I predict there will be more emphasis on providing professional services that drive adoption and consumption of the platform. These new service activities will increase the percentage of revenue coming from professional services and may move companies like salesforce.com out of the product-provider profile.

Finally, we end this list of company examples with a snapshot of Sun Microsystems from 1999. With less than 14 percent of total company revenues coming from all service activities, it is pretty clear Sun was a hard-core product provider in 1999. However, companies do change their revenue mixes and hence their services-strategy profiles. In 2007, services represented 37 percent of total company revenues. Professional and education services have blossomed to 8 percent of total company revenues. Chapter 8: Bridging the Services Chasm will discuss this challenge of managing services strategy through shifting revenue mixes.

## UNIQUE CHALLENGES AND KEY METRICS

Companies who desire to execute a product-provider services strategy should be well aware of the unique challenges that will present themselves within the PS business:

### Keeping Partners Enabled

As defined in the previous section, product providers are counting on a robust environment of services partners to deliver the bulk of PS activities surrounding product sales. For this strategy to become a reality, services partners must be enabled. That enablement comes through developing service-delivery methodologies partners can execute and training those partners on those delivery methodologies. Professional services must fund and resource these critical partner enablement activities.

### Supporting PS-Intensive Product Offerings

Product providers do not have immense embedded PS capabilities. However, as mentioned earlier in this chapter, product companies can launch new technologies that require intense PS engagement to drive initial adoption. And with new product launches, the service partner environment is rarely fully enabled to support customer needs. When this perfect storm occurs, the embedded PS organization will be called upon to help support early product adoption directly. This may require additional resources of both corporate and local delivery staff.

### Keeping PS Costs Contained

The product provider must be ever diligent that PS expenses are not exceeding sales benefits. If the sales force becomes accustomed to having free, unbilled technical resources available for both presales and postsales, management staff must track how much unbilled PS activity is occurring per region, per account type, and ideally, per sales rep, and possibly even per engagement or delivery manager. By quantifying this cost, management can avoid the pitfall of ballooning PS expenses that are not associated with any customer revenue. Every product provider, regardless of how lucrative product sales are, has a limit to the amount of unbilled PS activity that can occur before overall company profits are impacted.

## Measuring Success

With these common friction points in mind, companies executing this services-strategy profile should consider a set of success metrics that map to the strategic objectives of the PS function. Specifically, product providers should gravitate to the following metrics when evaluating the success of PS:

**Customer Satisfaction**: Since professional services exists to drive product adoption and customer success, product providers will often attempt to quantify the impact of direct PS involvement on customer satisfaction with the company. This correlation analysis has had mixed success in the industry.

**Product Renewal**: Instead of focusing on the impact of professional services on customer satisfaction, product providers analyze the impact of professional services on long-term product renewal behaviors. This analysis is by no means common in the industry, but there are examples of companies that have completed this analysis.

**Solution Maturity**: To sell and deliver a technology PS engagement, tangible artifacts can support the effort (e.g., reference solution architectures and sample project plans). The concept of measuring solution maturity involves itemizing these artifacts and determining which artifacts are available for each solution in the PS solution portfolio. For example, if you believe there are 10 artifacts that can support a PS solution and you have 10 core service offerings, 100 artifacts would have to be documented to achieve 100 percent solution maturity.

**Size of Enabled Partner Environment**: For the product provider, the size and quality of the partner environment is actually more important than the size of the internal PS organization. Tracking the number of service partners enabled and the quality of those service partners is a metric that often no one tracks. Yet, the ultimate success of the PS organization for a product provider could be solely judged by the ability for PS to teach service partners to implement and integrate company products.

**Economic Impact Analysis**: TPSA is developing a framework with member companies to help analyze the total economic impact PS activities have on company success. The technology industry, historically, has been very immature at assessing how professional services influences product renewal rates, product adoption, and total account spending. This is beginning to change. Conducting basic economic impact analysis can be a significant tactic in communicating the value of professional services, even when PS revenues are small and margins are mediocre.

## SUMMARY

The concept of the services-strategy profile provides a mechanism for executive teams to frame the overarching role and objectives of the professional service organization. When a company is considering the adoption of a product-provider service strategy profile, the following points should be considered:

1.  **Cost Implications**: Can the company afford a product-provider profile? If PS revenues have exceeded 15 percent of total company revenues, this profile may no longer be economically viable.

2.  **Cost Containment**: With this profile in play, management teams must make sure mechanisms are in place to track the amount of PS activity that is discounted or given away for free. No product company has infinite dollars to apply to free service activities.

3.  **The Right Metrics**: With PS revenues and PS profitability a lower order concern for product providers, the executive management team and PS management team must define a set of nontraditional PS metrics that can be used to measure the impact and success of the PS organization on overall company success.

We have now two services-strategy profiles under our belt. The contrast between these two profiles could not be more dramatic. But these are not the only two options on the table for product companies. There are two more common services strategies we have yet to explore. The next one should be very interesting to any product companies that find their core product markets maturing.

# Chapter 5

# The Product Extender

Many product-centric companies are motivated to assume the product provider services-strategy profile outlined in the previous chapter. However, decreasing product revenues and increasing service revenues force traditionally product-centric companies to revisit their services-strategy profile. The product-provider profile is not well suited to product companies that are not generating a majority of their revenues from new product sales. As a case in point, let's examine Oracle Corporation, a $17B plus software behemoth of Silicon Valley. Figure 5-1 documents Oracle's license sales from 1999 to 2007. As can be seen, a dramatic pause occurred in new license sales after 2001, but the company seems to have rebounded nicely.

However, Oracle conducted significant acquisitions from 2003 through 2007 as documented in Table 5-1.

If we remap Oracle's license revenues and subtract the $1.3 billion of license revenue Oracle gained through acquisition, the ending picture looks very

Figure 5-1 Oracle License Revenues

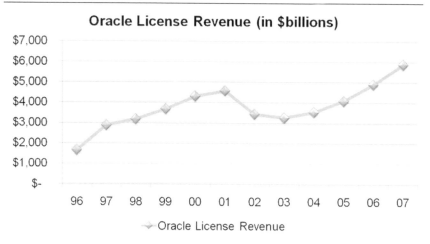

97

Table 5-1  Oracle Acquisitions

| Company | Acquisition Announced | Last Reported Annual License Revenues (millions$) | Source |
|---|---|---|---|
| Peoplesoft | Dec. 2004 | $538,400 | 2003 10-K |
| Seibel | Sept. 2005 | $487,127 | 2004 10-K |
| Hyperion | March 2007 | $295,117 | 2007 10-K |
| | **TOTAL LICENSE** | **$1,320,644** | |

different as shown in Figure 5-2. From 1996 to 2000, Oracle license revenues had a compounded annual growth rate (CAGR) of 27 percent. However, from 2001 to 2007, even with acquisitions, the CAGR was only 8 percent. Doing the very rough calculation of subtracting license revenues acquired, the CAGR on license growth from 2001 to 2007 was basically zero.

Regardless of the exact breakdown of organic vs. acquired license growth, it is clear overall license growth has slowed for Oracle. When product companies face a maturing marketplace for their core product offerings, they must reexamine the role of service revenue streams. Many companies delay this conversation and remain in denial. They believe robust product growth is just one new product release away. As we stated in the overview of services-strategy profiles, the appropriate services-strategy profile is driven not just by management team desire but also by the maturity of the product set and the requirements of the marketplace being served. Management teams serve the best interest of customers, employees, and investors by aligning the appropriate services

Figure 5-2  Oracle License Revenues

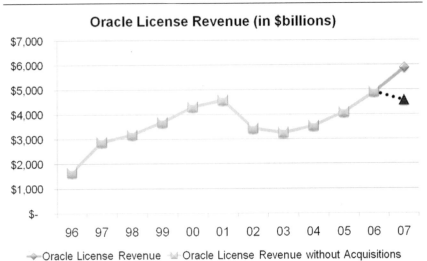

**Oracle License Revenue (in $billions)**

strategy to the realities of the marketplace. What follows are the same tools we used with the solution-provider and product-provider profiles to help management teams discuss what services-strategy profile makes the most sense for their company.

## PRODUCT-EXTENDER LITMUS TESTS

**This services-strategy profile is well suited for companies with a significant install base that is receptive to new, value-added services offerings.** This profile is extremely common for mature software companies that have successfully penetrated their target market and now have a natural opportunity need to keep these existing customers committed to the platform. Oracle and its main competitor SAP are classic examples of very successful product extenders. Mature hardware companies may not fit this profile, only because they have not identified or pursued a services portfolio that helps secure ongoing commitment to their hardware platform.

### Some Simple Questions

Perhaps your company once was a classic product provider as outlined in the previous chapter, with product sales rapidly rising. However, as you review the past few years, you see evidence your core market is maturing and, although product sales continue to grow, they are not growing anywhere near the rate they were growing. Once again, the strategy for the PS organization serves as the canary in the coal mine. Is it time to consider a product-extender services strategy? As a starting point for the management dialogue regarding this decision, the team can individually answer the twelve questions outlined in Table 5-2.

If a majority of the management team comfortably answered 9 to 12 of these questions with a resounding "yes," then the company is most likely already executing a product-extender services strategy. The information provided in this chapter should provide guidance regarding the optimization of that services strategy. If a large disparity exists in some of the answers from manager to manager, the team is not aligned around executing a product-extender strategy and this chapter should be used to better understand what it means to truly execute this profile.

### Guiding Principles of Professional Services

A second tactic management teams can use to determine how closely they are aligned regarding services-strategy profile is to review the guiding principles of

Table 5-2 Product-Extender Alignment Questions

| Question for the Management Team | YES | NO |
|---|---|---|
| 1. Are PS revenues more than 15% of total company revenues? | | |
| 2. Are PS revenues more than 25% of the total deal when professional services and product are sold together? | | |
| 3. Are PS revenues growing faster than product revenues? | | |
| 4. Have you decided the company cannot afford to give professional services away for free? | | |
| 5. Have you put policies in place to restrict the discounting of professional services? | | |
| 6. Is executive management concerned about the profitability of professional services? | | |
| 7. Is professional services encouraged to capture more of the service opportunity surrounding the sale of your products? | | |
| 8. Is there a dedicated sales force selling professional services or have your product sales reps been given quota targets for professional services? | | |
| 9. Is professional services increasingly taking prime responsibility for large integration projects involving service partners? | | |
| 10. Are local PS hiring decisions coordinated on a global basis to maximize the profitability of the global PS organization? | | |
| 11. Is a product dollar worth more than a PS dollar to your company? | | |
| 12. Is professional services spending more time with install base customers—not just customers that are in a buying cycle? | | |

the PS organization. The following guiding principles would be very appropriate for PS organizations within a product-extender strategy:

- Professional services accelerates and deepens adoption of company products in both new and existing customers.

- Professional services develops and offers services that secure product renewal with existing customers.

- Professional services develops and offers services that are profitable for the company.

- Professional services enables account expansion by delivering valuable, fee-based services to existing customers.

- Professional services owns the development of service methodologies for implementing company technology.

- The success of professional services will be evaluated by customer renewal rate, total customer spending with the company, and the profitability of PS engagements.

If the management team cannot agree on the guiding principles of professional services, the services-strategy profile needs work. Product companies often have established guiding principles of the PS organization that are aligned with a product-provider profile, even though the economics of the company now require a product-extender approach. One way this misalignment presents itself is disagreement on what guiding principles make sense for the PS organization.

## Product Maturity

A third tactic management teams can use to determine how closely they are aligned regarding services-strategy profile is to discuss the maturity of the product portfolio. Companies most suited to execute a product-extender service strategy profile have successfully taken their product to "main street," where a significant install base now exists. Product sales may still be growing, but at a much slower pace than in previous years. These economic dynamics force the company to rethink the role of professional services in securing additional revenue streams and truly contributing to the overall profitability of the company. Figure 5-3 shows the natural strike zone during the product-adoption life cycle when a product-extender services strategy makes sense. Companies can execute the product-extender profile a little left or right of this strike zone.

Figure 5-3  Product-Extender Strike Zone

In general, the worst scenario is confusion within the management team regarding the services-strategy profile the company is attempting to execute. Perhaps the company wishes it was a classic product provider with fast-growing product sales (section B on Figure 5-3). Perhaps the company was a product provider but markets matured and customer expectations changed. This framework should be used to help align the management team to current market realities and current customer expectations regarding service capabilities.

### Special Cases

All of the discussion to date regarding services-strategy profile has been focused on the overarching, or aggregate, services-strategy profile of the company. We are trying to define the role of professional services in a majority of the go-to-market scenarios for company products. However, a product company may have a hot product offering that requires less PS involvement to drive adoption, or conversely a new, complex product that requires heavy customization and integration work. In this case, the answers to some of the questions above may be different:

- Professional services is much less than 25 percent of the total deal when this new product is sold.

- Many partners are enabled to deliver the required PS activities.

- Product revenues are still growing very fast for this product.

These special cases will always exist. It does not mean the company is changing its aggregate services-strategy profile. **The clarifying question for the management team is simple: When this hot product matures, do we want to assume more service responsibilities? If the management team agrees services will become more involved by design as the product matures, the product-extender profile is still in play.**

## SERVICES-STRATEGY VARIABLE SETTINGS FOR THE PRODUCT EXTENDER

As introduced in the previous chapters, for each services-strategy profile, we expect the variables of the PS strategy to be set a little differently. For example, the charter of a PS organization within a product extender is very different from the charter of PS within a systems provider. The same can be observed for financial targets and the services-partner strategy. This section overviews how product extenders should set nine critical service-strategy variables to maximize the impact of the PS businesses.

Figure 5-4  PS Charter for Product Extender

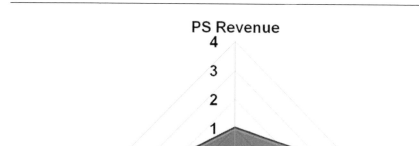

## Charter, Business Model, and Financial Objectives

For product extenders, the PS charter shifts toward securing continued customer satisfaction and executing the PS portfolio profitability. Compared to the product-provider profile, there is a shift from giving professional services away simply to drive product share. The product extender has the market share, now they need to maintain it profitably. Ranking the four reasons professional services exists, where 4 is the most important factor and 1 is the least important factor, product extenders will have a charter that is weighted as shown in Figure 5-4. Figure 5-5 compares the charter of PS within the product provider to the charter of PS for the product extender.

After setting the charter, the management team should review the target financial business model of the PS organization. Of course, the business model should be 100 percent aligned with the charter. TPSA benchmarks PS business models and actually segments that data by services-strategy profile to understand what differences exist between service-strategy profiles. Table 5-3 shows the business model for product extenders compared to industry averages for the PS businesses within hardware and software companies. The table also shows the performance of PS Pacesetters. These are the top 25 percent PS organizations, in terms of financial performance, that have benchmarked with TPSA.

Figure 5-5  Product Extender vs. Product Provider

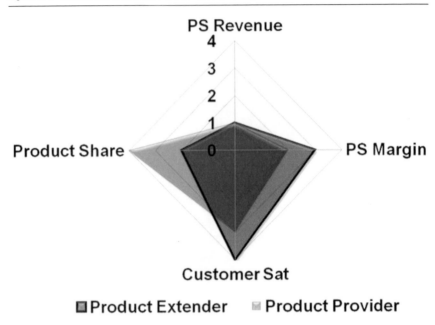

Table 5-3  Product-Extender Business Model

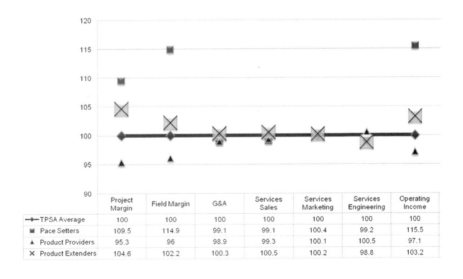

| | Project Margin | Field Margin | G&A | Services Sales | Services Marketing | Services Engineering | Operating Income |
|---|---|---|---|---|---|---|---|
| TPSA Average | 100 | 100 | 100 | 100 | 100 | 100 | 100 |
| Pace Setters | 109.5 | 114.9 | 99.1 | 99.1 | 100.4 | 99.2 | 115.5 |
| Product Providers | 95.3 | 96 | 98.9 | 99.3 | 100.1 | 100.5 | 97.1 |
| Product Extenders | 104.6 | 102.2 | 100.3 | 100.5 | 100.2 | 98.8 | 103.2 |

As can be seen, product extenders are driving better project margins than the overall benchmark average and much better project margins than product providers. Product extenders also have a tendency to invest less in services marketing. They are extending their services presence into the install base, so perhaps fewer marketing activities or promotion for the sake of awareness need to occur. It is also interesting to observe that the product extenders seem to spend much more on nonbillable field management than the highest performing PS organizations. High nonbillable field costs are usually a symptom of a geo-centric management approach where there is little synergy between each geography, and each geography is performing redundant tasks to support their local PS business. Product extenders often have an opportunity to centralize various aspects of their PS business to drive global efficiencies. A stove-piped approach to managing each region is a legacy of a product-centric approach to services.

With the charter and target business model in place, the third strategy variable to review is financial objectives. What are the growth expectations for the PS business? For product extenders, the expectation is that PS will grow at least as fast as product revenues because product revenues are not growing substantially. If customers desire the services, product extenders may grow professional services faster than product revenues. Figure 5-6 maps an expected strike zone for PS growth within a product-extender services strategy.

At this point, the management team has reviewed the charter of the PS organization, the financial business model, and the growth objectives. Clear definitions surrounding the financial expectations of the PS business now exist. But

Figure 5-6  Target Growth Rate for PS in a Product Extender

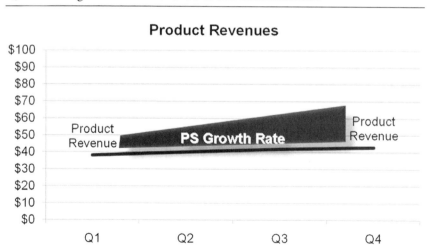

where, specifically, will PS revenues come from? That is the focus of the next three strategy variables.

## Target Markets, Offerings, and Sales Channels

What customers will the PS function focus on first? **For product extenders, all install-base customers and strategic prospective customers are in play. However, professional services will spend a majority of its time serving the existing install base.** PS in the product-extender profile will play a critical role in securing new customers and accelerating the adoption of new products. But most importantly, PS will focus on services that drive the install base to renew and upgrade. Two simple metrics that can be used to assess is the effectiveness of PS in this profile are *renewal rates* and *release adoption*. Are existing customers renewing their commitment to the product platform? Are existing customers upgrading to the latest release of your product? If the answers are yes, PS is being leveraged correctly in this profile. A common frustration of software companies is that customers are not implementing the latest release of the product. Soon, portions of the install base find themselves multiple releases behind. This is a symptom of a company stuck with a product provider PS strategy (PS secures the new deals) when a product-extender approach (PS drives adoption in the install base) would drive larger returns. Figure 5-7 documents where product extenders direct PS engagement. Figure 5-8 compares the market focus of product extenders to product providers.

The second variable in the services pillar concerns target offerings. **For product extenders, the focus is on implementation, integration, and technology consulting. In addition, the product extender will take on various custom integration projects within the install base. Finally, the product extender should enhance the service portfolio to include business domain consulting offerings designed to increase product usage among long-term customers.**

Although, the product extender is not attempting to become a full-blown system integrator, it will provide services that are applicable throughout the customer engagement life cycle. The product extender is capturing more of the total service opportunity than a product provider will. **Yet a natural limit exists to how much service opportunity should be captured. If the product extender begins capturing more than 25 to 40 percent of the total service opportunity generated by all product sales, service partners may begin feeling the product company is too competitive.** To be clear, for some customer types considered strategic by the company, the product extender may attempt to capture 80 to 100 percent of the services required when the product is sold. However, the product extender is not attempting to achieve this capture rate for all customers that buy the product. Otherwise, PS would

Figure 5-7  Market Focus of PS in a Product Extender

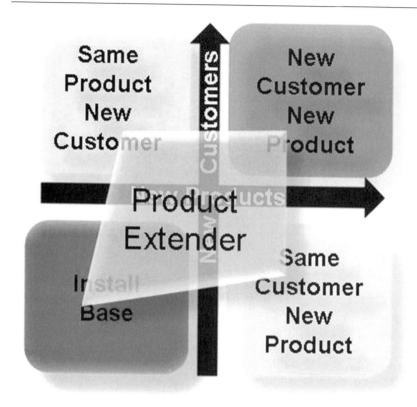

Figure 5-8  Product Extender vs. Product Provider

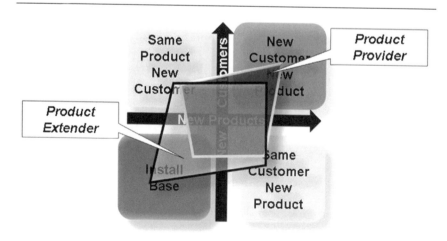

Figure 5-9  Product-Extender Direct Customer Engagement

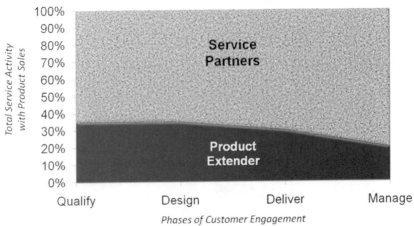

become a much larger percentage of total company revenues and this is not a driving objective in this services strategy. Figure 5-9 provides a logical view of where the product extender is engaging the customer with direct-service offerings and what portion of the total service opportunity (for all product sales) is being captured by the product extender vs. service partners. Figure 5-10 contrasts product extenders to product providers regarding the total portion of service opportunity captured.

Figure 5-10  Product-Extender vs. Product-Provider Service Capture

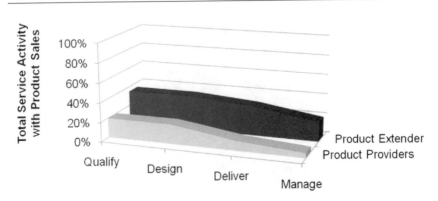

The final variable in the services pillar concerns sales channels. How are PS offerings sold by a product provider? To sell their professional services, product companies can turn to several channels.

**For product extenders, the preferred sales channel for direct professional service engagements is a combination of the product sales force, specialized service sales reps, and telesales.** Because professional services plays a larger role in the economic engine of the company, the company cannot afford for PS resources to be underutilized or PS deals to be poorly scoped. The overlay services sales force works closely with product sales to drive PS activities. **The presence of an overlay sales force dedicated to selling services is especially critical if a product company is migrating from a product provider to a product-extender profile.** A transaction-driven product sales force will not naturally be adept at selling intangible services. This point has been proven again and again by the failed attempts of long-time product providers to unsuccessfully attempt to force new services offerings through their product-centric sales force. Always a train wreck in the long term and never a success in the short term. If and when the product sales force becomes competent at selling professional services, the overlay services sales force may no longer be required. Telesales resources are used to sell standard service packages designed to drive product renewal into the install base. Figure 5-11 documents these sales channel preferences.

Figure 5-11  Product-Extender Services Sales Channels

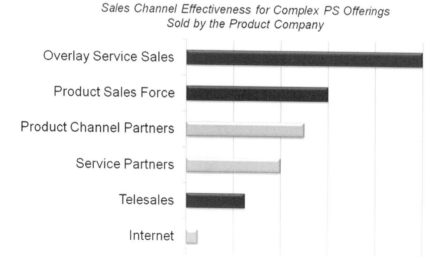

The target markets, target offerings, and preferred sales channels have now been reviewed for the PS business strategy. This provides a solid baseline for where the company expects PS service revenues to come from. But we have not discussed how product extenders deliver their service portfolio.

## Core Skills, Partners, and Scalability

The final pillar of a mature services strategy concerns skills. How will the company source the skills required to execute the PS business?

**For the product extender, the focus is on the solution architects and senior consultants that live in the middle of the PS hourglass and the demand generation resources required at the top of the hourglass.** The product extender, like the product provider, will have a delivery force that is still weighted toward senior architects and consultants. There are just more of them. There is also an increased emphasis on project or program management. Some product extenders like to refer to these specialized resources as providing "expert services" around the core product. This title helps differentiate from the more generic implementation and integration work performed by services partners. More junior roles may be subcontracted. Figure 5-12 highlights the positions that are core to the product extender.

After understanding what skills are core to the execution of the PS strategy, a management team must consider how it will leverage partners. Product

Figure 5-12  Core PS Skills for the Product Extender

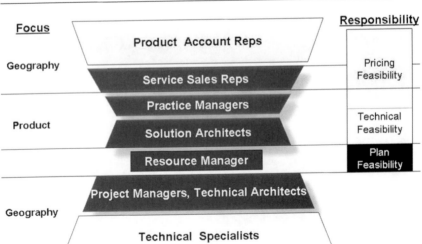

extenders must establish clear lines of demarcation between where they want to provide services and where service partners will be engaged. For product extenders, service partners not only provide staff to augment service engagements booked by the product company, but these service partners continue to be the primary vehicle for delivering the PS services required when products are sold. This leads to the final strategy variable of scalability and resourcing strategy.

**In the product-extender profile, like the product-provider profile, the ultimate key to service scalability is partner enablement. The product extender needs to keep PS resources utilized, but also needs a healthy partner ecosystem.** Yes, the product extender is providing more services directly, but a majority of all the PS activity required to integrate a company product will be delivered by the partner ecosystem. An example target delivery mix for a product extender is represented in Figure 5-13. The delivery mix for the product provider is shown to demonstrate the subtle shift in the resourcing mix. As can be seen, the product extender is pushing more of the total service opportunity toward direct delivery, but there is no total land grab in mind.

For the PS activity delivered directly, the product extender, like the product provider, is always looking for ways to leverage hard-to-find technical skills.

Figure 5-13  Resource Mix for all PS Activity

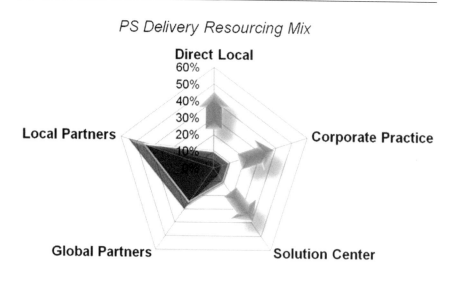

The product extender should be aggressive with centralized solution centers providing technical skills to multiple geographies. Also, global delivery partnerships should be negotiated and leveraged to provide qualified subcontracting resources. Local delivery partners favored by local account teams will be the most threatened as the product extender establishes a more efficient and scalable resourcing models. Figure 5-14 shows a logical resource mix for the PS engagements delivered directly by the product extender.

## ORGANIZATIONAL STRUCTURE OF THE PRODUCT EXTENDER

Now, for the organizational structure of PS within the product extender. For every embedded PS organization, four fundamental organizational design decisions must be optimized:

1. Where does global leadership PS report?

2. Where does local, or geographic-specific, PS leadership report?

3. Who makes decisions on local PS hiring?

4. Where does the overlay PS sales organization report?

Figure 5-14  Resourcing Mix for PS Engagements Delivered Directly

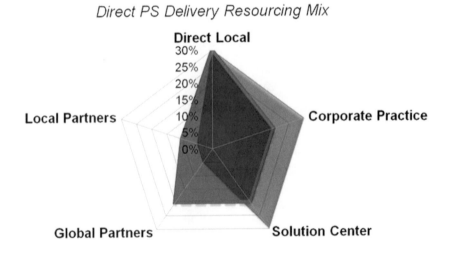

From the organizational structure surveys conducted by TPSA to date, it is difficult to state what the optimal organizational structure should be for a high-performing product extender. In fact, product extenders seem to successfully adopt two fundamentally different organizational structures.

## MODEL 1: Sales-Centric

In this first model, the following organizational parameters are put in place:

- Global PS leadership reports to the head of global sales.

- Local geographic PS management reports hard line to the local country manager and dotted line to global PS management. Companies do this to maintain tight alignment within countries.

- There is a PS-specific sales organization in play. It can report hard line to PS management or hard line to sales management.

Putting this all together, the sales-centric model is often structured as shown in Figure 5-15. We know that this organizational structure has limitations in scaling PS capabilities and supporting PS-intensive product offerings on a consistent, global basis. However, for some product extenders, these limitations are worth the benefits of keeping a closed economic loop between country managers and PS staff.

Figure 5-15  PS in a Product Extender, Sales-Centric Model

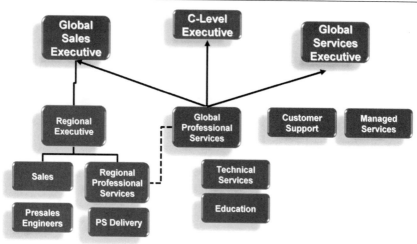

## MODEL 2: Service-Centric

In the second model, PS reporting is extracted from the field organization, and the following organizational attributes are put in place:

- Global PS leadership reports to the head of all global services, or a CXO executive.

- Local geographic PS management reports hard line to global PS management and dotted line to local country management. Companies do this to drive consistency and scalability around the PS business.

- Local PS managers make the final decision on what PS staff are hired within the country. The PS managers have ultimate responsibility for the profit and loss of their region. PS has its own profit and loss.

- There is a PS-specific sales organization in play. It can report hard line to PS management or hard line to sales management.

For the second model, PS in a product extender is often structured as shown in Figure 5-16. This organizational structure offers more opportunities for sharing of practices and centralized resources across geographies. However, it requires the product company to break the tight profit and loss ownership held by the regional executives.

Figure 5-16  PS in a Product Extender, Services-Centric

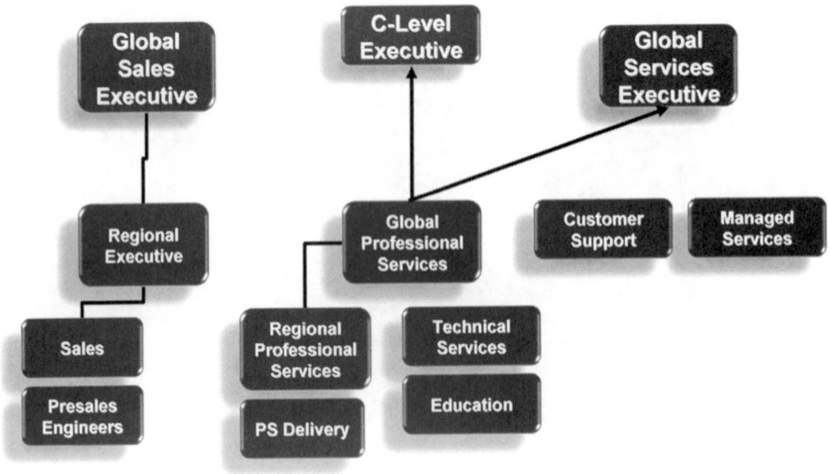

# THE ECONOMIC ENGINE OF THE PRODUCT EXTENDER

At this point, we have reviewed the product-extender services strategy in detail. But how does this profile play out regarding company economics? Once again, companies with the product-extender profile are hoping to extend their service capabilities into the install base to secure the customer stays on the product platform. Product extenders are all about maintaining a dominant market position. The ramification is that product extenders have more revenue coming from both professional services and traditional support services. Figure 5-17 documents the typical revenue mix for a product extender.

As can be seen, in the product-extender profile, the largest gear in the economic engine is most likely going to be support revenues. Product revenues are critical to overall health of the economic engine, but they will represent only a third to half of total company revenues. The product remains the economic gear that typically is used to start the conversation with the customer, as indicated by the chevron arrow in the above graph. The product extender leads new product sales with the feature functionality of the product offerings but maintains the install base with the service gears.

Figure 5-17  Economic Engine of the Product Extender

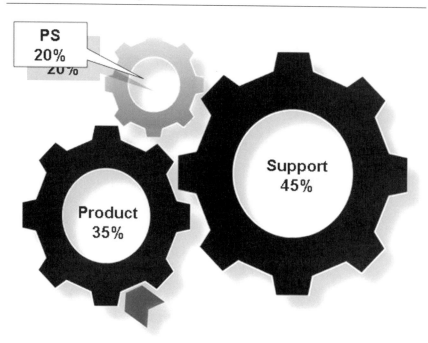

## EXAMPLE PRODUCT EXTENDERS

So what product companies execute a product-extender services strategy?
This strategy is very common among successful software companies. However, some hardware companies have adopted and maintained this strategy
profile. Table 5-4 provides a snapshot of the revenue mix for five companies
that have executed a product-extender services strategy. This table references
public data available from the company and compares product revenues to all
service revenues. Very few product companies break out the individual revenue
streams for support services and PS revenues. However, it is a safe assumption
that a majority of the service revenue being experienced by these companies in
these snapshots is related to support services, not project-based professional
services.

BEA is a software provider that has been acquired by the software company
Oracle Systems. It is important to note that many of the software companies
that have been acquired for the past several years are hard-core product extenders. For software companies such as PeopleSoft and Mercury Interactive, new
license revenues became less than half of total company revenues. These product extenders, like BEA, became attractive acquisition targets for the annuity
support service revenue streams they represent—not new license sales.

Table 5-4  Example Product Extenders

| Company Name | Data Source | Total Annual Revenues | Net Income % | % Revenue from Products | % Revenue from ALL Services |
|---|---|---|---|---|---|
| BEA | 10-K, March 28, 2008 | $1.5B | 13.6% | 36% | 64% |
| IKON | 10-K November 29, 2007 | $3.6B | 20.9% | 46% | 54% |
| Oracle | 10-K June 29, 2007 | $17.9B | 24% | 33% | 67% |
| SAP | 20-F April 2, 2008 | $14.9B | 19% | 33% | 67% |
| Sun Microsystems | 10-K August 29, 2007 | $13.9B | 3.4% | 62% | 38% |

IKON Office Supplies was not a traditional product company but a value-added reseller (VAR) of products made by other companies. However, VARs can assume different services-strategy profiles based on corporate strategy and market needs. IKON, before being acquired by Ricoh in 2008, reported 20 percent of its revenues were coming from professional and managed services, and was clearly a product extender. These value-add services made IKON attractive to Ricoh as an acquisition target.

Oracle, as highlighted at the beginning of this chapter, has experienced slowing license sales over the years. This maturation the enterprise software industry has made both Oracle and its global competitor SAP classic product extenders.

Finally, we end this list of company examples with a more recent snapshot of Sun Microsystems from 2007. When we profiled product providers, we showed Sun's revenues in 1999 when product revenues were 86 percent of total company revenues. Over time, product revenues have slowed and service revenues have expanded. Based on 2007 10-K report, professional services still represents a little less than 10 percent of total company revenues, so Sun is really an emerging product extender. However, the march from product to service revenues is clear. And the pain this transition can incur is evident in Sun's decrease in net income from over 13 percent in 1999 to 3.4 percent in 2007.

## UNIQUE CHALLENGES AND KEY METRICS

Companies who desire to execute a product-extender services strategy should be well aware of the unique challenges that will present themselves within the professional service business.

### Soothing Partners

Product extenders need a robust services-partner ecosystem to help support all the service requirements surrounding the product portfolio of the company. However, as the product extender expands some of its service capabilities, service partners naturally become pensive. Product extenders must create clear rules of engagement for service partners to avoid channel conflict. We will discuss this challenge of partner conflict in more detail in Chapter 11: Services Partner Strategy.

### Enabling Partners

Closely related to the issue of working with partners is a process of enabling these service partners. Product providers have a good relationship with service partners. Product extenders have a strained relationship. Despite this tension, professional services should continue to own the enablement of these critical service partners. It is a mistake for PS to remove itself from this role.

### From Free to Fee

Product providers have a tendency to give professional services away to secure product sales. Product extenders can no longer afford this luxury. Yet many product extenders were once product providers, and old habits die hard. Product extenders must establish sales processes that minimize the discounting of PS capabilities.

### Measuring Success

With these common friction points in mind, companies executing this services strategy profile should consider a set of success metrics that map to the strategic objectives of the PS function. Specifically, product extenders should gravitate to the following metrics when evaluating the success of PS:

> **Product Renewal**: Product extenders should analyze the impact of PS on long-term product renewal behaviors. This analysis is by no means common in the industry, but examples exist of companies that have completed this analysis.

> **Total Account Revenue**: Is PS involvement increasing the total amount of money the customer spends with the company?

> **Project Profitability**: Are PS project margins acceptable to the company? Or, is PS still engaging in low-margin, discounted projects that will drain profits from the company as PS activities expand?

> **Field Margin**: Is the PS organization finding economies of scale across geographies so that nonbillable activities within each regional are kept at a minimal level. This drive for global efficiency will be a new endeavor if the company is moving off of a product-provider profile.

## CLOSING THOUGHTS

Product companies do not start their lives as product extenders, they evolve into this profile. Evolution within companies is painful. Successful evolution requires different processes and skills. When a company is considering the adoption of a product-extender services strategy profile, the following points should be considered:

1. **Profile Alignment**: Using the strategy settings outlined in this chapter, a management team can determine if this is indeed the services-strategy profile that best aligns with overall company objectives and market maturity.

2. **Cost Implications**: Can the company afford a product-extender profile if PS does not achieve certain profitability targets? Product extenders increase the amount of services they intend to deliver to customers. Is the company still giving away too much PS to afford a product-extender profile?

3. **Skills Implications**: To successfully execute a product-extender profile, a product company needs the right skills in service management in place. Otherwise, the PS gear becomes a financial sink hole for the company.

4. **The Right Metrics**: PS profitability has to become a larger concern for product extenders. In addition, PS must become more adept at modeling the impact of PS engagement on total company and customer account success.

Three services strategy profiles defined; one to go. The last profile is pursued by those product companies that blur the line between what it means to be a product vs. a services company.

# Chapter 6

# The Systems Provider

There comes a point in the life cycle of some product companies when it is fair to ask the following question:

*Is this company a product company or a services company?*

Since 2004, TPSA has been tracking the largest technology-services providers on the globe. Every quarter, without fail, IBM tops our list based on total services revenues. Table 6-1 documents technology services revenues for the fourth quarter of calendar 2008. As shown, IBM dominates with over $14 billion in quarterly revenues from services—twice the services revenues achieved by Accenture, one of the largest global pure services companies in existence. Sixty percent of IBM's total company revenues came from services during this particular quarter. So, is IBM a product company or a services company?

To be honest, I would argue IBM is first and foremost a product company. Despite all the revenue coming from services, IBM continues to use hardware and software innovation to anchor their economic engine. As I write this

Table 6-1  Technology Services Revenues, Fourth Quarter Calendar 2008

| Rank by Services Revenue | Company | Services Revenue | Services % of Revenue |
| --- | --- | --- | --- |
| 1 | IBM | $14,764 | 60% |
| 2 | HP | $ 9,678 | 29% |
| 3 | Fujitsu | $ 6,970 | 52% |
| 4 | Accenture | $ 6,019 | 100% |
| 5 | CSC | $ 4,239 | 100% |
| 6 | Oracle | $ 3,981 | 71% |
| 7 | Capgemini | $ 2,727 | 100% |
| 8 | Hitachi | $ 2,718 | 9% |
| 9 | SAP | $ 2,490 | 70% |
| 10 | Xerox | $ 2,126 | 51% |

chapter, IBM has begun a new marketing campaign focused on the tagline of creating "a smarter planet." Visiting the IBM website, we see that IBM's vision of smarter water management is based on *"advances in technology—sophisticated sensor networks, smart meters, deep computing and analytics."* Smarter public safety is based on *"sophisticated analytics and search capabilities to make connections across multiple databases."* And smarter health care is based on digitizing patient health care records. The company leads with technology innovation. However, they follow with a heavy dose of complex services that help companies realize the business value of the technology. This is the hallmark of a systems provider, and this is the final services strategy we will be profiling.

## SYSTEMS PROVIDER LITMUS TESTS

**This services-strategy profile is pursued by companies that are willing to provide a blend of hardware, software, and services to solve complex business problems.** This profile is uncommon for product companies because of the intense commitment to services that is required. IBM pursued this profile only when the only other alternative appeared to be bankruptcy. Xerox, another systems provider, also faced potential extinction before pursuing this profile. The same is true for Unisys. Hardware companies are more likely to drift into this profile than are software companies. But to be sure, no product company should pursue this profile unless it is convinced service-revenue streams have become mission critical to the survival of the company.

### Some Simple Questions

Perhaps your company once was a classic product provider or a product extender as outlined in the previous chapters. However, your core product market has either evaporated or commoditized. For IBM it was both—the evaporation of the closed mainframe market and the commoditization of the PC market. For Xerox, it was the commoditization of copiers. To survive, your company must radically restructure the economic engine. Services may no longer be nice to have, but a must-have for survival. Is it time to consider a systems provider services strategy? As a starting point for the management dialogue regarding this decision, the team can individually answer the seven questions outlined in Table 6-2.

If a majority of the management team comfortably answered five or six of these questions with a resounding "yes," then the company is most likely already executing a systems provider services strategy. The information provided in this chapter should provide guidance regarding the optimization of that services strategy. If a large disparity showed in some of the answers from manager to manager, the team is not aligned around executing a systems-

Table 6-2 Systems-Provider Alignment Questions

| Question for the Management Team | YES | NO |
|---|---|---|
| 1. Are PS revenues more than 20% of total company revenues? | | |
| 2. Are PS revenues more than 40% of the total deal when professional services and product are sold together? | | |
| 3. Are professional services and managed services revenues growing faster than product revenues? | | |
| 4. Do you believe services revenues are the most likely source of revenue growth for the company? | | |
| 5. Do you feel the company should offer more services that take a greater responsibility for the customer's environment? | | |
| 6. Is executive management just as concerned about the profitability of services as they are about products? | | |
| 7. Do you believe your company is now required to offer hardware, software, and services to successfully deliver the value proposition to the customer? | | |

provider strategy, and this chapter should be used to better understand what it means to truly execute this profile.

## Guiding Principles of PS

A second tactic management teams can use to determine how closely they are aligned regarding services-strategy profile is to review the guiding principles of the PS organization. The following guiding principles would be very appropriate for PS organizations with a systems provider strategy:

- Professional services accelerates and deepens adoption of company products *and services* in both new and existing customers.

- Professional services develops and offers services that secure *account* renewal with existing customers.

- Professional services develops and offers services that are profitable for the company.

- Professional services enables account expansion by delivering valuable, fee-based services to existing customers.

- Professional services will capture and deliver as much of the services opportunity within a customer account as possible.

- The success of PS will be evaluated by customer renewal rate, total customer spending with the company, and the profitability of PS engagements.

If the management team cannot agree on the guiding principles of PS, the services-strategy profile needs work. The above guiding principles for a PS organization are atypical for most product companies. They represent a sea change in the role of PS. The systems provider is not looking for services partners—the systems provider desires to be the primary services provider for the customer. Discussing these guiding principles can test the willingness of a management team to truly embrace a systems-provider profile.

### Product Maturity

A third tactic management teams can use to determine how closely they are aligned regarding services-strategy profile is to discuss the maturity of the product portfolio. Companies most suited to execute a systems-provider services-strategy profile have successfully taken their product to "main street" but now face a commoditizing market. This pressure is almost a requirement for a product company to be willing to consider the complexity of this profile. Today, IBM has many products in various stages of maturity. However, when the decisions were made to become aggressive in the services area, product revenues were under immense pressure. Figure 6-1 shows the natural strike zone during the product-adoption life cycle when a systems-provider services strategy is considered. Companies can execute the systems-provider profile a little left of this strike zone. Attempting to pursue this profile too late can result in company bankruptcy or being acquired. SGI and Sun Microsystems, providers of high-end UNIX servers, prove classic examples of this error.

As always, confusion within the management team regarding the services-strategy profile the company is attempting to execute is problematic. For companies flirting with this services strategy, confusion can be catastrophic. This

Figure 6-1  Systems-Provider Strike Zone

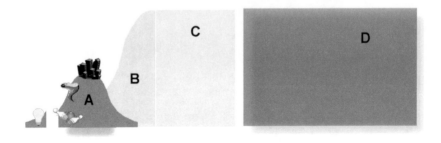

framework should be used to help align the management team to determine if this is truly the right profile to pursue.

## No Special Cases

The services-strategy profile framework is used to define the role of services in a majority of the go-to-market scenarios for company products. In previous chapters, we discussed how a product company may be pursuing one services-strategy profile while, on special occasions, it wraps a different services strategy around specific products. For example, product providers may temporarily act like solution providers for emerging product lines until they are established. Systems providers may have some legacy products that do not require intense services. However, when a product company crosses the line and becomes a systems provider, all the service options are on the table for all the product offerings. The goal is to maximize services opportunities. In a sense, potential confusion is less. Product providers temporarily acting as solution providers for specific product lines is a tricky act and may confuse both customers and partners. The systems provider never has to sweat this type of services-strategy schizophrenia.

## SERVICES-STRATEGY VARIABLE SETTINGS FOR THE SYSTEMS PROVIDER

As introduced in the previous chapters, for each services-strategy profile, we expect the variables of the professional services strategy to be set a little differently. For example, the charter of a PS organization within a systems provider is very different from the charter of PS within a product extender. The same can be observed for financial targets and the services partner strategy. This section overviews how systems providers set nine critical services-strategy variables to maximize the impact of the PS businesses.

### Charter, Business Model, and Financial Objectives

For systems providers, the PS charter shifts toward maximizing services revenues and profits. Compared to the product-extender profile, there is a shift from leveraging PS to secure product renewal to pursuing PS opportunities—period. The systems provider wants to leverage existing product market share to create new service opportunities. Ranking the four reasons PS exists, where 4 is the most important factor and 1 is the least important factor, systems providers will have a charter that is weighted as shown in Figure 6-2. Figure 6-3 compares the charter of PS within the product extender to the charter of PS for the systems provider.

Figure 6-2  PS Charter for Systems Provider

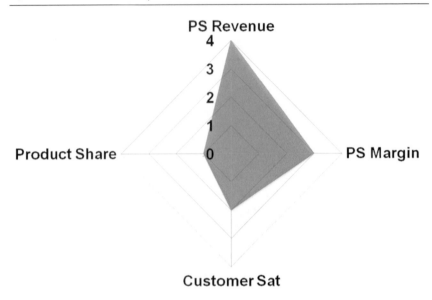

Figure 6-3  Systems Provider vs. Product Extender

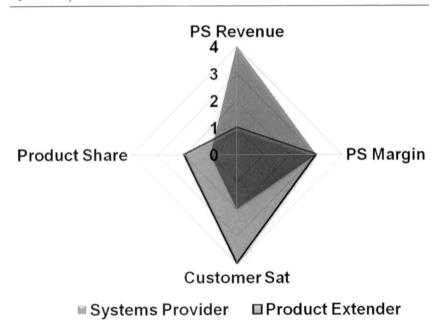

After setting the charter, the management team should review the target financial business model of the PS organization. Of course, the business model should be 100 percent aligned with the charter. TPSA benchmarks PS business models and actually segments that data by services-strategy profile to understand what differences exist between services-strategy profiles. Unfortunately, the systems-provider profile does not occur commonly in the industry. For this reason, we do not have enough data points to outline a typical business model for systems providers. However, for the systems providers we have benchmarked, we know they do not operate PS as a cost center with a break-even or negative-operating income.

With the charter and target business model in place, the third strategy variable to review is financial objectives. What are the growth expectations for the PS business? For systems providers, the expectation is that PS will grow at least as fast as product revenues because product revenues are not growing substantially. However, systems providers are actually aggressively pursuing incremental service opportunities. This means professional services may grow faster than product revenues. Figure 6-4 maps an expected strike zone for PS growth within a systems-provider service strategy.

At this point, the management team has reviewed the charter of the PS organization, the financial business model, and the growth objectives. A clear definition surrounding the financial expectations of the PS business now exists. Now we focus on where the services-aggressive systems provider will search for new services revenues.

Figure 6-4  Target Growth Rate for PS in a Systems Provider

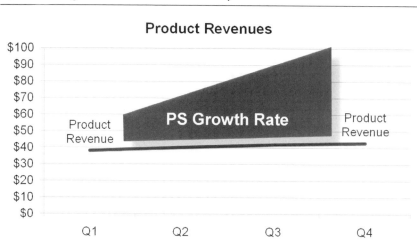

*Target Markets, Offerings, and Sales Channels*

On which customers will the PS function focus first? **For systems providers, all product-install base customers and strategic prospective customers are in play. In addition, PS will spend a significant amount of its time searching for new services customers.** These are customers that may not currently have any company products installed. They may not even be product prospects at this point in time. However, they have a services need the systems provider can satisfy. This divergence from the product-install base and product prospect list is unique to the systems provider. Figure 6-5 documents the aggressive nature of PS within the systems providers. Figure 6-6 compares the market focus of systems providers to that of product extenders.

The second variable in the services pillar concerns target offerings. **Systems providers will create services for the entire customer life cycle. The systems provider will start with business and technology consulting and end with managed and outsourcing services.**

Figure 6-5  Market Focus of PS in a Systems Provider

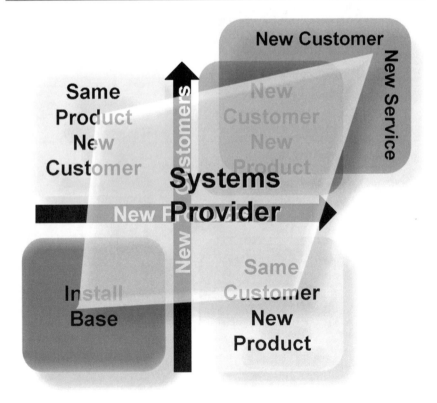

Figure 6-6  Systems Provider vs. Product Extender

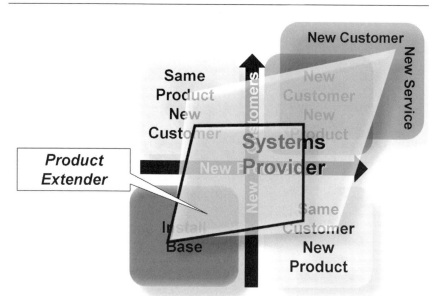

The systems provider is indeed attempting to become the primary services provider for the customer and will attempt to capture a maximum percentage of the total service opportunity. The systems provider may even take responsibility for products and services it does not provide directly, but resells or subcontracts. This willingness to take responsibility for the products and services of others is another unique attribute of this services strategy. Figure 6-7 provides a logical view of where the systems provider is engaging the customer with direct service offerings and what portion of the total service opportunity is being captured by the systems provider compared to the service partner. Figure 6-8 contrasts systems providers with product extenders and product providers regarding the total portion of service opportunity captured. As shown, systems providers are offering services that increase their account presence in the latter stages of the customer life cycle. Systems providers are very interested in being heavily involved in the ongoing management of the overall IT environment. This is polar opposite of the desires of product providers and even solution providers.

And finally, how will a product company executing this profile get its services offerings to market? **For systems providers, the preferred sales channel for direct PS engagements is a specialized services sales force**. Because advanced service offerings play a critical role in the economic engine of the company, the company must assure the services are positioned early in the

Figure 6-7 Systems-Provider Direct Customer Engagement

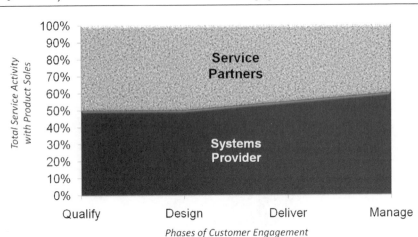

sales cycle and scoped profitably. The overlay services sales force works closely with named account managers assigned to the task of overall account coordination. **The presence of an overlay services sales force dedicated to selling services is especially critical if a product company is migrating from a**

Figure 6-8 Systems Provider vs. Product Providers and Product Extenders Service Capture

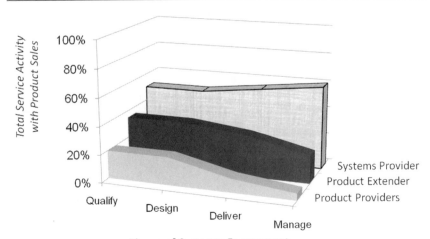

Figure 6-9  Systems Provider Services Sales Channels

product-extender to a systems-provider profile. A transaction-driven product sales force will not naturally be adept at selling intangible services. Figure
6-9 documents the sales channel used to drive the complex services portfolio
of the systems provider.

Preferences for the target markets, target offerings, and preferred sales channels of a systems provider have been reviewed. This defines where the services
revenues will come from (everywhere). Now, how does the systems provider
deliver on this aggressive services strategy?

## Core Skills, Partners, and Scalability

The final pillar of a mature services strategy concerns skills. How will the company source the skills required to execute the professional services business?

For the systems provider, the focus is on everything but the commodity skills sets of the PS hourglass. Services sales representatives, solution
architects, project managers, and senior consultants are all critical resources
to the systems provider. Systems providers, depending on the cost structures,
may even develop large pools of technical and analyst skills located toward
the lower half of the hourglass. Only specialized, niche technical skills or low-
margin technical skills are subcontracted. Figure 6-10 highlights the positions
that are core to the systems provider.

Figure 6-10  Core PS Skills for the Systems Provider

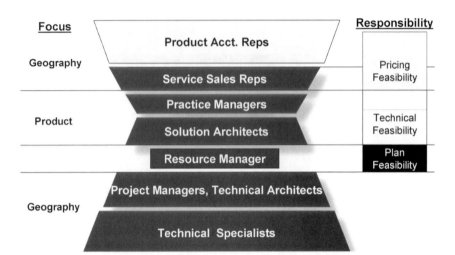

After understanding what skills are core to the execution of the PS strategy, a management team must consider how it will leverage partners. Systems providers are clearly not as partner friendly as are product providers or product extenders. **The systems provider will only leverage partners to provide niche or commoditized technical skills.** Niche technical skills may be required to support the implementation of a third-party product. If demand is not large and global for this product, it makes no sense for the systems provider to ramp up delivery resources directly. The example target delivery mix for a systems provider is represented in Figure 6-11. The delivery mix for the product extender is shown to demonstrate the shift in the resourcing mix. As can be seen, the systems provider is aggressively grabbing more of the total service opportunity.

The tactic of leveraging resources across geographic boundaries can be challenging for systems providers. Why? The geographic regions of a systems provider will aggressively hire services delivery resources to meet services growth objectives. Once those geographic capabilities are in place, it can be challenging to convince geographies to share resources or leverage centralized resources. Despite this cultural challenge, the systems provider should be aggressive with centralized solution centers providing technical skills to multiple geographies.

Figure 6-11  Resource Mix for all PS Activity

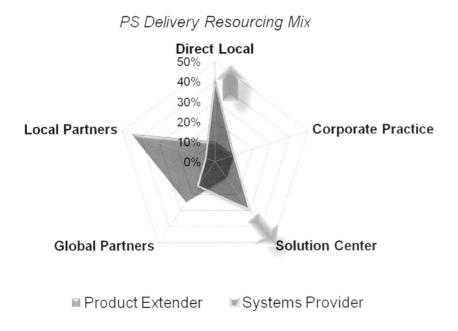

## ORGANIZATIONAL STRUCTURE OF THE SYSTEMS PROVIDER

In discussing the three previous services-strategy profiles, we identified four fundamental organizational design decisions that are considered in the effort to optimize the structure of the PS organization:

1. Where does global leadership for PS report?

2. Where does local, or geographic-specific, PS leadership report?

3. Who makes decisions on local PS hiring?

4. Where does the overlay PS sales organization report?

Systems providers are a rare breed, so it is impossible to state what the typical organization structure should look like to optimize these four parameters. However, we know from direct observation that systems providers implement very matrix-oriented organizations. The ramifications of this approach are as follows:

- Because services are a significant revenue stream, global PS reports into a global services executive.

- Regional PS leadership and may have a dual reporting structure to both the global services organization as well as to the geographic regional office.

- Local hiring decisions are made by regional PS, not by the regional country manager.

- The overlay services sales force may also end up with a dual reporting structure. Quota targets will be rolled up and resolved from two perspectives: the sales target for the region and the sales target for global services.

A sample of this matrixed organization is shown in Figure 6-12.

Figure 6-12  PS in a Systems Provider

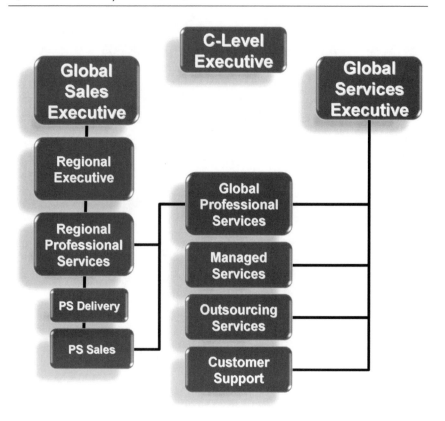

## THE ECONOMIC ENGINE OF THE SYSTEMS PROVIDER

Companies with the systems provider profile lean on services as a critical source of both revenue and profit. Services not only help the company maintain dominance in existing markets, but services also help the company gain traction in new markets. The ramification is that systems providers often lead with professional services and then pull through not only product but additional services such as outsourcing and managed services offerings. Figure 6-13 shows an example revenue mix for a systems provider.

In the representations of the other three profiles, one gear is clearly dominant. For solution providers, it is professional services. For product providers, it's the product. For product extenders, it's maintenance. **In the systems-provider profile, there may be no dominant revenue gear. Revenues are distributed across multiple revenue sources: hardware, software, project-based PS, annuity-based support, and outsourcing. However, I would argue, as with product extenders, the health of product revenues still are critical to overall health of the economic engine in the systems-provider profile.** The customer conversation may begin with consulta-

Figure 6-13 Economic Engine of the Systems Provider

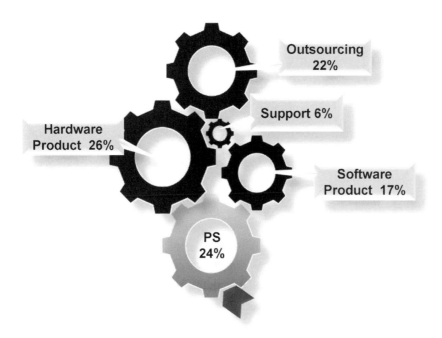

tive services, but the ongoing source of company differentiation remains in product innovation.

## EXAMPLE SYSTEMS PROVIDERS

So what product companies execute a systems-provider services strategy? This is indeed the hardest and most complex services-strategy profile to maintain. For that reason, not many true systems providers are roaming the planet. Like elephants, they are large and require lots of market space to sustain themselves. To date, systems providers have been the byproduct of large hardware companies that diversified into software and services. However, with Oracle's acquisition of Sun Microsystems in 2009, a new trend may be emerging. Table 6-3 provides a snapshot of the revenue mix for three companies that currently execute a systems-provider services strategy. This table references public data available from the company and compares product revenues to all service revenues.

IBM is the $100 billion behemoth that describes its business model in this way:

> *The company's global capabilities include services, software, hardware, fundamental research and related financing. The broad mix of businesses and capabilities are combined to provide business insight and solutions for the company's clients.*

> *The business model is flexible, adapting to the continuously changing market and economic environment. The company has divested commoditizing businesses like personal computers and hard disk drives, and strengthened its position through strategic investments and acquisitions in higher value segments like business intelligence and analytics, virtualization and green solutions. In addition, the company has transformed itself into a globally integrated enterprise, which has improved overall productivity and is driving investment and participation in the world's fastest growing markets. As a result, the company is a higher performing enterprise today than it was several years ago.*

> *The business model, supported by the company's long-term financial model, has enabled the company to deliver consistently strong earnings, cash flows and returns on invested capital in changing economic environments.*[1]

---

[1] SEC 10-K filed Feb. 24, 2009.

Table 6-3  Example Systems Providers

| Company Name | Data Source | Total Annual Revenues | Net Income % | % Revenue from Hardware Technologies | % Revenue from Software & Other | Revenue from PS | % Revenue from Outsourcing | % Revenue from Maintenance | % Revenue from Other Services |
|---|---|---|---|---|---|---|---|---|---|
| IBM | 10-K, Feb. 24, 2009 | $103B | 16.4% | 19% | 21% | 19% | 19% | 7% | 15% |
| Unisys | 10-K March 2, 2009 | $5.2B | -5% | 10% | 2% | 28% | 38% | 7% | 17% |
| Xerox | 10-K Feb. 13, 2009 | $17B | 1.3% | 23% | | | | 21% | 56% |

Despite supporting a revenue mix of complex services, the company significantly values technology innovation. This commitment is important to keeping the systems-provider profile healthy. Read another excerpt from the 2009 annual report:

> *In addition to producing world-class hardware and software products, IBM innovations are also a major differentiator in providing solutions for the company's clients through its services businesses. The company's investments in R&D also result in intellectual property (IP) income of approximately $1 billion annually. Some of IBM's technological breakthroughs are used exclusively in IBM products, while others are licensed and may be used in either/both IBM products and/or the products of the licensee.*

Not all systems providers have kept their eye on innovation. Unisys, like IBM, was a successful provider of mainframes. Like IBM, Unisys migrated into services as the mainframe market matured. In fact, in its 2009 annual report, the company's own description of its business strategy could serve as a classic definition for a systems provider:

> *Unisys brings together services and technology into solutions that solve critical problems for organizations around the world.*
>
> *In the services segment, we design, build, and manage IT systems and provide services that help our clients improve their competitiveness, security, and cost efficiency. Our services include outsourcing, systems integration and consulting, infrastructure services and core maintenance.*
>
> - *In outsourcing, we manage a customer's data centers and end-user environments as well as specific business processes, such as check processing, insurance claims processing, health claims processing, mortgage administration, citizen registry and cargo management.*
>
> - *In systems integration and consulting, we design and develop innovative solutions for specific industries—such as check processing systems, public welfare systems, airline reservations and communications messaging solutions.*
>
> - *In infrastructure services, we design and support customers' IT infrastructure, including their networks, desktops, servers, and mobile and wireless systems.*

- *In core maintenance, we provide maintenance of Unisys proprietary products.*

- *In the technology segment, we design and develop servers and related services and products that help clients modernize their data-center environments to reduce costs and improve efficiency.*

However, as the company became more services intensive, it struggled to release new technologies that captured market share. Instead, the company became heavily reliant on providing only commodity technology services. In 2008, IBM had a banner year. The financial results for Unisys in the same year are overviewed in their 10-K:

> *For 2008, the company reported a net loss of $130.1 million. Revenue for 2008 was $5.23 billion, down 7 percent from 2007 revenue of $5.65 billion. The results include pretax charges of $103.1 million related primarily to cost-reduction actions announced in the fourth quarter of 2008. The company's 2008 financial results also reflect the global economic slowdown in the second half of the year. The company saw this slowdown particularly in its financial services business, but also in other key commercial industries, as clients reacted to economic uncertainties by reducing information technology (IT) spending. Reduced demand for the company's services and products impacted the company's revenue and profit margins for the year.*

Looking at the similarities and differences between the IBM and Unisys mix, one can't help but notice that IBM, a systems provider, still acquires 40 percent of total revenues from hardware and software. Unisys, on the other hand, acquires only 12 percent of total revenues from technology sales. Product companies—even systems providers—can become too services intensive. When this happens, they lose the core gear of their economic engine—technology innovation and product sales.

Xerox made its money in copiers. Then, everyone started making copiers. Today Xerox makes less than 25 percent of its revenue on equipment sales. The rest comes from an array of services—everything from document management optimization to outsourcing and equipment leasing services. Xerox describes themselves as "a technology and services enterprise and a leader in the global document market, developing, manufacturing, marketing, servicing and financing the industry's broadest portfolio of document equipment, solutions and services." The 21 percent of maintenance revenues listed in Table 6-3 actually come from paper and other supplies Xerox is providing to customers where Xerox manages the printing environment. Not an insignificant source of revenue. It is also interesting to note that Xerox never breaks out the mix of services in revenues in their 10-K. In other words, it is not clear how much of Xerox's revenues come from outsourcing vs. consulting or document management. Everything has to be lumped in the "other services" revenue category. Finally, Xerox's skinny operating income is not a good sign for a systems provider. Like Unisys, Xerox must be careful it is not building its economic engine around commoditized technologies.

Beyond IBM and Xerox, there is an emerging list of technology product companies that could potentially migrate into the systems-provider profile. HP's acquisition of EDS clearly puts the classic product provider on a path to eventually become a systems provider. HP's commitment to growing both software and "cloud" offerings help accelerate the trend. However, the revenue mix has a long way to shift. Oracle's purchase of Sun creates the first instance of a software company buying a multi-billion dollar hardware company. With Sun's shrinking product revenues and legacy maintenance revenues, this is really the merging of two product extenders. However, this could serve as the springboard for Oracle to become a provider of software, hardware, and a slew of value-added services that migrate the company into a systems provider model.

## UNIQUE CHALLENGES AND KEY METRICS

Very few technology companies will have the wherewithal to migrate to this services-strategy profile. Companies who do make it should be well aware of the unique challenges that will present themselves within the professional services business.

### Product Atrophy

As highlighted in the overviews of both Unisys and Xerox, systems providers must be every diligent that they do not lose their product innovation edge. They do not have to be the first to market with new technologies, but they must continue to provide technology solutions that offer some distinct advantage to customers. A systems provider with no product gears is simply a services provider that used to be a product company. This is not the end game product companies typically desire to achieve.

### Tension Between Gears

The services organizations within systems providers become very focused on driving services revenues and profits. This is a requirement because services are so important to the economic growth of the systems provider. However, services organizations can sometimes become tethered from their product brethren—to the point where the services organization may happily sell competitive products in order to secure large service deals. This behavior will frustrate the produce executives within the company to no end. **Systems providers must implement checks and balances that help guide the services organization to build offerings that drive company products. This sounds like a no brainer, but I have heard the frustration of product managers within systems providers when the services organization does not focus on driving the products of the company.**

## The Account Pig Pile

Because the systems provider is supporting so many product and service lines, specialized sales resources are created to support the primary account managers. There may even be separate sales forces to represent different services lines. All of this sales specialization can create a "pig pile" of sales bodies within customer accounts. Both the cost and coordination of this challenge needs to be managed by the systems provider.

## Services Stigma

Finally, systems providers sit precariously on the dividing line between product companies and services companies. A majority of the revenue for a systems provider comes from services. Analysts and investors may begin viewing the company as a services company. If the product gear shrinks too much, the perception is magnified. In Chapter 7, we will discuss the negative attributes analysts and investors attach to services-revenue streams. Being classified as a "services company" is not what most product company executive teams aspire to achieve. Especially when they consider the low price–to–earnings multiplier applied to services companies.

## Measuring Success

Systems providers execute a complex business model that requires a diverse set of metrics to measure the success and health of multiple business lines. However, a few success metrics are particularly important to services providers:

> **Total Account Revenue**: As with the product extenders, systems providers should understand if PS involvement is increasing within an account, if the total amount of money the customer spends with the company is increasing?

**Project Profitability**: Systems providers cannot afford to engage in lots of poor performing projects.

**Global Sourcing**: To be cost competitive, systems providers must drive economies of scale across geographies so that nonbillable activities within each region are kept at a minimum.

**Product Pull**: How much company product is the services organization selling as part of its services contracts? This may seem like a metric much more suited for product providers, but tracking this ratio will help keep services tethered to the company product portfolio.

## CLOSING THOUGHTS

Just as product companies do not start their lives as product extenders, they do not start as systems providers—they evolve into this profile. The evolution to a systems-provider strategy is painful. Lou Gerstner documented the challenges very well in his book *Who Says Elephants Can't Dance?* This profile is suitable only for companies that have the following attributes:

1. Significant install base where new services can be sold.

2. Significant revenue and capital to support the funding of new service businesses.

3. A willingness to provide hardware, software, services, and third-party products to deliver end-to-end business solutions to customers.

Once again, only a handful of companies in any product industry are realistically in a position to assume this profile. However, if done successfully, this profile can transition a company from a struggling, has-been provider of aging products to an industry giant.

And there we are. All four services-strategy profiles defined. A fact that should be apparent by now is that each of these profiles has unique strengths and unique challenges. This is why choosing a services strategy is by no means a simple decision. When a product company does not fall neatly into one of the profiles, executives can agonize over the process of choosing the appropriate services strategy. It is this debilitating uncertainty that creates the topic of our next chapter.

# Chapter 7

# The Services Chasm

At this point in the journey, we have presented four distinct services strate-gies product companies have a tendency to assume. The previous chapters also provided examples of product companies crisply executing one of these services strategies. Cisco as a product provider, Oracle as a product extender, and IBM as a systems provider. However, product companies are not always so clear regarding their services strategy—especially when the needs of the market shift. This confusion in services strategy can make a product company thrash in a horrid place we call the services chasm.

## INTRODUCING THE SERVICES CHASM

In Chapter 2 we mapped services-strategy profiles to market maturity. This picture is shown again in Figure 7-1.

In Chapters 3 through 6, the details of each services-strategy profile were provided. In that information, it becomes clear why different profiles are more effective in different states of market maturity. For example, it is hard to assume a product-provider approach when product sales are still emerging and no services partner ecosystem exists for your product. What was not discussed in Chapter 2 is how a product company manages its services-strategy profile

**Figure 7-1** Services-Strategy Profiles and Market Maturity

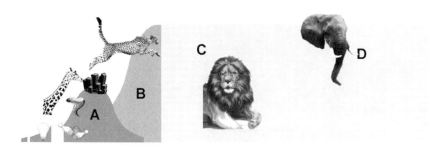

as a market matures. There is a painful reality. As a product market matures, a product company will be forced to face a critical strategic decision:

### Does the company change market or change mix?

In other words, does the company find a new, high-growth product market to pursue *or* does the company begin pursuing new service opportunities that exist in the maturing product market? This is a very difficult decision for executive teams to make. Pros and cons are associated with either choice.

If a management team decides to change markets, it must successfully identify a hot new product market to pursue. This may involve the pursuit of both new technologies and new customer relationships. What if the market does not mature quickly enough to satisfy the growth objectives of investors?

If the management team decides to change mix and pursue service opportunities, the strategy, structure, and culture of the historically product-centric company must be altered to support and value the pursuit of the services business. It is difficult to change the DNA of a company. Also, by increasing the percentage of total revenues coming from lower margin services, a change will occur to the overall financial model of the company—not an easy change for any company to endure.

Despite the challenges faced with either a "change market" or "change mix" strategy, the alternative is far worse. When a company does not make an explicit, well-defined choice, it will drift into a place we are defining as the *the services chasm*. The location of this no-man's land is shown in Figure 7-2.

Companies can thrash in this chasm for years. In essence, companies are lingering in the middle phases of the disruption-to-demise life cycle described

Figure 7-2  The Services Chasm

in Chapter 1. During one quarter, a push to pursue service opportunities may be the focus. Six months later, there will be renewed hope that the next release will reinvigorate lagging product sales. For a study in this thrashing behavior, recall the antics of Siebel Systems as discussed in the Chapter 1. A review of the press releases associated with Siebel Systems, the once high-flying enterprise software provider that was bought by Oracle in 2005, shows a company deeply mired in the services chasm. With the economic downturn of 2001, Siebel experienced a dramatic decrease in product license sales. From total revenues of $2 billion in 2001, the company had shrunk to almost half that size by 2004. How should a company respond to this type of abrupt slowing in its legacy market? Should Siebel have developed new product or platform offerings to reinvigorate product sales (change market), or should Siebel have focused on adding higher value services to its existing and substantial installed base (change mix)? There are pros and cons to either strategy. What is not sustainable is to thrash between strategies. Table 7-1 documents the news headlines that clearly signal the indecision being exhibited by the company during its final year.

Siebel provides the perfect example of a company clearly caught in the services chasm, which is naturally created when a product market matures. However, it is not always so crystal clear when a company is actually in the chasm. The next section will provide some tactics for helping to identify when product companies are being sucked into this precarious place.

Table 7-1   Siebel in the News

| Headline | Date Published | Source |
| --- | --- | --- |
| **New Siebel CEO Shifts Company Focus from Products to Services** | October 14, 2004 | *AMR Research* |
| **Charting a New Course at Siebel** | March 30, 2005 | *Business Week* |
| **Siebel Is Stuck on the Seesaw** | April 8, 2005 | *Business Week* |
| **Siebel Board Ousts Chief as Market Share Declines** | April 14, 2005 | *New York Times* |
| **Siebel Shows Off New CEO, New Products at User Conference** | April 19, 2005 | *InformationWeek* |
| **License Revenues Sink Siebel** | April 27, 2005 | *Internetnews* |
| **Siebel Continues Its Slide** | July 8, 2005 | *Forbes* |
| **Oracle to Buy Siebel in $5.9 Billion Deal** | September 12, 2005 | *Business Week* |

## SYMPTOMS OF THE SERVICES CHASM

**Product companies have a tendency to naturally experience a disconnect between their services-strategy profile and the actual state of their marketplace. It occurs because services-strategy decisions lag actual market requirements.** We believe that as the technology industry continues to mature in general, more and more historically product-centric companies will find themselves facing this disconnect. To assist companies in self-assessing their current state, there are three tell-tale signs that indicate a product company is in or near the services chasm:

### *Mix ≠ Message*

If the actual revenue mix of the company does not support the messaging to the marketplace, the company is in or nearing the services chasm. If a company is telling customers "We are a solutions company," which implies a certain commitment to service capabilities, but it is geared like a hard-core product provider, the services strategy is not appropriately aligned. This scenario is common in two instances. The first is when the company has a new product that requires a significant amount of services to drive initial market adoption, but the company does not want to provide these services. In other words, the market is looking for a solution provider, but the company is geared like a product provider. The second instance is when a market is maturing, product revenues are slowing, and the product company begins promoting services capabilities to secure new revenues. In this scenario, the company is promoting itself as a product extender or systems provider but may indeed still be geared like a product provider.

### *Mix ≠ Market*

As a market matures, many customers turn to product providers for one-stop shopping. Customers want one place to purchase both the products and services required to maintain a particular business solution. When this occurs, cheetahs must decide if they are willing to transform into lions or elephants to satisfy customer needs. A disconnect occurs when the product provider keeps pushing product enhancements that drive little incremental value to the customer and do not satisfy the requests for services. This motion pushes the product provider toward the services chasm as product revenues slow and new services revenues are not pursued.

### *Market ≠ Margin*

Finally, as a market matures, product volumes could decrease, product margins could decrease, or both things could happen. If a company is geared like a product provider, but the product gear is rapidly decreasing, the entire economic engine grinds to a halt. This motion slams the company into the services chasm. Top-line revenues decline and, more importantly, bottom-line profitability drops out. In this scenario, the product provider may desperately seek product refreshes in hopes of regaining higher product margins. However, not enough differentiation exists in the eyes of the marketplace, product margins continue to erode, and the company business model is no longer sustainable.

When these symptoms appear, why don't management teams immediately become motivated to better align their services strategy? Why would companies delay their response and hold on to product centric business models that may be a dead man walking? For that answer, we have to turn to Wall Street. But before we drag Wall Street into the discussion, we need to provide one clarification to the application of services-strategy profiles. We need to highlight the difference between the overall company profile and the unique needs of specific business units or product offerings.

## MARKET VS. PRODUCT NEEDS

The three common disconnects described previously occur when the overall services strategy of the company is disconnected with the needs of the major markets the company is serving. For example, if a majority of customers who buy storage are paying less for pure hardware capacity but are willing to pay more for services to help manage the storage environment, this market has crossed to the other side of the services chasm. A hardware storage provider must now seriously contemplate the change-mix or change-market decision. However, let's say customers in the storage marketplace are still infatuated with simply buying lots of capacity (think 1999). At this time, a storage hardware provider launches a new product that has some neat features that no one else offers. However, the product is very complex to implement. For this one new product, customers are going to need a lot of implementation and integration assistance. Does that mean the company needs to change its services-strategy profile?

There can be real differences between the overall services-strategy profile of a company, one of the company's business units, and the services needs of a specific product offered by the company. To visualize this landscape, think of the company whose services-strategy needs are documented in Figure 7-3. This figure shows a company that is, overall, executing a product provider profile. This is because the largest business unit in the company supports a product-provider services strategy. However, there is a second, much smaller business unit that is actually exhibiting a product-extender revenue mix. One of the products in this business unit actually requires a solution-provider revenue

Figure 7- 3  Multiple Services Strategies in One Company

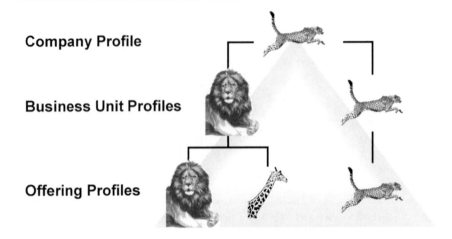

**Company Profile**

**Business Unit Profiles**

**Offering Profiles**

mix. Getting lost? This is where those animal icons come in handy to help map the services needs!

Can one company simultaneously sustain so many diverse services strategies? Absolutely. Think of Hewlett Packard. It produces a wide array of products that range from simple printers to complex servers. These products have diverse services needs. The services-strategy profile of the printing and imaging business unit will look very different than the services-strategy profile for enterprise servers. When a company must support multiple services-strategy profiles, this framework is helpful at two levels:

1.  Aligning the services strategy for specific products and business units

2.  Aligning the overall (or aggregate) services strategy of the company

The first application is straight forward. Using the concepts introduced in this book, the company can assign the appropriate services strategy to specific products or business? The more specific taxonomy of services-strategy profiles breaks out as follows:

- **Company Profile**: The aggregate services-strategy profile of the company. Profile is based on total company revenues.

- **Business Unit Profile**: The services-strategy profile of a specific business unit within the company. Profile may be different than the aggregate profile.

- **Offering Profile**: The services-strategy profile a company has applied to a specific company offering. Profile may be different than the business unit or aggregate profile.

For a company with a diverse product portfolio, the second application is a little trickier. Does the overall services-strategy profile matter for a product company that, underneath the covers, is executing multiple services strategies? The short answer is *yes*. Product companies need to be as clear as possible regarding the overall revenue mix they expect to receive from products vs. services. Overall, is the company a product provider, product extender, or a systems provider? The overall services-strategy profile provides "revenue bumpers" that set expectations for investors. This concept is visualized in Figure 7-4. Why are these revenue mix bumpers so important? The answer to this question lies with the perceptions of Wall Street analysts and how companies are valued—which is the topic of our next section.

## THE ROLE OF WALL STREET

Since late 2008, Wall Street has become the popular scapegoat for many of our business woes. However, long before mortgage debts soured, Wall Street has had a very real influence on services strategy within product companies. Historically, analysts and investors reward high-growth product companies with high price-to-earnings ratios. Hence, it behooves product company executives to have their companies assume a product provider profile. This gearing is optimal for driving high-margin, highly scalable product revenues. Yet even though the highest market capitalization for a company will occur on the left

Figure 7-4 Services Revenue Bumpers

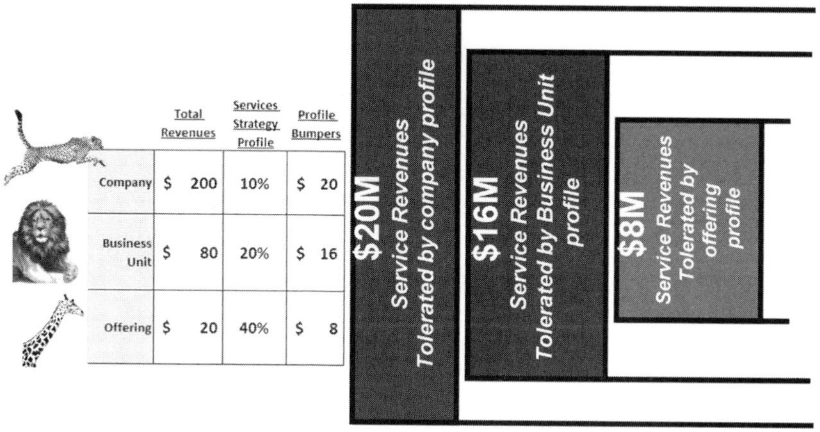


| | Total Revenues | Services Strategy Profile | Profile Bumpers |
|---|---|---|---|
| Company | $ 200 | 10% | $ 20 |
| Business Unit | $ 80 | 20% | $ 16 |
| Offering | $ 20 | 40% | $ 8 |

side of the services chasm, the long-term revenues and profits will occur on the right side of the services chasm. Think of IBM with a typical P/E ratio in the high teens, but revenues hitting $100 billion. What if IBM were to have remained focused on mainframes and PCs? Would the company ever have grown to its current size on the back of product revenues alone? Unlikely. Yet, a services-aggressive strategy for product companies is not viewed favorably. Turn back to the crazy days of the late 1990s, when every technology stock was overvalued—except IBM's. Read the observations of a *Business Week* reporter, posted in December of 1999:

> *Total all three of these valuations (hardware, software, and services), and you get a market capitalization for IBM of $462 billion. IBM's current market capitalization is $190 billion. That's a 150 percent undervaluation, which means that if this exercise made sense in the real world, IBM's stock should be worth about $250 a share, rather than $105.*
>
> *Of course, this scenario doesn't translate well in the real world. That's because the three divisions aren't separate, and IBM isn't about to split them up. Even if they did get their freedom, no one can say the units will be as successful as an Oracle or a Sun. Still, it's abundantly clear that IBM's stock doesn't get the same respect from Wall Street that its Silicon Valley competitors do.[1]*

For a more recent example of Wall Street's reaction to a product company increasing services revenues, we can turn to HP's acquisition of pure services company EDS. Here is how one *Wall Street Journal* blogger saw the transaction:

> *Why is the stock market so cranky about Hewlett Packard Co.'s $13.3 billion purchase of Electronic Data Systems Corp.? Investors have already knocked off about $12 billion in value of H-P shares since Monday.*
>
> *What a crummy deal, right?*
>
> *No. It's got less to do with H-P the company and everything to do with H-P the stock.*
>
> *It's no surprise that H-P's shares fell upon the announcement of the acquisition of EDS. An acquirer's shares typically do. It is unusual, however for the acquirer's shares to fall more than the purchase price of*

---

[1] IBM Sure Is One Undervalued Net Stock at least compared to Internet pure plays. So how do you put a proper value on Big Blue? Here's one attempt at www.businessweek .com/1999/99_50/b3659007.htm.

*the acquisition. You can argue all day whether this is the right deal for H-P. In EDS, H-P is buying a domestic, low-growth "body shop"... But the market hates the EDS deal, because now it must confront the reality of what H-P has become: A behemoth with a projected annual growth rate of 5 percent acquiring another massive company with 3 percent projected growth, according to Capital IQ figures.*

*If H-P had bought Salesforce.com or another growth engine, H-P may have retained some element of mystery, no matter how much it may have overpaid. And it's that element of mystery that keeps the momentum in certain stocks.[2]*

Clearly this analyst would have been much more excited about an acquisition that would have accelerated product growth. The perspective from another analyst:

*Clearly, the Street is not crazy about Hewlett-Packard's (HPQ) plan to acquire Electronic Data Systems (EDS). In two days, the Street has knocked about 10 percent off HP's stock price, chopping its market cap by about $12.5 billion, almost equal to the $13.9 billion deal price. The obvious question is, why?*

*And the answer is, there are several reasons. For starters, this is a large deal—EDS has 135,000 employees—and has the potential to create all kinds of distractions for HP CEO Mark Hurd and his team. Two, $13.9 billion is a lot of cash, and some people wonder if they are overpaying for a company that has not been a good performer in recent years. **Three, there is concern about dilution of both revenue growth and margins. And four, there are some who wonder if HP might not have been better off beefing up its software arm**, or snapping up an Indian outsourcing firm rather than adding a U.S.–focused body shop like EDS.[3]*

These analysts are very concerned about the dilution of margins brought about by increasing services revenues. Also, the low growth rate of services revenues vs. product revenues reduces the future potential for high growth. A

---

[2] May 14, 2008, 12:35 p.m., Why H-P's Stock Is Stuck, Evan Newmark, http://blogs.wsj.com/deals/2008/05/14/why-h-ps-stock-is-stuck/.

[3] May 13, 2008, 3:14 p.m., Why HP's EDS Deal Makes The Street Nervous, Posted by Eric Savitz, http://blogs.barrons.com/techtraderdaily/2008/05/13/why-hps-eds-deal-makes-the-street-nervous/.

Figure 7-5  Wall Street Perceptions

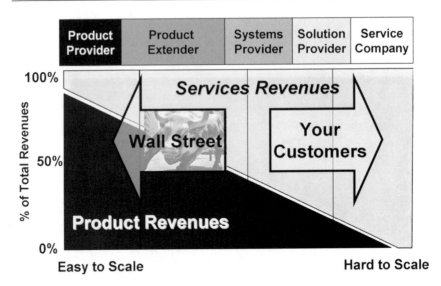

way to graph this Wall Street bias is provided in Figure 7-5. Companies with revenue mixes appearing on the left-hand side of the graph are viewed as more scalable and more profitable. They are rewarded with higher stock price per earnings ratios by investors. Companies on the right-hand side are viewed as hard to scale and lower margin.

The question not adequately addressed by the Wall Street analysts concerns the synergy between product and service offerings. What if the purchase of EDS successfully positions HP to become a $150 billion systems provider as opposed to a $90 billion product provider? **More importantly, what if the purchase of services know-how from EDS enables HP to transition from delivering customer premise equipment–based (CPE-based) product offerings to subscription and cloud services offerings?** And what if annuity services revenues from long-term services contracts help offset a decrease in product revenues during a global economic downturn? These considerations do not map to the one dimensional mentality documented in Figure 7-3. All of those benefits are too long term. Those benefits speak to HP's viability beyond four quarters. Where's the exponential, high-product growth baby? The point here is that Wall Street perceptions can contribute to product companies extending their stay in the services chasm as they thrash around, desperately attempting to avoid any strategy that may involve increased services revenue— even if that is the appropriate strategy to pursue.

## ECONOMIC CONSEQUENCES

Even though Wall Street has a clear preference for product companies to stay on the left side of the services chasm, that is not always an option. As the last section of this chapter will verify, markets do mature. If companies do not effectively navigate market maturity with crisp services-strategy decisions, company success is jeopardized.

### Complete Failure

The failure pattern outlined in Chapter 1 occurs when companies delay their services-strategy decisions. This delay sends the product company into the heart of the services chasm, where the company thrashes. Eventually it makes belated services-strategy decisions that come too late to save the company from a downward spiral. As a reminder, the death march occurs in eight steps:

1. **Disruption**: Product market matures or disruptive technology enters the market making current product offering less competitive. This pushes the product company to the left edge of the services chasm.

2. **Denial**: Company focuses on old technology and old consumption models too long by staying locked in a product-provider profile, even though product revenues and margins are on a steep decline.

3. **Decline**: Top-line revenues stagnate or shrink, and operating income begins to shrivel.

4. **Services Focus**: In an attempt to shore up top-line revenues and profits, the executive management team belatedly announces a focus on services opportunities. This is a belated attempt to rapidly transition to a product-extender or systems-provider profile.

5. **Services False Positive**: Service revenues do become a larger portion of total company revenues, but that is largely due to continued maintenance streams on top of a shrinking product installed base. The company is a support-centric product extender with an underdeveloped PS gear.

6. **Services Failure**: Despite the belated focus on services, total company revenues continue to flatten or fall off. Support revenues are shrinking as the install base shrinks. Lack of significant replacement revenues from new product offerings or new services offerings cause total company profitability to tank.

7.   **Demise**: Finally, there is an abrupt change in corporate direction. Services leadership or overall company leadership is suddenly changed. The company does one of three things: declares a renewed focus on product innovation, declares bankruptcy, or is acquired. In essence, the company has reached the bottom of the services chasm.

## The Services Buffer

Fortunately, not all product companies find themselves strewn on the jagged rocks jutting from the bottom of the services chasm. Some companies muddle through services-strategy decisions in a way that allows the company to survive, just not in a financially optimal way.

Our benchmarking work in the industry associations allows us to model the revenue mix and margins of product companies. Using this real-world data, we can create example revenue scenarios. The classic scenario we can use to quantify lost revenue and margin opportunities is based on an enterprise software company. The scenario is modeled over twelve data points. These data points could be months, quarters, or years—it is not relevant for this example. In the first seven data points, the company is successfully growing license revenues. In the eighth period, the company begins experiencing a slight decline in license revenues as the next generation of the product is geared up for release. After four periods of declining license revenue, the new product does get released and license revenue begins increasing again. Throughout this twelve-period cycle, the company never invested aggressively in services capabilities beyond maintenance. The revenue mix for the company is shown in Figure 7-6 and the financial data is documented in Table 7-2.

Figure 7-6   Software Company with Limited Services

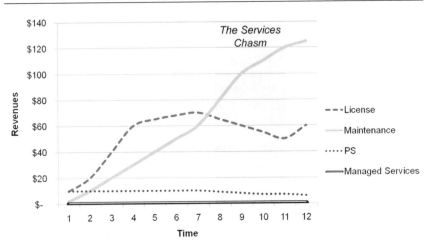

Table 7-2 Software Company, Limited Services

|  | 1 | 2 | 3 | 4 | 5 | 6 | 7 | 8 | 9 | 10 | 11 | 12 | TOTAL |
|---|---|---|---|---|---|---|---|---|---|---|---|---|---|
|  |  |  |  |  |  |  |  | *The Services Chasm* | | | | | |
| License | $ 10 | $ 20 | $ 40 | $ 60 | $ 65 | $ 68 | $ 70 | $ 65 | $ 60 | $ 55 | $ 50 | $ 60 | $ 623 |
| Maintenance | $ 2 | $ 10 | $ 20 | $ 30 | $ 40 | $ 50 | $ 60 | $ 80 | $ 100 | $ 110 | $ 120 | $ 125 | $ 747 |
| PS | $ 10 | $ 10 | $ 10 | $ 10 | $ 10 | $ 10 | $ 10 | $ 9 | $ 8 | $ 7 | $ 7 | $ 6 | $ 107 |
| Managed Services | $ - | $ - | $ - | $ - | $ - | $ - | $ - | $ - | $ - | $ - | $ - | $ - | |
| Total Revenue | $ 22 | $ 40 | $ 70 | $ 100 | $ 115 | $ 128 | $ 140 | $ 154 | $ 168 | $ 172 | $ 177 | $ 191 | $ 1,477 |
| Margin $ | $ 12.40 | $ 27.00 | $ 52.00 | $ 77.00 | $ 88.50 | $ 98.20 | $ 107.00 | $116.30 | $ 125.60 | $127.90 | $130.40 | $142.70 | $ 1,105 |
| Margin % | 56% | 68% | 74% | *77%* | 77% | 77% | 76% | 76% | 75% | 74% | 74% | 75% | |
| Service Margin $ | $ 4.10 | $ 10.50 | $ 18.50 | $ 26.50 | $ 34.50 | $ 42.50 | $ 50.50 | $ 66.25 | $ 82.00 | $ 89.75 | $ 97.75 | $101.50 | $ 624 |
| Service Margin % | 19% | 26% | 26% | 27% | 30% | 33% | 36% | 43% | 49% | 52% | 55% | 53% | |

In this classic product-provider strategy, the software company exits its journey through the services chasm with revenues below $200 million. **As long as the next generation product gets traction, the company is not too much worse for the wear.** If the next release of the product does not gain traction in twelfth period of the cycle, the company will only have maintenance revenues to cushion the blow. Also, the company will not have internal services capabilities that could be engaged to accelerate adoption of the new product release. **In a sense, this is a high-risk strategy solely dependent on rapid adoption of new product releases.**

In contrast, we can look at the same type of enterprise software company, only this time the company invested in both professional and managed services to augment the product. The revenue mix of this company is shown in Figure 7-7 and the financial data is shown in Table 7-3.

In this scenario, the software company embraced a product-extender profile prior to entering the services chasm and leveraged that profile to secure over $200 million in additional revenues through the twelve-period cycle. In addition, the company exits the services chasm with over $250 million dollars in annual revenues as opposed to less than $200 million. These financial variances may seem subtle, but what is $30 to $50 million in revenue worth to a $200 million enterprise? Especially if the latest release of the product hits some bumps in the revenue road.

This type of modeling can be done for all types of products and markets. Obviously, some markets and technologies lend themselves more aptly to building value-added services. Regardless of the size of the services opportunity, the internal debate is always the same: Do we really need to mess with these services businesses? **Can't we simply weather the dip between product**

Figure 7- 7  Software Company with Services Buffer

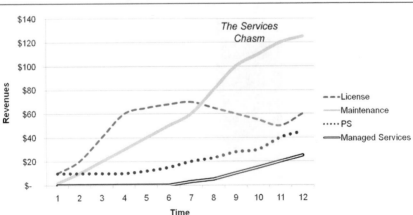

Table 7-3  Software Company with Services Buffer

*The Services Chasm*

|  | 1 | 2 | 3 | 4 | 5 | 6 | 7 | 8 | 9 | 10 | 11 | 12 | TOTAL |
|---|---|---|---|---|---|---|---|---|---|---|---|---|---|
| License | $ 10 | $ 20 | $ 40 | $ 60 | $ 65 | $ 68 | $ 70 | $ 65 | $ 60 | $ 55 | $ 50 | $ 60 | $ 623 |
| Maintenance | $ 2 | $ 10 | $ 20 | $ 30 | $ 40 | $ 50 | $ 60 | $ 80 | $ 100 | $ 110 | $ 120 | $ 125 | $ 747 |
| PS | $ 10 | $ 10 | $ 10 | $ 10 | $ 12 | $ 15 | $ 20 | $ 23 | $ 28 | $ 30 | $ 40 | $ 45 | $ 253 |
| Managed Services | $ - | $ - | $ - | $ - | $ - | $ - | $ 3 | $ 5 | $ 10 | $ 15 | $ 20 | $ 25 | $ 78 |
| Total Revenue | $ 22 | $ 40 | $ 70 | $ 100 | $ 117 | $ 133 | $ 153 | $ 173 | $ 198 | $ 210 | $ 230 | $ 255 | $ 1,701 |
| Margin $ | $ 13.00 | $ 28.00 | $ 53.50 | $ 79.00 | $ 91.50 | $102.45 | $ 114.05 | $ 126.00 | $ 139.50 | $ 144.75 | $ 152.00 | $ 167.75 | $ 1,212 |
| Margin % | 59% | 70% | 76% | *79%* | 78% | 77% | 75% | 73% | 70% | 69% | 66% | 66% | |
| Service Margin $ | $ 4.10 | $ 10.50 | $ 18.50 | $ 26.50 | $ 35.00 | $ 43.75 | $ 54.05 | $ 71.50 | $ 90.50 | $ 100.75 | $ 113.00 | $ 120.00 | $ 688 |
| Service Margin % | 19% | 26% | 26% | 27% | 30% | 33% | 35% | 41% | 46% | 48% | 49% | 47% | |

**releases and take our lumps in short-term revenue loss? If product revenues always rebound, I actually agree with staying true to the product provider strategy.** The challenge facing more and more product companies is that product revenues and margins do not rebound. Again, think Siebel, Sun Microsystems, Dell, and Xerox. When product revenue does not rebound, aligning services-strategy profile for flattening product-adoption curves can be the difference between viability and failure.

## SERVICES STRATEGY IN SIX WORDS

The services chasm can create significant financial hardship for a product company. Misaligned services strategy can accelerate the failure of a product company. This reality is clear. To put a finer point on this discussion of aligning services strategy for product company success, I want to boil the conversation down to three services-strategy challenges that can face a product company.

On Friday, February 13, 2009 (yes, Friday the 13th), I experienced a moment of synchronicity concerning services strategy. Synchronicity is the experience of two or more events that are causally unrelated occurring together in a supposedly meaningful manner. In order to count as synchronicity, the events should be unlikely to occur together by chance. The two separate and distinct events that occurred that day were as follows:

1.  I participated in a meeting where a person asked "What is your hypothesis regarding our services strategy?"

2.  I listened to a podcast from NPR where they discussed the book *Not Quite What I Was Planning: Six-Word Memoirs by Writers Famous and Obscure*. This is a compilation of six word sentences provided by folks that summarize their lives.

These two disparate events came together in my mind when I realized that I can, indeed, boil down the successful application of services strategy to product company success into to six simple words.

The importance of services strategy to a product company presents itself in three distinct situations. For each situation, we can summarize the importance of services in six words:

### First Scenario: Getting Products Adopted

#### Great product, forgot services, company fails

This six-word services strategy applies to the scenario when a product company needs services to help accelerate product adoption. The product is new to the market and has potential, but customers need help gaining the benefits of the new technology. If product companies forget to create enabling services directly or through partners, product adoption languishes and the company can fail. Not because the product was not solid, but because the required services were not in place. In this scenario, the error is to pursue a product-provider profile when a solution-provider or product-extender profile is required.

## Second Scenario: Buying Time

### Old product, services buffer, next product

This six-word services strategy applies to the scenario when an existing product is beginning to mature and a lull happens before the next generation product is really taking off. This is the classic "s-curve" described by Everett Rogers in his 1962 book, *Diffusion of Innovations*. During the slow portion of early product adoption, revenues from the existing product are flat or declining. To maintain the top line, the company needs a source of revenue. That source can be services delivered to the existing install base. This phenomenon is simplified in Figure 7-8. In this scenario, the error is to hold onto a product provider profile when a product extender profile could have provided much-needed services revenues until the next product was ready for prime time.

Figure 7-8  Old Product, Services Buffer, New Product

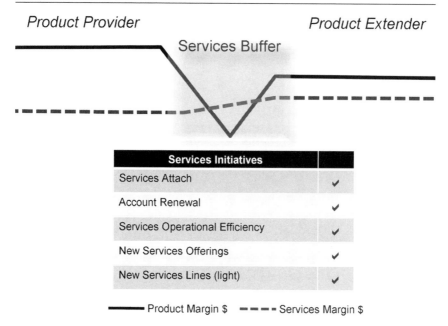

| Services Initiatives | |
|---|---|
| Services Attach | ✔ |
| Account Renewal | ✔ |
| Services Operational Efficiency | ✔ |
| New Services Offerings | ✔ |
| New Services Lines (light) | ✔ |

——— Product Margin $    ━ ━ ━ Services Margin $

## *Third Scenario: Changing Profiles*

### *Old market, new services, new company*

This six-word services strategy applies to companies that serve a market that is maturing. Despite new innovations in technology, customers are just not willing to pay more for the product. Think PCs, UNIX servers, hardware storage, printers, and so on. In this scenario, companies either find new product markets to explore or they create new ways to add value around commoditizing products. This shift in the value proposition creates a fundamental shift in revenue mix and a shift in the overall company strategy. This services strategy scenario has applied to many product companies, not just to IBM. Companies that have experienced "old market, new services, new company" include Xerox and EMC. The impact of this scenario on revenue mix is shown in Figure 7-9. In this scenario, the company may have been a product provider but migrates to becoming a product extender or systems provider.

This book covers the intricacies of setting services strategy within product companies. We cannot boil the essence of this entire body of work into three sentences, each with only six words. However, these three sentences accurately capture the three most common services-strategy challenges facing product

Figure 7-9  Old Market, New Services, New Company

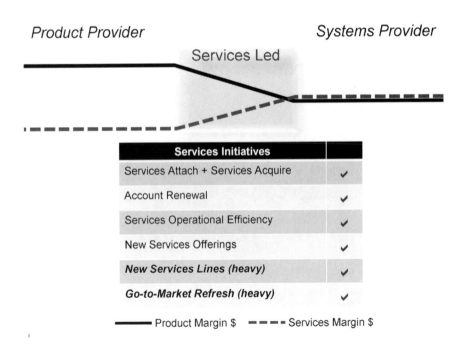

| Services Initiatives | |
|---|---|
| Services Attach + Services Acquire | ✔ |
| Account Renewal | ✔ |
| Services Operational Efficiency | ✔ |
| New Services Offerings | ✔ |
| *New Services Lines (heavy)* | ✔ |
| *Go-to-Market Refresh (heavy)* | ✔ |

━━━ Product Margin $   ▬ ▬ ▬ Services Margin $

companies. It is very probable one of these three apply to your product company right now. If that is the case, how does your company agree to one of these services strategies and align the company to successfully execute the strategy? That is the topic of the next chapter: Bridging the Services Chasm.

## ENDNOTE: MATURATION OF AN INDUSTRY

Before leaving this overview of the services chasm, I would like to close with a discussion of the current state of the software industry. Throughout our personal careers, the software industry has been predominantly focused on growth. Software companies are optimized to identify, attack, and dominate markets that can emerge overnight. However, the growth of software markets has slowed. Established and highly successful software companies like Oracle now grow by acquitting the install base of stagnant competitors. To emphasize this industry maturation, we can review a dataset assembled by Professor Michael Cusumano at MIT. He has been analyzing the product/service mix trends in the software industry. His team at MIT has identified 485 public software "products firms" under SIC code 7372 (prepackaged software). Reviewing the annual public financial reports of these companies from 1990

Figure 7-10  Product/Service Mix of the Software Industry

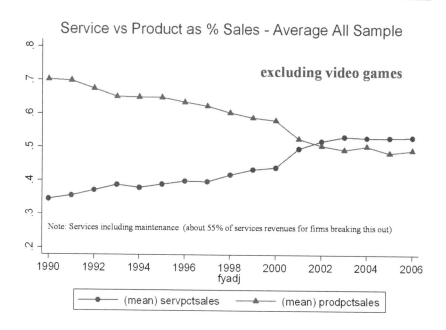

to today, Professor Cusumano's team has aggregated 3,386 data points on the product/service mix.

Reviewing this dataset, Professor Cusumano has mapped the march of the software industry from a product-centric to services-centric revenue mix. He summarizes his findings in an article titled "The Changing Software Business: Moving from Products to Services" published in January of 2008 by the IEEE Computer Society.

A graph from the article maps how much revenue the software companies in this dataset have been receiving from products vs. services from 1990 to 2004. The graph is republished as Figure 7-10. As can be seen, since 2002, a majority of the revenue generated in the product-centric software industry is actually from services. We do not see this trend reversing. The Technology Professional Services Association takes a quarterly snapshot of the product/service revenue mix for the largest software and hardware companies in the industry. This quarterly snapshot corroborates the 10-year trend documented by Cusumano and shows software companies in that index, depending on the quarter, are averaging 56 to 70 percent of revenues from services.

The article also discusses software companies that are "stuck in the middle" regarding their revenue mix. These are software companies that are unclear if they want to focus on product revenues or services revenues. This observation by Cusumano is directly related to our observation of companies caught in the services chasm.

This analysis and article on the software industry by an esteemed MIT professor places an exclamation point on our belief that the technology industry in general is maturing. Now, for the first time in the history of the industry, many technology companies must be optimized to serve maturing markets. These maturing markets are often service intensive. Product companies must decide if they will cross the services chasm to satisfy these maturing markets or push that requirement to partners in the market place. If service requirements in aging markets are sent to partners, product companies must work diligently to identify new sources of product growth. To be clear, those product opportunities still exist. Complex business problems requiring product innovations will never cease to exist. However, historically product-centric companies must realistically assess their current abilities to capture a shrinking volume of explosive product markets.

In Chapter 1, I began by stating I have the following bias:

> *Effectively aligning a company's services strategy to overall company strategy will become the defining discipline in any product company's success.*

Once again, I will remind the reader I am not claiming products no longer matter to the success of product companies. However, the approach of optimizing product economics in a vacuum devoid of services strategy is indeed outdated.

By understanding that common services strategies have already emerged, product companies can accelerate the process of mapping the appropriate services strategy to optimize product and company success. I also believe selecting the appropriate product/service mix has become critical to surviving in maturing marketplaces. In 5 or 10 years, we will know exactly how critical services-strategy decisions were to the technology industry players of today.

# Chapter 8

# Bridging the Services Chasm

an, it took us a long time to get here. Eight chapters into this book, and we are just now discussing the topic that is in the title: *bridging the services chasm*. It took us awhile to reach this point because context is everything. Without the context of services-strategy profiles, you can't understand the phenomenon of the services chasm. If you don't understand what creates the services chasm, you have no context for what you are attempting to bridge. **In fact, simply having a common taxonomy and framework for discussing services-strategy decisions is a significant step forward in crossing the services chasm**. But all of that context setting is behind us, and here we are. Ready to build bridges. Bridges that determine the success or failure of your services initiatives.

## THREE FACTORS TO FIND DIRECTION

The services chasm is very real. Every product company faces this as its product technologies mature. Thrashing in the chasm is not productive. Listening

Figure 8-1  Bridge Building

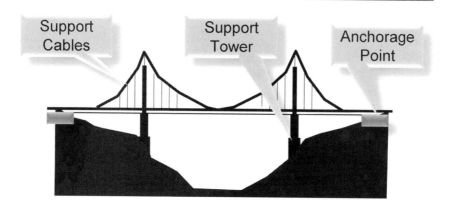

exclusively to Wall Street analysts is even less productive. If a product company finds itself in the chasm, how can the management team decide which way to move, forward or backward? In other words, does the company really need to change its services-strategy profile? **In case the perspective has been lost, I do not believe every product company should plow forward and change its revenue mix when faced by the services chasm. Some product companies should absolutely change product offerings.** But what makes sense for your company? I recommend management teams base their services strategy on three key factors:

1.  Business strategy of the company

2.  Maturity of the marketplace

3.  Maturity of the product set

## Business Strategy

To start the assessment of appropriate services strategy, a company should consider the overall business strategy of the company. The well-read article *Customer Intimacy and Other Value Disciplines* by Frederik D. Wiersema and Michael Treacy identifies three broad business strategies companies tend to pursue[1]:

> **Operational Excellence**: Strategy is predicated on the production and delivery of products and services. The objective is to lead the industry in terms of price and convenience.

> **Customer Intimacy:** Strategy is predicated on tailoring and shaping products and services to fit an increasingly fine definition of the customer. The objective is long-term customer loyalty and long-term customer profitability.

> **Product Leadership:** Strategy is predicated on producing a continuous stream of state-of-the-art products and services. The objective is the quick commercialization of new ideas.

What services-strategy profile a company is interested in adopting is greatly influenced by its overall business strategy. Expanded services capabilities often go hand in hand with a customer intimacy strategy. Product leadership fits nicely with a focus on product revenues. Table 8-1 maps the fit of different services strategies to the three common business strategies.

---

[1] Customer Intimacy and Other Value Disciplines, Jan 1, 1993, Frederik D. Wiersema, Michael Treacy.

Table 8-1  Mapping Services-Strategy Profile to Business Strategy

|  | Product Leadership | Operational Efficiency | Customer Intimacy |
|---|---|---|---|
| **Solution Provider** | WEAK FIT | STRONG FIT | STRONG FIT |
| **Product Provider** | STRONG FIT | STRONG FIT | WEAK FIT |
| **Product Extender** | MODERATE FIT | STRONG FIT | STRONG FIT |
| **Systems Provider** | MODERATE FIT | STRONG FIT | STRONG FIT |

## Market Maturity

After identifying the general business strategy the company is pursuing, a management team should consider the current realities of the technology marketplace the company is serving. Is this an emerging market with high-growth potential? Is this an aging marketplace with fewer new customers to conquer? What is more important to the customers buying the solution: feature functionality or total cost of ownership? Understanding the maturity of the marketplace creates a second sync point in understanding what services-strategy profiles are feasible for future growth. For example, a product-provider profile will generate little growth in a mature market where product sales are waning. Table 8-2 maps services-strategy profiles that generate revenue growth to Geoffrey Moore's four stages of product market maturity.

## Product Maturity

Finally, a management team should consider the maturity of the product around which the company is building the services strategy. A marketplace could be in high growth mode, but the product the company is releasing is

Table 8-2  Revenue Growth Opportunities

| Services | Market Maturity | | | |
|---|---|---|---|---|
| Strategy Profile | A | B | C | D |
| **Solution Provider** | HIGH GROWTH | MODERATE GROWTH | MODERATE GROWTH | MODERATE GROWTH |
| **Product Provider** | LOW GROWTH | HIGH GROWTH | NO GROWTH | NO GROWTH |
| **Product Extender** | MODERATE GROWTH | HIGH GROWTH | MODERATE GROWTH | MODERATE GROWTH |
| **Systems Provider** | MODERATE GROWTH | MODERATE GROWTH | MODERATE GROWTH | MODERATE GROWTH |

relatively immature. This means the company may need to assume a solution-provider profile in the short term, even though the marketplace is supporting product-provider profiles from other companies.

## *Putting It All Together*

It is no accident I recommend management teams first consider business strategy, then market maturity, and finally product maturity. I have found management teams have a strong sense of their desired business strategy. They have less understanding of the overall maturity of the markets they are serving, and they have even less certainty concerning the actual maturity of their own products. Yes, companies tend to overestimate the maturity of their products (and hence underestimate the services requirements for emerging products). Even with these limitations in place, management teams can use these three factors to tease out what services strategy makes the most sense. There are certain combinations of business strategy, market maturity, and product maturity that point to a clear services strategy that is optimal. These examples are documented in Table 8-3.

This approach of analyzing business strategy, market maturity, and product maturity can identify where a significant disconnect exists between current services strategy and optimal services strategy. If it is clear the company needs to change services-strategy profile, the reader can proceed to the section on bridge building. However, some management teams cannot successfully ascertain from discussing these three parameters if a services-strategy shift is in order. A second mechanism managers can use is more of a "bottoms up approach" to choosing a target services strategy.

## THREE GATES: REVERSE-ENGINEERING SERVICES-STRATEGY PROFILE

Analyzing business strategy, market maturity, and product maturity is a relatively strategic approach to setting services strategy. Let's be blunt, some companies are not that strategic. To them, the approach outlined in the previous

Table 8-3  Optimal Services-Strategy Profiles

| Business Strategy | Market Maturity | Product Maturity | Optimal Profile |
|---|---|---|---|
| Product Leadership | A | LOW | Solution Provider |
|  | B | HIGH | Product Provider |
| Customer Intimacy | A | LOW | Solution Provider |
|  | B, C | HIGH | Product Extender |
| Operational Efficiency | D | HIGH | Systems Provider |

section will seem academic and esoteric. In the final chapter of this book, I will make the economic case why I believe all product companies will be forced to become very strategic in their product-services planning. However, **product companies may find themselves against a financial wall, where revenues and profits need to be improved almost immediately. For those seeking a more tactile approach to calibrating services-strategy profile that results in short-term financial improvements, you can follow a three gates model.**

## First Gate: Services Dilutive?

In the first gate of this process, the management team examines the profitability of each distinct services line within the company. For example, support services, professional services, education services, and managed services. For each services line, the company reviews current financial performance and determines if the services are dilutive to company profitability. In other words, are the services generating low or no margin dollars for the company?

## Second Gate: Divest or Invest?

For services that are dilutive, the second gate in this process will be to identify tactics for divesting the company from delivering these services. Services can be migrated to partners, and services delivery staff can be reallocated.

For services that are additive to company profitability, the management team can identify tactics for expanding these services revenues. Tactics such as sales training to increase attach rates can be itemized. In addition, the management team will want to identify opportunities for improving services profitability through operational efficiency initiatives. These first two gates are documented in Figure 8-2.

After passing through the first two gates of dialogue, the management team understands if the general intent is to contract or expand the services portfolio. This leads to the third gate.

## Third Gate: New Services-Strategy Profile?

Finally, the management team can take stock in the previous decisions and leverage the information on services-strategy profiles. The team can determine if these decisions are causing the company to alter its fundamental services-strategy profile. In other words, is the company now moving from a product-provider profile to a product-extender profile? If the services-strategy profile

Figure 8-2  Gates One and Two

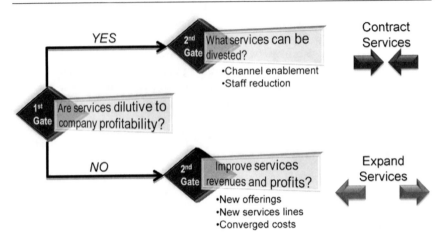

is changing, the management team should begin discussions on initiatives required to support the new profile. Figure 8-3 documents the third gate.

These three gates in services-strategy conversations emerge when product revenues suddenly come under duress, as they did in the global economic downturn that began in 2008. Company executives look for ways to trim the ship. Low margin, human-capital-intensive services are a natural target. At the same time, higher margin services become attractive to offset product short-falls.

One point of caution. **There is a known risk in this three gates approach**. A product company may require certain services capabilities to ultimately achieve market adoption of a new product—even if those services offerings are unprofitable to deliver. If no competent services partners exist, the prod-

Figure 8-3  Gate Three

uct company will need to hold on to these offerings. If the company is under incredible financial duress, this scenario can prove fatal. Either the company needs to secure additional funding or the company will need to quickly acquire the ability to deliver these required services profitably.

## BRIDGE BUILDING

Up to this point in the journey, we have spent a great deal of time and energy to clearly define exactly what constitutes the services chasm, this thrashing on the target services strategy for a company with a blended portfolio of products and services. We have also spent a great deal of time clearly defining alternative service strategies a product company can choose. All of this framing serves as an accelerator for solving the challenges presented by the services chasm. Clearly understanding the challenge is the prerequisite for successfully addressing the challenge.

Now, what if a management team has made the decision it wants to cross the services chasm. In other words, the executive team wants to pursue a "change mix" strategy where the amount of revenue coming from services will increase. For example, a product provider decides it wants to change into a product extender. When this decision has been made, a management team must begin orchestrating significant organizational change. We are now into the dark art, I mean science, of change management. There are numerous reasons companies fail to manage change in their business lines. Clayton Christensen's *Innovator's Dilemma* highlights several factors that are applicable to product companies creating new service lines:

> **Company resources are allocated to the current revenue streams that pay the bills**. In the case of product companies attempting to cross the services chasm, company resources are heavily allocated to the development and selling of products.

> **Company processes and skills reinforce current revenue streams**. Regardless of resource allocation, a product company is optimized to make and sell product. Entering new service markets requires the development of new skills and processes. Always easier said than done.

> **Initial revenue streams are trivial.** A company may be generating millions or billions of dollars from product sales. Initial services revenue streams appear microscopic in comparison. This lack of size makes it challenging to recruit top managers within the company to become part of this new business endeavor. Without top leadership talent, change management becomes even more difficult.

Despite these known challenges, some companies do successfully manage change. And some companies do cross the services chasm. The most apropos metaphor for describing how companies successfully cross the services chasm is bridge building. Management teams approach the edge of that services chasm and peer across to the other side. How do we get there? This is no different than the challenge facing an Inca Indian, 3,000 years ago, looking across a river gorge and wondering how to traverse the gap. The Incas learned how to build suspension bridges. The same general concepts they applied to cross a physical gap can be applied by organizations when attempting to cross an organizational gap:

1. Set anchorage points on the far side.

2. Thread support cables.

3. Surface the bridge.

The next three sections will define these bridge-building tactics as they relate to navigating service strategy change.

## SETTING THE ANCHORAGE POINT

The first step in building a suspension bridge across a chasm is establishing an anchorage point on the far side of the chasm. This anchorage point is used to secure all future efforts in building the bridge. If the anchorage point is not solid, the bridge-building process collapses. **For an organization crossing the services chasm, setting the anchorage point is all about aligning the executive team on the target services-strategy profile.** This alignment answers the question "where is the far side?" What target state is the company trying to reach with the service business? If the management team does not have a clear vision of the target state (the other side), no one knows how long or strong the bridge needs to be. Also, if the anchorage points are weak (unclear vision), the new bridge will collapse under the weight of employees and processes that need to cross it.

Unfortunately, setting a strong anchorage point is not as simple as *picking* a target services-strategy profile. To move an executive team toward a common vision they can truly internalize will require the use of multiple tactics. Howard Gardner, out of Harvard, wrote a great book titled *Changing Minds*[2]. Gardner studied the tactics that organizations can employ to drive change in behaviors. He discusses three tactics that are very relevant when working to align a management team on a common vision:

---

[2] Howard Gardner, *Changing Minds*. Boston: Harvard Business School Press. 2006.

**Clear Reasons:** First of all, a management team needs to understand why change must occur. Why does the organization need to build a bridge and move to a new target state? If a set of compelling reasons have not been clearly itemized, executives can lose their will to change. The framework on services-strategy profiles provides some of the compelling reasons a company would decide to change services-strategy profile.

**Representations:** Gardner found that a change of mind becomes easier to the extent that it lends itself to representation in multiple forms. For example, frameworks, graphs, and pictures help tell the story of why the change needs to occur and what the target state looks like. These representations help executives internalize where the organization needs to go. Once again, the services-strategy profiles and services-chasm framework are example representations for setting services strategy.

**Real-World Examples:** Finally, Gardner found that the more real-world examples that can be cited, the easier it becomes for the executive team to understand the change at hand. IBM has been the poster child for a company that successfully crossed the services chasm, but the series on services-strategy profiles cites many more examples.

Strong common vision equates to a strong anchor point to secure the pending bridge. You know the management team has established a solid anchorage point for services strategy when multiple executives and managers answer the services-strategy profile quizzes provided in Chapters 3 though 6 with consistent responses. In addition, senior leaders should be able to accurately describe the following parameters of the services strategy:

- How important is service profitability to the overall profitability of the company?

- Does the company need to increase, decrease, or sustain the amount of total revenue coming from services?

- What new service capabilities is the company investing to build?

- In the selling cycle, when does the company want services to be engaged?

- When (and why) does the company use internal service resources vs. service partners?

To be clear, the answers to these questions will differ greatly based on the target services strategy. The importance is in the consistency of the answers.

Before moving to the next step in building the bridge across the services chasm, I want to discuss the challenge of crossing a very large chasm.

### Establishing Support Towers

If the gap to be crossed is large, a simple suspension bridge will not do. Towers need to be built in the gap to support the bridge. Think of the bridge spanning the Golden Gate in San Francisco. This same dynamic applies to companies that want to undergo a significant change in services strategy. For example, the company needs to transition from being a hard-core product provider to a systems provider. To achieve this large of a transition, the company should establish change milestones. Each milestone is equivalent to a supporting tower. Change milestones should be defined by achieving target metrics. For example, a company may realize it has achieved a significant step forward when sales people attach service engagements to at least 50 percent of all new product installations.

Before closing this section on setting the anchorage point, I want to comment on the book that preceded this one: *Mastering Professional Services*. The catalyst for that body of work was the disparity I saw in management teams when they would discuss their professional services strategy. I designed a set of frameworks for executives to align their expectations regarding the parameters of the PS business. In essence, the frameworks are designed to help management teams anchor their services strategy by agreeing on the parameters for nine critical services-strategy variables. Regardless of the mechanisms employed, once a management team has established a strong anchor point on the far shore, it can move onto the second step in the bridge-building process.

## THREADING CABLES

After the anchorage point is established on the far side, a new suspension bridge requires cables to be carried across. These cables will actually bear the weight of the bridge surface and any traffic the bridge must support. There are two main cables supporting the Golden Gate Bridge. Within each cable are 27,752 steel wires—over 80,000 miles of wire. When building an organizational bridge, the supporting wires are people, or the human capital required to support the new services strategy.

In *Changing Minds*, Gardner also highlights the importance of resource allocation and reward systems to motivate change within an organization. These two tactics are now critical as a company reinforces its efforts to cross the services chasm. Specifically, three tactics exist that companies should employ to begin threading human capital to the other side:

### First Tactic to Support Change: Breaking Down Geo-Centric Boundaries

The first tactic a company can use to thread supporting cables across the services chasm relates to organizational structure. To sell and deliver services, the company will need skilled service professionals close to the customer. For many companies, this means local country or regional managers would have to support the hiring of service personnel. If these new employees hit the profit and loss line for the regional managers, the hiring may never be done. Proof of this challenge is shown from the results of questions asked at a TPSA industry summit in 2007. One hundred twenty PS leaders were asked to respond to the following statement:

> **PS business plans have failed because resources have not been hired in a timely manner.**

The audience responses are documented in Figure 8-4.

Figure 8-4  Delayed Hiring Impact Services Success?

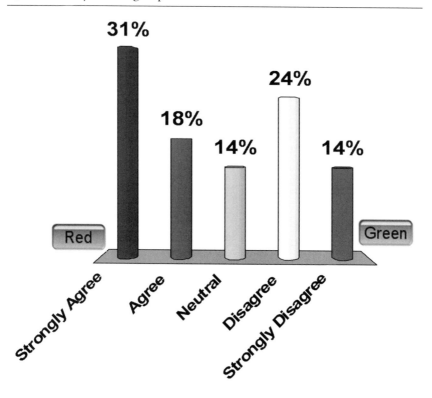

The data from this sample of industry veterans shows that if hiring is not in sync with new services-strategy requirements, the services strategy is a dead man walking. After all, how can you build a human-capital-intensive business if no one wants to hire the human capital? An effective response to this challenge is to place the hiring responsibilities into the hands of the global services team. The global team needs the latitude and authority to hire new skills ahead of the pending demand. If these geo-centric and localized hiring models are not broken down, the bridge-building process collapses.

In Chapter 10, the various strategies for scaling resources in a services organization will be discussed in more detail. In today's world of globalized delivery, multiple resource pools must be leveraged to optimize both scalability and profitability. The key point at this time is hiring and resourcing must be coordinated on a global basis to accelerate the development the new skills required to support the new target services strategy. But what happens after the folks are hired or transferred into the services organization?

### The Second Tactic to Support Change: Hiring and Developing New Services Skills

The new state of the services business will most assuredly require skills not currently present in the human capital of the company. Sample skills required in service organizations but not required in product companies include:

- Ability to successfully sell the value of intangible services

- Ability to accurately estimate the effort required to deliver complex service projects

- Ability to profitably manage scope change and changing customer requirements during longer service engagements

- Familiarity with managing a services P&L

- Expertise in creating compensation for services staff

These are just some of the skills unique to a services business. Some of this expertise can be rented through consultants. However, the organization must eventually develop the skills required to manage the services business. Some of the skills required to sell, deliver, and manage the services business will be brought in through key hires. However, invariably, existing staff will need services skills developed. McMann-Ransford is a consulting firm that specializes in helping companies develop the processes and skills required to manage a services organization. The firm has made the following observations regarding skills development for PS organizations:

*PS teams are constantly forming, norming, storming, and performing around customer projects. As consultants move in and out of projects, success requires not losing valuable project time on the forming, norming, and storming activities. Effective PS skills development focuses on "behavioral change" that enables quick assimilation of PS teams. This enables external hires or internal transfers to embrace "one culture," and deliver one voice/approach in managing customers and projects to quickly deliver value. Developing a high-performance PS organization is not an overnight transition. PS staff will need to leverage multiple development methods:*

- *Self-Improvement*

- *Classroom Training*

- *Experience*

- *Coaching*

- *Mentoring*

*It is a combination of low-risk classroom approaches (tools and best practices, role playing exercises) and moderate to high risk approaches (customer site) to help staff develop confidence, that enables the development of PS staff while engaging, they continue to engage in billable work.[3]*

By investing in a formal skills evaluation and skills development programs, the company begins migrating staff capabilities from one side of the chasm to the other. But investing in new skills will not provide enough support. One more step needs to be taken.

## The Third Tactic to Support Change: Rewarding Change

Finally, the compensation systems of the company will need to be adjusted. The compensation system of product companies is optimized to profitably sell products. If the services strategy is being modified to increase services revenues, the compensation system should mirror this change. Account managers will need to be rewarded to sell complete solution sets that include both products and services. Services delivery managers may need compensation that emphasizes customer satisfaction *and* profitability.

---

[3] *Strategies in Professional Development,* Ford, Lah, McMann, April 2008, TPSA Update.

A specific example concerning changes in compensation is related to rewarding services delivery staff for meeting billable utilization targets. PS compensation is an area TPSA has researched for several years. The data shows two consistencies regarding the compensation of PS delivery staff within embedded PS organizations:

1. Billable utilization is a relatively low percentage of overall compensation for delivery staff (typically less than 2 percent of total compensation for delivery staff in embedded PS organizations).

2. Solution providers concentrate more heavily on billable utilization than product providers.

If a product company is going to shift revenue mix and rely more heavily on services revenues, delivery staff will need to be more motivated to achieve billable utilization targets.

Regardless of the dollar amounts assigned to variable compensation levers, it is the message that matters. Compensation practices should help drive behaviors to support the new target services strategy.

### The Fourth Tactic to Support Change: Cautious Acquisition

Gardner does not discuss acquisition as a tactic to accelerate change, but this is clearly an option. A common desire can be found in product companies to jump start the threading process by acquiring a services organization. Rarely does this big bang approach prove successful. A short list of failed "big bang" acquisitions of services companies by product companies includes Lucent Technologies purchase of International Network Services (INS) in 1999, Novell's purchase of Cambridge Technology Partners in 2001, and Nortel's purchase of PEC solutions in 2005. IBM's purchase of PWC has even been questioned by some analysts. **A company needs to build supporting cables of services skills and services processes before attempting to support the weight of an acquired services business.** A more prudent approach is acquiring targeted services capabilities once the core services DNA is in place. Another more cautious approach is one that was taken by EMC. They leased services expertise from Accenture for 5 years with an option to buy as opposed to acquiring a large services company outright.

## SURFACING

New organizational structures, skills, and compensation policies will create the initial threads of change. However, the change needs to be institutionalized. For this to occur, two tactics will be used to surface this bridge of change:

1. New business practices (processes) will be developed and deployed.

2. New success metrics will be defined, tracked, and celebrated.

## Services Processes

Several business processes exist that are of minimal importance to product companies and maximum importance to services organizations. For illustrative purposes, we will highlight three such process areas.

> **Resource Management:** Resource management involves all the processes required to allocate human capital to the delivery of services engagement. Just like supply chain management applies to optimizing product inventories, resource management processes are designed to optimize the allocation of the right skills to customer projects. Immature resource management processes result in poor services profitability and frustrated customers.

> **Project Management:** To deliver complex services projects, organizations need defined project-engagement processes that navigate effort estimation, project reporting, and scope change. Product companies may have historically ceded project management responsibilities to services partners. However, to cross the services chasm, these processes need to become part of the product company repertoire.

> **Services Development:** Every product company has a defined product-development life cycle (PDLC). This cycle identified key gates for deciding when investment is made in new products and how products are successfully brought to market. Services also require a defined development life cycle. TPSA has found the investment cycle for a successful services-development life cycle (SDLC) is fundamentally different than that of a PDLC. The SDLC does not require the levels of front-end investment required in a PDLC. However, for services to be launched and scaled, a defined SDLC needs to be in place. Also, the SDLC needs to be mapped to the PDLC.

In Chapter 12, we will discuss the concept of monitoring the practices and results required to drive the financial success of a services organization. A multitude of services processes are required to ultimately scale and optimize a services business. These are just three key areas that product-centric companies will typically not have developed. These are processes that can be used to solidify the bridge to a new services-strategy profile.

## Services Metrics

Over the years, I have written several chapters and articles on services metrics. I subscribe to the management truism that what does not get measured does not get managed. When bridging the services chasm, metrics take an even more significant role in success. Why? In bridge building, accurately understanding the current state is critical. Workers need to understand what has been done and what needs to be done. Broadcasting the current state to all parties involved is just as critical. Citizens need to know when they can start driving across that bridge.

At TPSA, we documented over 70 metrics that an organization can use to understand the health of a PS business. In *Mastering Professional Services*, I provided a framework for categorizing services metrics to create a portfolio that provides leading indicators on the health of the business. In addition, TPSA has surveyed services executives to determine the 10 most commonly used metrics. Pulling all of this together, there are metrics beyond services bookings and utilization rates we recommend services leaders begin tracking early in the bridge-building process:

> **Attach Rate:** How often are the new services being offered by the company being attached to product sales? Ten percent of the time? Fifty percent of the time? Services attach rates tell the story of company commitment to an expanded services portfolio.
>
> **Project Margin:** When product companies first begin offering new services, overall services margins may drop. Look at the IBM example in the next section for a dramatic example of this phenomenon. However, as services processes and skills mature, project margins should improve.
>
> **Discount Rate:** Discount rate is the delta between your list price for a service and the realized price. Discounting rate is a proxy metric for how well the sales force is able to articulate the value of services to customers.
>
> **Repeat Rate:** Repeat rate tracks how many repeat customers the services organization has for new services capabilities. This is a proxy metric for customer satisfaction that is easier to calculate and speaks directly to the customer's experience with services.
>
> **Solution Maturity:** Solution maturity is the measurement of a company's ability to deliver a specific services offering consistently and profitability. Solution maturity is calculated by inventorying the artifacts required to support services delivery and determining which ones

are in place for key offerings. Artifacts include delivery engagement methodologies, delivery skills profiles, and sample customer deliverables. The more artifacts in place, the higher the solution maturity rating. This metric helps track progress of the maturity of the overall services portfolio and the maturity of the services organization in general. The metric can also be used to help instill confidence in the product sales force that the company truly has the ability to deliver new services offerings.

By tracking and communicating these five metrics, services leaders are both informing and promoting. They are informing the company on the maturity of the bridge-building process. They are also promoting the fact that the effort is having a real impact on services financials. In the next chapter, we will discuss the process of connecting services activities to overall company success, but that is a discipline that goes beyond the basic metrics highlighted here.

## TIME FRAMES FOR BRIDGE BUILDING

The final section in this chapter on bridge building concerns time. A very common question we receive is "how long?"

- How long will it take for our company to be more services led?

- How long will it take for us to be able to sell solutions instead of just technology?

- How long will take for our account managers to care about attaching services?

These are all fair questions. My answer is always unpopular. "Twice as long as you expect, three times as long as you hope." Why is that my answer? Companies embark on the services chasm crossing with a one-year perspective. They announce new services initiatives with the hope the company will migrate to a new services-strategy profile within a calendar year. Privately, they know it may take a little longer—maybe a full 18 months for the change to really get traction.

**In reality, shifts in services strategy are 3-year journeys—minimal. The first year is all about threading cables with new staff and new services-related skills. The second year is surfacing, when processes are truly matured to support new services activities in a more scalable fashion. The third year is when the organization begins seeing the results of its efforts, and the change laggards are either converted or catapulted.** I told you—an unpopular answer!

I stick to this 3-year guidance because no empirical data exists supporting faster transitions. In *Building Professional Services,* I documented four distinct phases companies experience as they transition their product services mix:

> **Phase 0: Support Services:** Product company provides support services aligned closely to the core product.
>
> **Phase 1: Implementation Services:** Product company expands services offerings to accelerate product adoption. Services still aligned closely to product.
>
> **Phase 2: Integration Services:** Product company expands services to incorporate the integration of products and services not developed directly by the company.
>
> **Phase 3: Consulting Services:** Product company provides true consulting services related to business insights.
>
> **Phase 4: Converged Services:** This is a newly named, emerging phase, where the product company begins merging product and services into subscription or utility offerings. Traditional boundaries between product and distinct services lines blur, which creates unique opportunities for improved margins on offerings.

The services mix and services margins experienced during these four phases was initially modeled in *Building Professional Services.* An example transition curve was provided and is recreated in Figure 8-5. As can be seen, as services revenues grow as a percentage of total revenues, services margins temporarily dip down. This is a function of investing in skills, processes, and so on.

Figure 8-5  Four Phases of Building Services

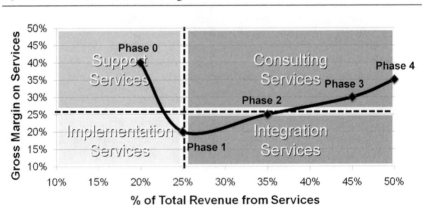

Since publishing *Building Professional Services* back in 2002, I have tracked the successful and failed services-strategy transitions of many product companies. IBM's journey from product provider to systems provider is an important one to note—only because they have served as the poster child for product companies attempting to become more services oriented. The graph in Figure 8-6 maps IBM's transition from product-centric to more services-centric revenues. **The bubble size represents the growth rate of the services revenues that year**. Clearly, this was at least a 5-year journey that constituted incredible organizational angst that almost culminated in the demise of the company. Lou Gerstner's book *Who Says Elephants Can't Dance?* tells the tale.

Other companies, such as EMC and Xerox, have worked through significant transitions in services-strategy profiles. These examples, and countless others less public, reinforce the story. Shifts in services strategy take time. Years, not quarters. Once again—for effect, it takes "twice as long as you expect, three times as long as you hope."

## SUMMARY OF BRIDGE BUILDING

This chapter provides a blue print for how product companies can build a bridge to cross the services chasm. In summary, the key steps in the process are as follows:

Figure 8-6  IBM Services Growth

1.  **Select a target services-strategy profile.** This can be done by mapping business strategy to market state or by responding to urgent profitability needs.

2.  **Set a firm anchor point.** Verify the senior management team has a clear understanding of the parameters of the target services strategy.

3.  **Thread the supporting cables.** These supporting cables come in several forms:

    Organizational structure: Shift from geo-centric to global

    a.  Skills: Hiring an development of services management skills

    b.  Compensation: New emphasis on services-related metrics

4.  **Surface the bridge.** Mature the processes and metrics required to scale and optimize the new services offerings. Key process areas include resource management, project management, and services development. Key metrics include services attach rates, project margins, services discount rates, customer repeat rates, and solution maturity.

5.  **Allocate enough time.** The time allocated to build the bridge and cross the services chasm should be allocated in years, not quarters.

As a company navigates bridging the services chasm, there will be missteps along the way. Progress will be made, only to be undone. One discipline that serves services leaders well during the bridge building is the ability to clearly understand the impact new services capabilities are having on product success and overall company success. After all, any company with a strong heritage in product development and innovation will quickly lose its appetite for services if they are not ultimately helping to maximize the success of the product portfolio. The discipline of connecting service activity to product and company success is the topic of the next chapter.

Chapter **9**

# Maximizing Product Success

t took us eight chapters to reach the core topic of the book: how to bridge the services chasm. In this ninth chapter, we will reach the topic of the book's subtitle: aligning services strategy to maximize product success.

## DEFINING SUCCESS

Product companies want to sell products. I have no confusion on this premise. So, when you ask product company executives what they want from their services business, the answer is pretty straight forward: Help sell more products. The answer may not always come out quickly and directly. Executives may beat around the bush by saying "services are a strategic weapon to assure customer satisfaction and account success." But the reason you keep customers happy is very simple: You want them to buy more product. **I agree that the home run for services organizations within product companies is to accelerate product sales.** However, a significant disconnect exists between where services activities can maximize products sales and where product companies attempt to measure the impact of services on product sales. The disconnect between where services has the largest impact on product success and where product companies typically look for the impact can be expressed by the image shown in Figure 9-1. Let me explain.

### Current Perceptions of the Impact of Services

When you think about services influencing product success, four simple buckets can be used to discuss the influence:

**Sell:** Services capabilities help accelerate the product sales cycle.

**Buy:** Services help the customer in their initial implementation of the product.

**Adopt:** Services help the customer master product capabilities and fully realize the business benefits from having purchased the product.

185

Figure 9-1  Understanding the Impact of Services on Product Success

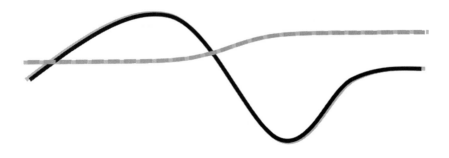

**Renew:** Services presence helps to increase the number of customers that stay on the product platform and do not defect to competitive offerings.

Where do product companies believe services capabilities have the greatest impact on product success? It depends on the type of service. For maintenance and managed services, clearly companies believe solid execution of these supporting services equates to product repurchase. For project-based professional services, the influence is believed to occur on the front end during the initial sell and buy phases.

These four phases of customer engagement and the perceived influence of services capabilities on product success are summarized in Figure 9-2. This graph shows the belief that professional services capabilities help sell the product and support services help with product repurchase. **In between the buy**

Figure 9-2  Perceptions of Services and Product Success

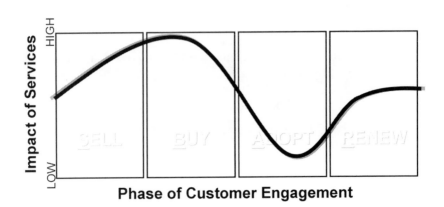

and renew phases is a no-man's land where the customer is often on his own to drive successful product adoption.

Why is the graph painted this way? Because our efforts within the service industry associations to definitively quantify the influence of services on product success have led us to these conclusions. Over the past 4 years, TPSA has been working with member companies to analyze the impact of services on product success. We refer to this discipline as *economic impact analysis*. From this work, we know the most common metrics used to assess the influence of services on product success. We also have a very good sense of what percentage of product companies actually track these metrics. The information on these metrics is shown in Table 9-1. As can be seen, even though these are the metrics most product companies would like to understand regarding the impact of services, a clear majority of product companies do not track any of these metrics. In addition, this short list of metrics is focused on the sell, buy, and renew phases of customer engagement.

This combination of a short list of metrics and a poor track record of actually measuring them has led to a significant disadvantage for services executives. My favorite analogy is borrowed from the movie *The Untouchables*: These services executives are showing up to a gun fight armed with a blunt butter knife. **Services executives are being asked to demonstrate how services maximize product success, but they don't have any data. To add insult to injury, they are most likely looking in the wrong places to make the case.**

Table 9-1  Common Economic Impact Metrics

| Metric | Description | Percentage of Product Companies Tracking this Metric |
|---|---|---|
| Product Pull | Services engagement "pulls through" the sale of a product. | 24% |
| Customer Satisfaction | Services engagement improves overall customer satisfaction ratings in the account. | 16% |
| Product Renewal | Services engagement improves the percentage of customers that repurchase product from the company. | 14% |
| Product Margins | Services engagement improves the margins achieved when selling company products to the customer. | 12% |

## WHAT PRODUCT COMPANY EXECUTIVES REALLY NEED TO KNOW ABOUT SERVICES

When services executives cannot link their offerings to product success, they fall back to business performance metrics. Multiple data points are extremely important to optimizing services profitability. For example, PS managers can report what bill rates and utilization rates are being achieved by PS resources. And how project margins are trending. Or how the backlog is big enough to make the upcoming quarter. These are all important points to the services executive. For the top management of product companies, however, these data points have little relevance. These items represent operational minutiae to an executive trying to conquer new markets and raise the stock price. So what does the executive staff need to know about the services business?

First of all, executives do care about overall service revenues and profits. No real business unit gets out of reporting those data points to executive management. These numbers have a direct impact on earnings per share. However, services executives in product companies need to successfully link their business to the overall success of the product. Back in 2006, TPSA documented a list of over 20 economic transactions the services organization has the potential to influence. This system of economic transactions is documented in Figure 9-3.

**The problem with Figure 9-3 is that it is overwhelming. Also, we have not seen many of these influences quantified by *any* product company.**

Figure 9-3  Economic Transactions Services Can Influence

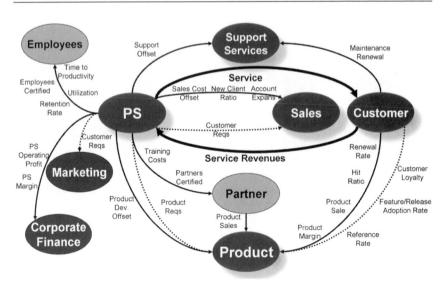

What services executives need is *focus*. They need to focus on a tight subset of metrics that have the biggest buck for telling the services story.

Of the multiple economic transactions the services organization could be influencing, there is a subset we have found that almost every product company cares about. Also, these metrics have the greatest potential for demonstrating the positive influence of services on product success:

1. Product revenues

2. Product renewal rates

3. Total account revenue

4. Total account profitability

The first two metrics of product revenue and product renewal were listed in the previous section. These metrics speak to the health of product sales. Metrics three and four speak to the overall success of the company within the account. What is clear from our work in this area is that services organizations have a much greater chance of demonstrating the influence of services activity on the long-term performance of an account as opposed to attempting to show how services secured an initial deal. Figure 9-4 represents this reality graphically. This figure shows that service activities are actually generating the greatest economic benefit for product companies during the product adoption and renewal phases, not the initial selling or buying phases. The current crime is that services organizations have historically focused their offerings to help out in the sell, buy, and renew phases, leaving the adoption phase as a no-man's land to be served by partners or the customer themselves. As the next section will show, this is a massive miss regarding services opportunity to maximize product success.

Figure 9-4  Ability of Services to Influence Product Success

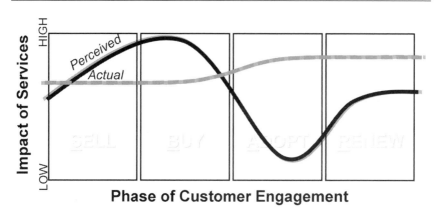

## REAL WORLD EXAMPLES

As previously stated, the discipline of mapping services activity to product success is in its infancy. However, there are companies making real progress on this front. The next section overviews analysis performed by three companies. The specific numbers have been modified to protect the actual datasets provided by these companies, but the positive correlation between services engagement and product success remains the same.

### *Software Company: Adoption of New Products*

Our first example comes from a software company with revenues over $400 million. The company had a new product offering that was slow to be adopted. The company separated customers that bought the new product without PS engagement from customers that leveraged PS to help adopt the product. Figure 9-5 shows how accounts performed with no PS engagement. The customers spent an average of X dollars with the company. A majority of the customer

Figure 9-5   Account Economics without PS

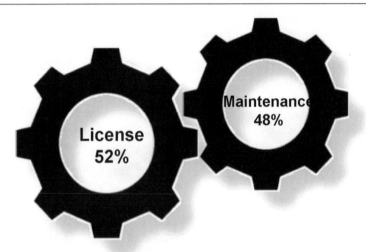

Average Revenue Per Account: (X)
Total Margin $: (Y)
Product Renewal Rate: 56%

dollars were spent on the software license. The remaining dollars were spent on a maintenance contract for the software. The sum of the initial license and maintenance contracts generated Y margin dollars for the company. **However, only a little over half of the customers that bought the new software were renewing their license after the first year.**

Now, for the same product, Figure 9-6 documents how accounts that engaged the company's professional services organization behaved. First, **customers that used professional services spent almost three times as much money with the company.** That's the key metric of total account spending! A chunk of those expanded revenues went to software licenses fees. The customers were spending more money on the software, either buying more licenses or

Figure 9-6  Account Performance with PS

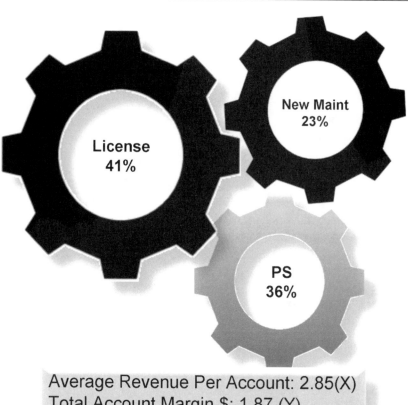

more features. Yes, these customers bought professional services that are lower margin than license or maintenance and can dilute the profitability of an account, but they also spent more money on licenses. In fact, these customers actually generated 1.87 times the amount of total margin dollars as the other customers. Finally, **the customers engaging professional services renewed their maintenance contracts at almost twice the rate of accounts with no PS engagement**.

This example is only one product offering within one product company. However, the point being made is universal: Services engagement can dramatically improve the key metrics of product spending, product renewal, total account spending, and total account profitability. **The ultimate test of success for product companies selling complex solutions is the overall economic performance of the entire account**. By focusing simply on the product gear, a product company limits the total revenue and profit potential of the company. This type of economic impact analysis that models the overall performance of the account enables this type of systems thinking.

### Software Company: Growing Recurring Revenues

Our second example comes from a software company with revenues over $800 million. The mantra of the executive team within this company was simple: Maximize monthly recurring revenue. Executives were fixated on growing the monthly recurring revenues within strategic accounts. Over 90 percent of company revenues came through software subscriptions. Professional services revenues were a rounding error. In fact, the executive team was wondering why any incremental resources should be applied to the PS group. "Why can't partners be used to help customers integrate our product?" Facing the potential of a long, cold hiring freeze, PS leadership embarked on the journey of economic impact analysis.

The PS team worked with executive management, sales management, and finance to segment the customer base and PS activity levels into meaningful categories. How customers and PS engagement levels are segmented can greatly impact the results of this type of analysis. As a starting point, TPSA recommends the following segmentation when analyzing the impact of professional services on account performance.

#### Customer Segmentation

**Large Customers:** The top 20 percent of the customers based on total spend with your company.

**Small Customers:** Bottom 20 percent of customers based on total spending with your company.

**Medium Customers:** All the customers that don't fit into the first two categories.

### PS Engagement Segmentation

**No PS:** PS has not been involved in the customer account.

**Light PS:** PS is involved 1 to 5 days in the account (40 hours or less).

**Moderate PS:** PS is involved 6 to 20 days (41 to 160 hours).

**Heavy PS:** PS is involved more than 20 days (160+ hours).

With the categories in place, the PS team analyzed the impact of certain levels of PS engagement on monthly recurring revenue. They analyzed and presented the data in multiple formats.

## Correlation Analysis

The PS organization aggregated multiple data points to determine whether a statistical correlation existed between level of PS engagement and monthly recurring revenue. An example of the presentation format they used is shown in Figure 9-7. The analysis conducted by this company showed positive correlation increasing PS engagement and higher monthly recurring revenues.

Figure 9-7  Correlation Analysis

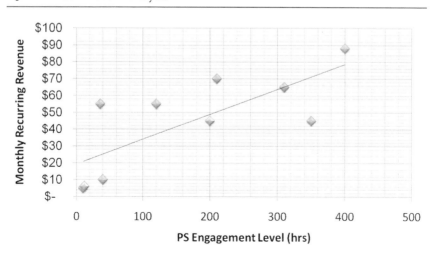

*Growth and Retention Analysis*

After correlation analysis, the PS team analyzed the impact of PS engagement on the two key metrics of account revenue growth and account retention. The analysis demonstrated, like the previous company example, that customers engaging with PS were much more likely to grow or at least provide stable revenues. Figure 9-8 was used to communicate the relationship between high-growth customers and the role of PS. Ninety percent of accounts that were high growth for the company engaged with PS at some level. Figure 9-9 was used to communicate the other side of the coin. Seventy percent of accounts that experienced shrinking monthly recurring revenues had no engagement with PS. The combination of these two figures was used to send simple messages to the sales force: If you want your accounts to grow, consider engaging PS. If you have an account this is high risk of shrinking, consider engaging PS.

*PS Value Matrix Analysis*

Finally, this very thorough PS team created a "PS Value Matrix" to help the executive management team see where PS investment had the greatest impact

Figure 9-8  Involvement of PS in High Growth Accounts

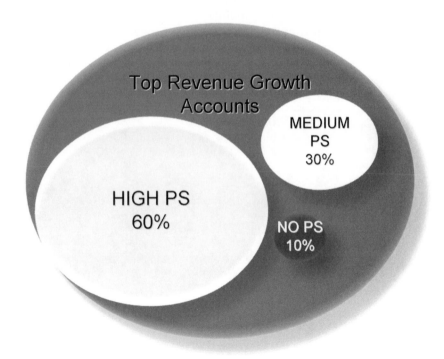

Figure 9-9  Involvement of PS with Shrinking Accounts

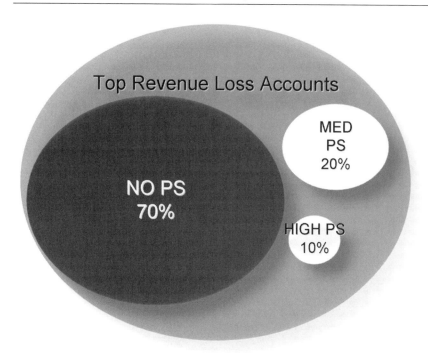

on monthly recurring revenue. The matrix, which is shown in Figure 9-10, helped communicate how different account types responded to different levels of PS engagement. Figure 9-10 shows that small accounts that receive moderate PS investment grow an average of 175 percent, and that small accounts that receive heavy PS involvement grow 200 percent. Using this type of table, companies can make educated decisions on where to target limited PS resources to create the biggest economic bang for the company. And yes, this table could be converted from percentages to absolute dollars to help determine where the largest dollar impact is to the company.

## Hardware Company: Protecting Legacy Revenues, Growing Emerging Revenues

Our third and final example of economic impact analysis comes from a multi-billion dollar hardware company. Because TPSA had documented the approaches pursued by the previous two companies, this company hit the

Figure 9-10  PS Value Matrix

| PS Engagement Level | Customer Segmentation | | |
|---|---|---|---|
| | Small | Medium | Large |
| Heavy PS | 200% | 120% | 90% |
| Moderate PS | 175% | 150% | 105% |
| Light PS | 125% | 90% | 70% |
| No PS | 70% | 65% | 55% |

ground running and focused like a laser on analyzing the impact of consulting on product revenue and account growth. The company's legacy hardware products were feeling the effects of commoditization. Customers were spending less with the company to receive the same (or more) capability. The consulting team found, however, that the largest and most important customers were much more likely to maintain their spending levels with the company if consulting was involved with the customer. The analyst working the data used the graph shown in Figure 9-11 to communicate the impact of consulting on account revenues. So in this case, the important factor surrounding account revenues was not growth but shrinkage. The analysis clearly showed that consulting engagement was protecting millions of dollars in legacy product revenue.

In additional analysis, this hardware company also determined that engagement from consulting dramatically changed the mix of overall spending by the account. Accounts that engaged consulting resources spent twice as much on new, emerging products as did accounts with no consulting. In other words, legacy accounts spent most of their money on legacy products unless consulting was involved to help introduce new product offerings.

All three of these companies, when conducting thorough economic impact analysis, found the same fundamental truth to exist:

*The increased presence of services increases account revenues over time.*

These companies found the impact of services was significant in the later phases of the customer relationship: in adoption and renewal. How many

Figure 9-11  Impact of PS on Legacy Product Revenues

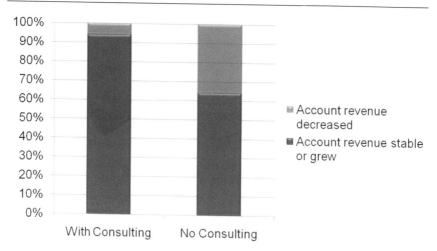

new deals did services close for any of these companies? I'm not sure. In fact, I'm not sure any of them could quote that number because it is difficult to prove what deals closed due to service involvement. However, by using analysis that separates a large number of accounts into two categories, those that have services engagement and those that do not, all three of these companies could clearly document the difference in ongoing account performance when services is engaged. They could also make a fact-based argument that the "services variable" was most likely having a significant impact on this delta in performance.

Service executives *know* their services business can have a positive influence on the key economic metrics of new product sales, product adoption account growth, and account profitability. But, unlike these three companies highlighted, a vast majority of services organizations have failed to quantify the impact. These three case studies are wonderful, but it has taken us years to tease them out of the industry. And for each one of these three companies, there are hundreds more out there that have not conducted any economic impact analysis. Why?

## WHY SERVICE ORGANIZATIONS DON'T TELL THE STORY

There are multiple reasons service organizations fail to quantify how services maximize product success. However, three factors commonly cripple this effort:

1.  Resourcing

2. The approach

3. The power of sales

First, service organizations rarely have the expertise available to conduct this analysis that links services activities to product success. Service organizations work hard to keep nonbillable support staff to a minimum. This makes economic impact analysis a lever few services organizations are resourced to pull. In addition, this type of analysis requires someone on staff that can conduct comprehensive data analytics. A dedicated data analytics resource will have the following responsibilities:

- Own, schedule, design, and manage all aspects of data analysis for the service organization.

- Communicate with internal and external stakeholders data analysis objectives and design survey instruments to meet project objectives and analysis goals.

- Coordinate with finance and IT to secure required data streams.

- Tabulate and analyze data and determine appropriate presentation of results, and synthesize data into succinct, actionable results to address project objectives.

- Oversee/direct integration of multivariate analysis, when appropriate.

- Develop internal reports/presentations that deliver strong implications to the business.

- Present findings internally to the senior team and across the company.

This type of data analytics resource has the following profile:

- Strong analytical skills, with the ability to turn business problems into researchable questions, oversee data collection, then analyze, interpret, and communicate actionable results.

- Expertise in quantitative research (web, phone, and mail), including survey design, data analysis and interpretation, report writing, and presentation of key findings.

- Strong communication skills, managing multiple outside research partners and marketing agencies as well.

- MBA and 3 to 5 years work experience post-MBA, with a related math/statistics background preferred.

How many service organizations have this type of resource assigned with these responsibilities? Not many. Without analytical cycles available, the service organization is handicapped in its ability to conduct credible economic impact analysis.

Not having the right resource is one common failure point. Yet, service organizations that have allocated resources to economic impact analysis still have failed in their attempt to model the influence of services on product success. The most common approach is when the service organization bites the bullet and conducts analysis on a few key customer accounts to find examples of services engagement impacting a key economic metric like increased product sales. When the service executive presents the analysis demonstrating that services engagement has increased product sales, the executive staff becomes skeptical and the analysis is discounted. Why? The services organization is showing how product sales at a specific customer have increased, but the executive team will wonder aloud if services engagement was actually the root cause of the increase. By focusing on a few key accounts, the services team opens the analysis up for this type of criticism. In addition, the executive team is often shown the end results of analysis without being engaged in the process itself. This adds to the executive suspicions.

An approach to economic impact analysis that focuses on too few accounts and has little executive engagement is almost always doomed. And the nail in the coffin will be delivered by sales. When reviewing PS impact on certain customer accounts, the sales executive will point to the product account team on that account. "That's our best team, that is why product sales improved, not because of any services sold into the account." **In fact, it becomes very difficult to dislodge the sales organization as the source of almost all the account successes the service organization would like to claim**. The dynamic of the sales organization being the ultimate source of account success should not be a surprise. The sales organization is highly motivated to be the source of account success and growth. In addition, in a product company, the sales organization has exponentially more political clout than the services organization. The ending result is service executives are stymied as they attempt to use specific customers to make their case.

So services organizations limp along, knowing their work is contributing to the overall success of the company, but failing to make their argument credible. But does it really matter? So what if the services staff can't crow about all the product dollars they are pulling? In fact, many product companies have come to the following conclusions regarding their professional service investments:

- Someone has to do the work required to install and integrate products into a customer's environment. This "glue work" is required to assure products are adopted by customers.

- Any partner services organization does not always have the right skills or adequate capacity to perform the glue work.

- As a product company, we need to deliver some level of glue work directly.

- It is better to have this glue work done by PS than by the pre-sales or engineering teams. If the pre-sales team does all this work, the cost of sales skyrockets. If the engineering team does this work, service delivery methodologies that could eventually be leveraged by service partners are never properly developed.

- It is very difficult to determine who drove a product sale: PS or sales. So we will not attempt to model this dynamic.

- To make sure we are not losing too much money on PS, we will at least track the cost of using PS resources in the sales process.

This is a reactive, defensive approach, designed to minimize downside. **If a company truly understands the impact of services on products, the game becomes how to maximize upside, not minimize downside.**

## BUILDING THE SCAFFOLDING

This book has covered, in some detail, ways to align product and services strategy within a product company. The framework of services-strategy profiles accelerates the strategy decisions that must be made concerning professional services within a product company. The overarching theme is that managing these services-strategy decisions in shifting marketplaces is not easy for most product companies; there are chasms in thinking that must be crossed. It is fair to observe that most executives, both product oriented and service oriented, would have to agree with this assessment. Setting services strategy has always been a second-order discipline within product companies. Setting services strategy in today's service-intensive markets is even more daunting.

To overcome the cultural reality that setting services strategy is not the strength of most product companies, service organizations must provide as many forms of supportive scaffolding as possible. The concept of supportive "scaffolding" systems to support change has been explored by several change management researchers. Leveraging Harvard Professor Howard Gardner once again: He touches on the concept of scaffolding in his book *Changing Minds*. Gardner explains that scaffolding systems help organizations as they obtain new skills, and that the scaffolding should be removed when the skills have been mastered. For example, services-strategy profiles provide scaffolding as leaders of product-centric companies become more comfortable with the various roles services can play within their companies. As the company becomes more adept at aligning the correct services strategy to product strategy, the process of explicating, discussing, and deciding on a services-strategy profile becomes obsolete.

In addition to services-strategy profiles, there is a second form of scaffolding service management can develop to help their company cross a chasm in services-strategy thinking. This scaffolding is built by conducting economic impact analysis and creating data that reinforces the business reasons for driving changes in the services strategy. So, yes, proving that the appropriate services strategy maximizes product success is an important step in the journey. This data provides much-needed scaffolding as the services chasm is being crossed. The next section provides guidance on how to successfully navigate the process of economic impact analysis. This guidance is based on the tough lessons learned by TPSA member companies that have actually conducted economic impact analysis.

## ACCELERATORS TO MAXIMIZING PRODUCT SUCCESS

To be clear, economic impact analysis that *successfully* changes company behavior is still a nascent experience within product companies. However, tactics are emerging that seem to accelerate the success of this type of analysis.

### Let Executives Pick the Economic Impact Metrics

First of all, the services organization needs the executive management team of the company to identify what metrics are being used to measure the overall success of current company initiatives. Several metrics exist on which companies may be focused at any given point in time:

- Number of new customers acquired
- Total company revenues
- Percent of revenue from small and medium-size businesses (SMB) customers
- Product sales growth
- Account expansion
- Average monthly recurring revenue per customer

- Average customer profitability
- Competitive replacements
- Customer satisfaction

None of these metrics is inherently better than the other. The only thing that matters is what specific success metrics the executive team is focused on now. **The services organization must understand what metrics the executive team is trying to influence**. Earlier, we made the case that the following four metrics are the ones every product company should be tracking:

1. Product renewal rates
2. Total account revenue
3. Total account revenue
4. Total account profitability

These may resonate with your executive team, or they may not. Once the services team understands what metrics the executive management is trying to move, they can conduct analyses that determines how services engagement impacts those specific metrics. **The accelerator is the fact the executive team sets the agenda for what analysis is meaningful**. This makes them less defensive and skeptical when the results start flowing in.

## Segment Customer Base and Services Engagement Levels

The services organization should also work with executive management, sales management, and finance to segment the customer base and services activity levels into meaningful categories. How customers and services engagement levels are segmented can greatly impact the results of the analysis conducted in future steps. As previously documented, TPSA believes the following segmentation could be used as a starting point for understanding the impact of professional services in accounts:

### Customer Segmentation

**Large Customers:** Top 20 percent of customers based on total spending with your company.

**Small Customers:** Bottom 20 percent of customers based on total spending with your company.

**Medium Customers:** All the customers that don't fit into the first two categories.

### PS Engagement Segmentation

**No PS:** PS has not been involved in the customer account.

**Light PS:** PS is involved 1 to 5 days in the account (40 hours or less).

**Moderate PS:** PS is involved 6 to 20 days (41 to 160 hours).

**Heavy PS:** PS is involved more than 20 days (160+ hours).

By having company leadership agree to this segmentation *before* any analysis is conducted, the results will carry more credibility. The executive staff will see how services engagement impacts the customer segments they already care about and track.

## Leverage the Power Base

As previously highlighted, the sales organization within a product company typically has a great deal of political power. **To gain momentum with this modeling, the exercise should be positioned with the sales organization as a mechanism to secure the right amount of services resources for strategic accounts.** By mapping the right level of services investment to target accounts, the probability of these accounts growing and renewing are increased. Sales leadership, which is ultimately paid more when accounts grow, should be motivated to better understand how services engagement can facilitate this growth.

## Show It All

**To build trust and confidence in the results of any economic impact analysis, provide a full picture of what the analysis shows.** Perhaps services engagement is not improving account profitability with large customers. If this is true, show it. Also, if some of the analysis is inclusive regarding the impact of services activity on improving a specific economic metric like product renewal, do not hesitate to show those results as well. The stakeholders in the organization will have greater faith in the analysis if they believe there is full disclosure.

By following these tactics, a services team has better odds of actually creating economic impact analysis the executive team will buy into. If they truly believe there is a real correlation between services engagement and product success, lots of things gets easier, like the ability to secure new headcount or change sales compensation to encourage the attachment of services offerings. Let's face it, crossing the services chasm requires not only bridge building but glass breaking. Legacy approaches will have to be modified. Business leaders are more confident breaking glass when data supports their actions.

## ENDNOTE: SCAFFOLDING FOR THE INDUSTRY

This chapter outlines how services organizations can use data to build a bridge—a bridge from product-centric planning to holistic product and services planning. We have seen services organizations change executive perspectives by conducting analysis that proves services can clearly help maximize product success. Yet, we believe the real acceleration will occur when an industry baseline is in place. If you are a software company, what is the average improvement you should expect in product renewals if you sell advanced services into accounts? How much does account profitability typically increase if you are a hardware company now selling professional services to your customers? If there were well-researched industry averages in place, services organizations could reference them and grab the attention of the planning process before any specific economic impact analysis was actually conducted within the company. AFSMI, SSPA, and TPSA, as industry associations, are in a position to work with the services organizations to build this industry baseline. These associations can work with member companies to aggregate their actual economic impact data. This aggregated dataset could be used to determine what industry averages are in play and what positive impact product companies should expect from various levels of service engagement. Through its work aggregating successful examples of economic impact analysis, TPSA has published a recommended process companies can follow. Figure 9-12 is an artifact from that process overview. Our hope is more companies will embrace this discipline, execute this process, and contribute to this emerging industry baseline.

Figure 9-12 Process of Economic Impact Analysis

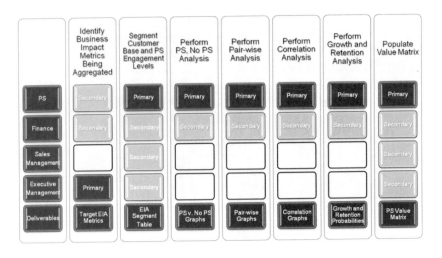

At some point in time, this type of data scaffolding may not be required in product companies. At some point in time, product companies may have ingrained the reality that service engagement increases critical account success factors. For now, building a bridge of data to facilitate executive understanding of the impact of services on product success is mandatory. We can't assemble these industry baselines fast enough.

Mapping the appropriate services strategy to current product strategy is the first step to maximizing product success. Tracking and understanding the impact services activities have on long-term product and customer account success is the second step to maximizing product success. The third step is optimizing the execution of the services business. The previous books *Building Professional Services* and *Mastering Professional Services* provide a set of frameworks for optimizing a technology professional services business. In some ways, this book should have preceded those two! Since the publication of *Building Professional Services* and *Mastering Professional Services*, some ground has shifted regarding the optimization of PS. Specifically, the increasing complexity of sourcing models and the growing importance of services partners. For this reason, I am including a chapter on sourcing strategies and a chapter on services partners. Let's begin with the emerging trends in sourcing models.

# Chapter 10

# Sourcing Services

## By Bo DiMuccio, Ph.D., and Thomas E. Lah

## THE SOURCING STRATEGIES DILEMMA

Despite advances in technology, the concept of self-service, and the emergence of "crowd sourcing" to solve complex problems, the delivery of technology professional services remains a very human-capital-intensive endeavor for product companies. Just to cite a few examples, data from a 2009 TPSA study on PS project performance shows that only two out of 10 projects include any hours billed to off-site or solution-center resources. **In other words, 80 percent of PS projects, according to this study, are delivered exclusively by traditional on-site consulting resources**. Even more interesting is that these numbers are largely unchanged from the 2007 TPSA PS project performance study.

So PS remains a hands-on, human-capital-intensive business. What's the problem? The fact is that complex services solving complex customer problems will increasingly require complex skill sets from increasingly complex sets of resource pools. The never-ending challenge for these companies is that it is always easier to burn another CD, build another mother board, or write more code than it is to hire, train, and deploy a competent professional services employee. Undoubtedly, some product companies are becoming much more aggressive and creative in the tactics they pursue to increase their ability to scale services capabilities. The reason for this is simple: The product and services synergies discussed throughout this book are clearly forcing the issue. **The conclusion is equally simple: To secure product adoption success or maintain account revenues, product companies need increasingly to be innovative in their delivery so that service offerings will be available on a global basis while being delivered in a consistent manner.**

## THE CURRENT STATE OF SOURCING STRATEGIES

Yet, as we've stated, sourcing strategies are remaining relatively static for many technology product companies. This is easily demonstrated by looking at just a few data points from the Q2 of 2009 snapshot of TPSA professional services benchmarking survey. On the topic of sourcing, the TPSA benchmark survey includes a key question about how companies manage the pool of human resources available for PS delivery. Most companies have a dominant approach for handling this core aspect of PS operations: by practice, on a global or centralized basis, and on a geographical or localized basis. As documented in Figure 10-1, the results may be somewhat surprising for anyone focused on services sourcing issues.

For all of the pressures ostensibly moving technology product companies toward a more centralized, globalized approach to resource management, this centralized approach remains the least common practice. In fact, from the first quarter 2008 (Q108) to the second quarter of 2009 (Q209), the proportion of companies with a centralized delivery pool management approach stayed pretty much flat, increasing only from 26 percent to 28 percent of all companies. What about for the larger companies, those with $1 billion in annual revenues or more? Would it not stand to reason that these larger more sophisticated companies might have very different practices than the average company and that they might have come a longer way since early 2008? Based on the data shown in Figure 10-2, the answer is: Not exactly.

The truth is that the large companies are even less likely to manage sourcing centrally or globally, and the percentage of these companies doing so actually declined marginally between Q108 and Q209. On the surface, these

Figure 10-1  Resource Management Practices

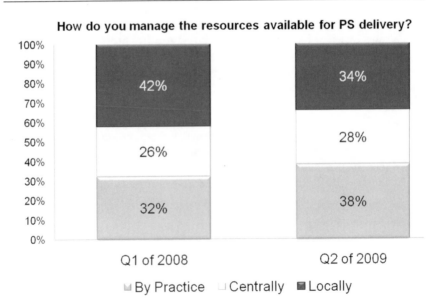

**How do you manage the resources available for PS delivery?**

Q1 of 2008 — By Practice 42%, Centrally 26%, Locally 32%

Q2 of 2009 — By Practice 34%, Centrally 28%, Locally 38%

⊔ By Practice    ⊔ Centrally    ▪ Locally

Figure 10-2  PS Resource Pool Management: Large Companies

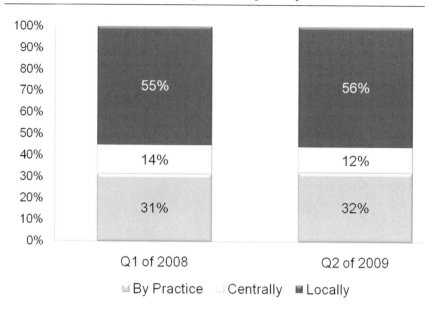

data points raise questions about the value of a more global or centralized approach. If there are so many pressures on companies to take advantage of global sourcing in all of its myriad manifestations and if it is so obviously beneficial for them to do so, why are more of them not doing it? The bulk of this chapter outlines the principles of complex sourcing for complex technology professional services. The remainder of this review of the current state of sourcing will look more in-depth at the data to discover what the potential benefits of a more centralized approach to PS sourcing might be.

One way to do this is to take a comparative look at some of the key sourcing-related practices and performance metrics in product companies that manage service delivery resources differently. One initial observation from the TPSA benchmark data is that PS businesses that employ a global or centralized approach to PS resource management are driving a larger percentage of total company revenues as documented in Figure 10-3.

Figure 10-3 leads us to believe that companies that manage their PS human-resource pool centrally are far more services-centric than those that don't. With such a drastically higher proportion of total revenue coming from technology professional services, we would also expect the financial performance of the same PS businesses to be very different, and in this case higher. Does the data support this expectation? Figure 10-4 provides a comparison of the business model performances for these three sourcing approaches.

Figure 10-3  Revenue Contribution of PS by Resource Management Approach

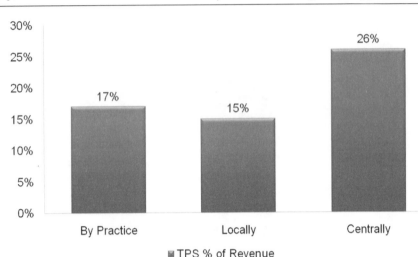

It stands to reason that the higher the revenue contribution of the business unit, the more profit it can be expected to contribute on average. This is definitely the case here based on the data in Figure10- 4. **PS businesses that employ a centralized or global resource management approach are far more profitable on average than those that use other approaches**. This greater profitability includes higher project margins, gross margins that are higher still than we see in the other groups, and average net operating incomes

Figure 10-4  PS Business Model by Resource Management Approach

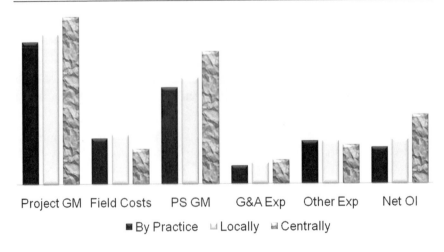

that as much as double the results achieved by companies that don't manage PS resources centrally. Of particular significance is the fact that costs for companies with central resource management compare very favorably in both absolute and relative terms, despite the fact that they are operating with more margin headroom. The key break point in any business model is gross margin. Costs required to deliver a service directly are called "above the line costs" and are subtracted to calculate the project margin achieved when delivering a service. Below the line costs are investments that must be made to sustain the business. Expenses such as marketing, selling, and general management costs. As shown in Figure 10-5, these companies have by far the lowest gross investment in field costs, about the same general and administrative (G&A) costs below the line of project margins, and a bit less in terms of all other below-the-line costs.

But even more interestingly, if we look at these costs (field costs and G&A costs) as percentages of the margin buckets out of which they are pulled, companies with centrally managed delivery-resource pools fare even better. Look, for example, at how much more efficiently they execute in the field relative to companies with other models! Field costs reflect, essentially, how much expense PS businesses have to account for above the line, purely as a function of nonbillable staff costs associated with services delivery. Centrally driven resource management is very likely accounting for at least a portion of these efficiencies.

Below-the-line G&A is often where costs associated with many aspects of PS operations are found. The finding in Figure 10-5 is that the much more

Figure 10-5  Costs Relative to Margins by Resource Management Approach

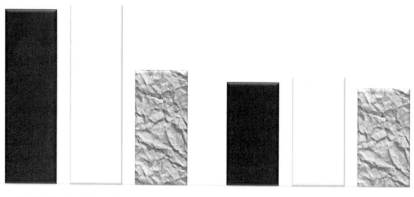

Field Costs % of Project GM            G&A Costs % of PS GM

■ By Practice   ⊔ Locally   ⊔ Centrally

profitable PS businesses with centrally managed resources are still invest-ing in operations below the line, though only slightly less as a percentage of gross margins relative to the other models. Still the question becomes, what does this investment buy for the companies with centrally managed human-resource pools, which can help explain why they are able to operate so much more profitably than the rest? To help address this question, let's look at two interrelated operations benchmarks that go straight to the heart of the issue:

1.  The ability to track staff availability

2.  The time it takes to source new engagements

A PS organization's ability to understand which delivery personnel are available or about to be available to staff a new engagement is a key indicator of sourcing efficiency. And based on the data in Figure 10-6, having a central-ized approach to resource management is an important enabler of this type of operational visibility. While small majorities (56 to 57 percent) of companies with other models also report having this ability, the vast majority (73 percent, or about 30 percent more) of companies that manage their human-resource pools centrally can track staff availability in real time. With this ability, PS organizations should be able to staff new engagements more efficiently and more quickly, thereby enhancing not only customer satisfaction, but also very likely, project profitability. The data in Figure 10-7 supports this premise.

Figure 10-6  The Ability to Track Staff Availability

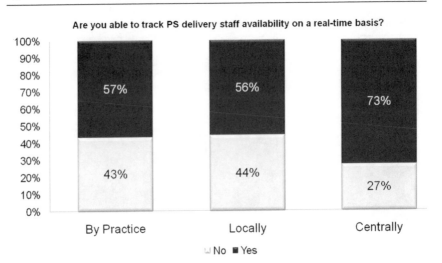

Figure 10-7 Business Days to Staff a New PS Engagement

How many business days on average does it take you to staff a new PS engagement?

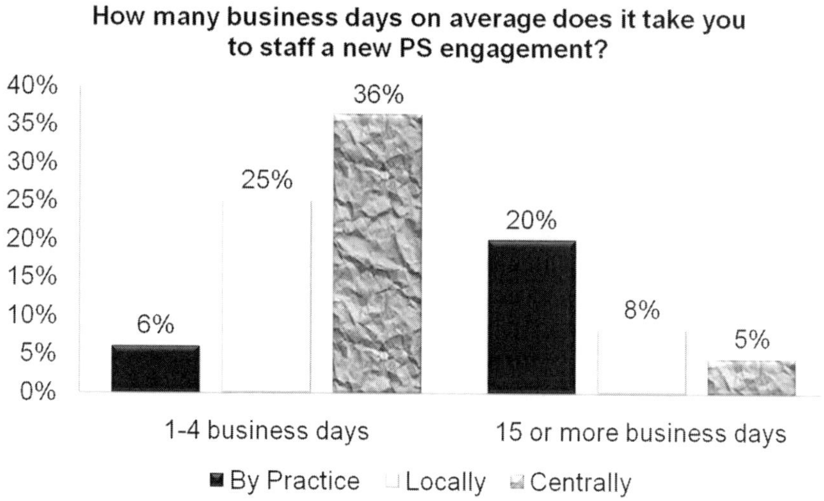

The TPSA benchmark study does not ask for specific numbers in response to the question about the number of business days to source a new project. Still the range data we have offers a compelling confirmation of our expectations as articulated in the previous paragraphs. PS businesses with a centrally managed human-resource pool indicate 1 to 4 business days far more frequently than the other groups and 15 or more business days far less frequently. In short, they staff new PS engagements much more efficiently. This is undoubtedly partly a result of the fact that they are more likely to have real-time staff availability capabilities specifically, and because more generally they manage the resource pool centrally.

**The point of this bit of PS benchmarking is simply to demonstrate that there are indeed potential benefits associated with innovation in the sourcing of professional services.** If increasingly complex services that are meant to solve increasingly complex customer problems do not employ increasingly complex tactics for optimizing resource management, what chance really does the PS business have of succeeding? In light of this contention, we will, in the balance of this chapter, cover three aspects of sourcing services that every product company should understand. For each item covered, we will introduce a framework management teams can use to help navigate challenges. By the end of the chapter, the reader should clearly understand, if nothing else, that the historical model of hiring local talent to serve local customers in a given geography is under immense pressure. Management teams must pull multiple levers to meet both customer needs and profit targets.

## CHALLENGE #1: THE PEAKS AND VALLEYS OF SERVICE DEMAND

First, product companies must understand the challenge of managing through the peaks and valleys of demand in a human-capital-intensive business. Yes, successful product companies understand how to align product inventory to match customer demand. In some ways, the challenge is no different in a services business. **However, the ability to scale services up and down is very different than the ability to scale product inventories up and down.**

In *Mastering Professional Services*, the challenge of matching the available resources in a services organization to customer demand is discussed. The ebbs and flows of service demand over time can wreck havoc on services profitability. If demand for your services spikes upward, your delivery staff will most likely respond by working more hours. The quality of their output may suffer, but they will address the increased demand. However, if demand continues to spike, they will eventually run out of hours in the day and revenue opportunities will be lost unless subcontractors can be found or new consultants quickly hired. On the flip side, if demand for your services falls below projections, profitability will be impacted. You are paying for staff hours that are not generating any income. Unless you can reduce the number of staff quickly, profits could be ugly for awhile as you adjust to the downturn. Services managers expect these peaks and valleys.

A baseline tactic used to manage PS profitability through the peaks and valleys of demand is to set a target billable utilization rate for delivery staff, knowing that at any given point in time staff may be a little above or below that utilization rate. By setting this target rate, services management can set expectations on both revenue and profitability for the business. This peak-and-valley challenge is shown in Figure 10-8. The line in the middle of the figure represents the *target utilization* just described. This line represents the capacity your services-delivery staff has in terms of hours.

*Mastering Professional Services*, raised a simple question: **"How quickly should a service organization be able to respond to fluctuations in demand?"** This is the fundamental challenge product companies need to model. If service deals start falling from the sky because a new product suddenly becomes hot, how much more business should you be able to address and still maintain profitability? 20 percent? 40 percent? More? At what point do you tap out the trained labor market and/or your ability to bring staff on board? We know through our benchmarking activities that a clear majority of PS organizations do not grow their revenues more than 25 percent year to year. Part of this could be market conditions, but we saw this cap in growth back in 2007 when the technology marketplace was doing well. In other words, there appears to be a real limitation to how fast most project-based services organizations are able to build capacity.

Figure 10-8  Peaks and Valleys

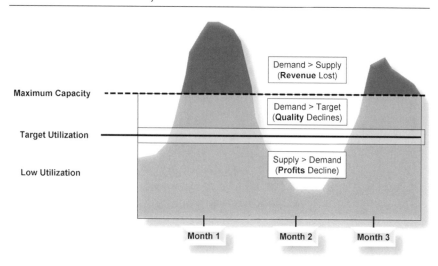

Let's go in reverse. What if the services forecast tanks and demand drops by 30 percent? Some of the projected deals did not come through and some existing customers have decided to delay the start dates of follow-on phases. I'm sure this was a common experience for companies at the end of 2008. You now have too many delivery employees. How much should you be expected to reduce your staff to project profitability now that revenue projections have plunged? By 5 percent? By 10 percent? More? Figure 10-9 is repurposed from *Mastering Professional Services* and shows this dilemma.

If a forecast is off, how quickly should a PS organization be able to respond and by how much? Plus or minus 40 percent of capacity? The answer is specific to the services you are offering and the labor markets you leverage. You will face clear limitations scaling both up and down. Those limitations are driven by several factors, including:

- Local labor laws
- The ability to find qualified resources to hire
- The capacity to train new employees
- The complexity of services offerings

This planning challenge is not insignificant. Pure services companies manage these peaks and valleys by using a sophisticated network of subcontacted, globalized, and sometimes centralized resource pools. Product companies are now just beginning to master these techniques.

Figure 10-9 The Capacity Strike Zone

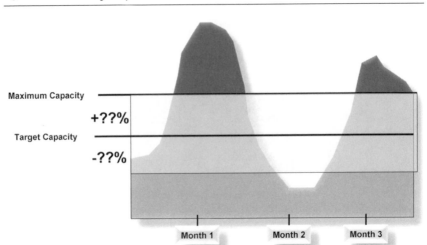

## CHALLENGE #2: THE SERVICES SUPPLY CHAIN

The second sourcing challenge product companies must understand is that services fulfillment involves more than simply hiring delivery staff. **Service fulfillment, like product fulfillment, involves a complex supply chain**. Traditional supply-chain management is the discipline of managing all movement and storage of raw materials, work-in-process inventory, and finished goods from point-of-origin to point-of-consumption. Product companies became good at this discipline when their supply chains became complex with multiple partners providing various components of a finished product. Also, robust software packages were created to support the supply-chain management processes. Oracle and SAP have come to dominate this enterprise resource management (ERP) software marketplace. Interestingly, SAP has begun to apply the concepts of supply-chain management to the business of services.

Back in the spring of 2007, a marketing team at SAP contacted TPSA to discuss current trends in the world of professional services. One of the challenges we lamented was the inability for services organizations to scale. The more we discussed the challenge, the more we realized it was the same type of challenge that faced many of SAP's ERP customers several years ago. Companies were struggling to cost effectively scale up (and down) product inventories. With the application of new business processes and technology, companies were able to drive incredible scalability and cost efficiency into the manufacturing process. Is that not what services organizations need to do today? Building on this realization, we crafted the concept of *Talent Supply Chain Management*. The following text is repurposed from a white paper TPSA published with SAP on the topic titled "Using Talent Supply Chain Management to Overcome Challenges in the Professional Services Market."

*First, we must clearly define what we mean by "Talent Supply Chain Management." Building off of the definition provided for supply-chain management, we apply the following definition to TSCM:*

> *Talent supply chain management (TSCM) is the complete and integrated process required to hire, retain, and resource professional services talent to successfully deliver customer engagements as efficiently as possible.*

*Now, to deliver on this vision of talent supply chain management, a project-based services organization must successfully manage five key business processes:*

1. ***Talent Management:*** *This is the discipline of selecting, recruiting, developing, and retaining staff. Because talent is the most important differentiator in the professional services business, firms must be clear on exactly whom they want to attract and retain within the organization. Hiring and retaining top talent is often cited as the most important aspect of managing a successful professional services firm.*

2. ***Resource Management:*** *Another area that most firms recognize as critically important is the ability to effectively manage resources. By integrating the process used to assign resources with both talent and demand management, firms can maintain the highest utilization levels. Typically, the information on opportunities and resource management is generated and managed in two different parts of the organization. In order to streamline capacity planning, these information silos must be integrated in a way that is meaningful and productive, so that the firm can easily balance demand and supply. They need a mechanism to compare the sales pipeline, resources, and current projects with an overview of their total talent pool. With this insight, they can determine whether they have the right resources—based on skill set, knowledge, and experience—to match their clients' expectations. If a gap develops between skills demanded and skills in the resource pool, a firm can proactively hire or partner to close the gap and improve both calendaring and booking.*

3. ***Demand Management:*** *Next, to manage the talent supply chain effectively, a firm needs to create visibility into the sales pipeline. Amid growing competition from offshore product companies and niche firms, a services director's goal is to sell more projects to both new and existing*

*clients. Accomplishing this requires a complete picture of committed projects and resources—a transparent view into the project pipeline, project schedules, future skill needs, and talent utilization. In addition, professional service firms need to become more adept at driving a service mix that maximizes demand for the most profitable service offerings.*

4. ***Supplier Management:*** *Increasingly, professional services firms are using subcontractors and cost-effective offshore resources to assist in the delivery of engagements. The Technology Professional Services Organization (TPSA) reports that a majority of I/T services companies benchmarked use subcontractors to deliver at least 20 percent of a services engagement. This 20 percent of partnered delivery creates both scalability and cost advantage. Managing this lever has become more complicated and critical with the advent of offshore resources.*

5. ***Offering Development:*** *Last but not least, the discipline of optimizing the talent supply chain must consider the specific services offerings of the firm. Different service offerings require different technical and industry expertise.*

*In any professional services organization, these five processes must map against three external entities:*

**Customers:** *The individuals and companies that consume your professional services.*

**Industry Talent:** *The pool of external talent from which your firm recruits professional services consultants.*

**Service Partners:** *The firms that can supply talent to help deliver your services engagements. This talent can be onshore or offshore.*

*Now, combining the five processes and three external entities, we can map the complete talent supply chain management environment as shown in Figure 10-10.*

*To source services effectively, a services organization would have mature processes established in all five of the areas outlined in this services supply chain. Looking at industry results and practices we have collected from 2005 to 2009, I would rate the maturity of these five process areas in the following order (from most mature, to least mature):*

1. ***Service Offering Development:*** *A clear majority of professional services organizations fund formal services development activities.*

Figure 10-10  Talent Supply Chain Management

Product companies typically invest 2 to 3 percent of PS revenues back into services development activities. In addition, a majority of organizations have defined a formal services-development life cycle (SDLC). To be sure, structured services development is still a relatively young discipline in many product companies. However, the funding is there. In addition, academics are publishing very rich research on effective services engineering processes and approaches.

2.  **Talent Management:** Most companies have mature HR processes to secure new talent from the industry. The friction point is that product companies are more optimized to hire product development talent than services delivery talent.

3.  **Resource Management:** You would think this area would be very mature, but it is not. Product companies are abysmal at developing and optimizing the skills they already have on board. Less than 35 percent of embedded services organizations have a formal skills evaluation process to help them track and develop the capabilities of staff. It takes over 20 business days (a calendar month) for most embedded PS organizations to get newly hired staff billable. And it takes over 15 days for them to source signed services engagements.

4.  **Supplier Management:** Our benchmark data shows that less than half of embedded services organizations have formal partner evaluation and certification programs in place. In addition, embedded PS organizations continue to source over 80 percent of their delivery activities

*directly. Often with local delivery staff. In the following sections, we will discuss why this approach is problematic in today's marketplace.*

5. ***Demand Management:*** *Finally, the most immature process area within embedded PS organizations (and perhaps all PS organizations) is demand management. PS organizations can define services offerings and the skills required to deliver them. However, if they have poor visibility from sales reps regarding what services will really book, it becomes difficult to staff the rights skills. This gap between forecast (what sales folks predict will be booked) and backlog (what is actually booked) can be significant. The wider the gap, the more challenged the services organization is to meeting it's sourcing and profit objectives.*

Product companies think in terms of supply-chain optimization. Internalizing the fact that service fulfillment requires the effective management of a complete supply chain is an important step forward for executives within product companies that do not have prior experience scaling services.

## CHALLENGE #3: EXPANDING RESOURCE POOLS

The third aspect of sourcing services that product companies should understand is that embedded professional service organizations are beginning to aggressively leverage multiple human-resourcing pools. As a quick reminder, five types of resource pools exist that can be leveraged to actually deliver a services offering:

1. **Direct Local Resources:** These are PS consultants employed directly by the product company and residing locally, close to customer engagement sites.

2. **Corporate Practice Resources:** These are PS consultants that have hard-to-find, specialized skills. They are leveraged across multiple geographies.

3. **Centralized Solution Center Resources:** These are delivery resources that can be leveraged to deliver portions of a PS engagement without being on the customer site. These resources are typically clustered where labor costs are lower.

4. **Local Delivery Partners:** These are services delivery partners that are identified and engaged by an individual country or specific region.

5. **Global Delivery Partners:** These are services delivery partners that are identified, selected, and enabled at a global level.

In the previous chapters that defined each services-strategy profile, a recommendation was made on what resourcing pools a product company executing that services strategy should leverage. These recommendations are made based on observations from industry data gathered in just the past 3 years. Historically, embedded PS organizations have leaned heavily on two of these resourcing pools to deliver services engagements booked directly with the product company: direct local resources and local delivery partners. In fact, our benchmark data shows a clear majority of embedded PS organizations deliver over 80 percent of service engagement hours with direct full-time employees (FTEs). A majority of those FTEs are located close to the customer. The historical delivery mix for embedded PS organizations is shown in Figure 10-11.

Today, a bifurcation is occurring with the sourcing models of embedded PS organizations. An emerging population of embedded PS organizations is following the relatively proven path of global system integrators such as Accenture and Wipro by leveraging additional resourcing pools. Specifically global delivery partners and centralized solution centers. By expanding the use of these human resource pools, product companies can decrease the number of staff that must be hired close to the customer. The direct local human resource pool will never go away, but the leverage it receives from the other four human resource pools is increased. By leveraging all five resource pools aggressively, product companies are addressing both the scalability and supply-chain challenges previously highlighted. Figure 10-12 shows the average sourcing mix 30 embedded PS organizations were targeting for 2010. In this same survey, some PS organizations reported sourcing mixes that were already much more leveraged than the average 2010 targets.

**Figure 10-11**  Traditional Sourcing Pools for Embedded PS

Figure10-12  Emerging Sourcing Mix for Embedded PS

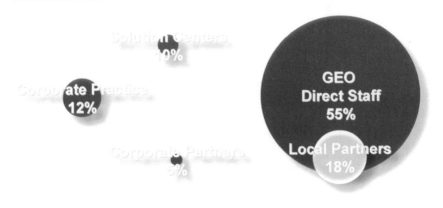

The key point is that product companies need to be thinking about how they can leverage multiple resourcing pools. SAP is a specific example of an embedded services organization that has come to the conclusion that global, consistent, scalable delivery will be based on access to all five of these resource pools. SAP services executive Bernd-Michael Rumpf delivered a keynote presentation at our 2008 Technology Services World conference in Las Vegas where he outlined SAP's vision for sourcing services. The five pools were unmistakable in the vision. Yet, one more aspect of sourcing exists that product companies must be aware of if they hope to compete in today's world of services.

## CHALLENGE #4: BREAKING DOWN THE GEO-CENTRIC MODEL

Realistic parameters for scalability, effective supply chains, and multiple resourcing pools—these are important concepts for sourcing success. The final concept ties all of these previous concepts together.

Mohan Sawhney is the Tribune Professor of Technology and the Director of the Center for Research in Technology and Innovation at the Kellogg School of Management. This Northwestern professor was kind enough to participate in an executive education session we hosted at Ohio State University in June of 2006. The topic of the session was "The Globalization of the PS Workforce." Mr. Sawhney was working with Indian services providers and he was studying the pending head-on collision that was about to occur in the marketplace between North American PS firms like Accenture and the offshore providers like Infosys and Wipro. **He was the first person I heard crisply articulate the fundamental shift from geo-centric to competency-centric sourcing models for technology professional services.** He presented a slightly different version of Figure 10-13 and explained how services delivery was migrating from on-site to a mix of on-site and off-site resources. To accomplish this shift, he argued services organizations would need to segment delivery tasks into those that can be done remotely and those that need to be done directly on the customer site.

When I first saw this graph, I was struck with three thoughts:

1.  Very few of the embedded PS organizations I knew were breaking apart delivery tasks into those that could be delivered remotely vs. those that had to be delivered on site.

2.  Very few of the embedded PS organizations I knew were working to establish competency centers of expertise that could be leveraged across multiple geographies.

3.  A vast majority of the PS organizations I knew still pushed all hiring and sourcing decisions for the PS business out to each geographic area.

In essence, embedded PS organizations build out their services capabilities in a traditional "partner model." When the product company needs services in a country or region, they hire a services leader. That leader is then responsible for determining how to source services engagements and meet financial targets in that region. This is very similar to how consulting firms traditionally would expand. They would assign a new region or practice to a partner and make that partner responsible for building a profitable business. As long as each partner hit its targets, the overall business was successful.

**The simplicity of the traditional partner model is attractive. It creates clear lines of responsibility for success and failure. However, it also**

Figure 10-13  Shift from Geo-Centric

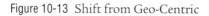

**results in a very geo-centric culture that sub-optimizes the use of scarce human capital.** In other words, every partner (or regional services leader) becomes fixated on optimizing its particular patch. There is little incentive to share resources or tactics across regions. This is not fertile ground for incubating competency centers or off-site resource pools that could be leveraged by multiple geographies. These limitations caught up with the Accenture's of the world and forced them to begin migrating from a geo-centric sourcing culture to a competency-centric sourcing model. It is this shift that has allowed them to remain competitive with the Indian services firms.

Embedded PS organizations are still in the process of learning that the geo-centric model is indeed out of gas. The migration of sourcing strategies up and to the right on Figure 10-6 is inevitable for any technology services organization that hopes to compete in a globalized marketplace. To successfully navigate this migration, product companies will need to break down traditional geo-centric organizational structures. This will not be easy. As a systems provider, IBM is one of the few product companies that was forced to the leading edge of this painful migration. Back in June of 2005, *Information Technology* published an article titled "Big Blue Shift" that described the radical transformation IBM was undertaking to move from a geo-centric to a competency-centric global organization. Read these compelling excerpts from the article. The concepts highlighted are highly aligned with the four concepts of sourcing strategy highlighted in this chapter:

> *What's all the hoopla about? IBM is sending the message that India and the rest of Asia are crucial to its future—as fast-growing markets and as pools of low-cost talent that IBM must tap to fend off pesky Indian competitors who are biting into its market share. IBM's India staff jumped from 9,000 to 43,000 in the past 2.5 years, making India No. 2 behind the U.S.*

> *But cheap labor is just part of the story. For IBM, globalization is about reorganizing its 200,000-strong services workforce along skill lines, not just geography, and about coordinating operations worldwide to deliver services that are better as well as cheaper. In essence, it's all about revamping the people supply chain.*

> *The transformation that's sweeping IBM could soon be showing up at companies everywhere. In the twentieth century, IBM was a pioneer of the multinational business model. It created mini-IBMs in each country— complete with their own administration, manufacturing, and service operations. But that approach is too top heavy at a time when lean Indian tech companies and Chinese manufacturers produce high-quality goods*

*and services for a fraction of what the multinationals charge. Now IBM is pioneering what it calls globally integrated operations. IBM aims to lower its costs and at the same time provide superior service so it can be more competitive, win more deals, and drive revenue and profit growth.*

*Here's how the thinking goes: In tech services, which account for half of IBM's $91 billion in annual revenues, low-cost labor is necessary but not sufficient. The company needs to bunch employees in competency centers (collections of people with specific skills) that are distributed around the world. That way it can take advantage of the low costs in some places, and in others have highly skilled employees in close proximity to customers. Rather than each country's business unit having its own workforce entirely, many people are drawn from the competency centers.*

I realize IBM is a $100 billion systems provider with incredible resources at its disposal, but the globalization of services delivery is not just impacting IBM and Accenture. This trend impacts any company delivering technology solutions—product providers and product extenders included. For this reason, product companies must quickly become comfortable and competent with these emerging sourcing strategies.

## FROM SOURCING TO PARTNERING

Sourcing strategy has become a critical lever to services success. This is why an entire chapter has been dedicated to the topic. Also, this is an area where the bar for success is moving higher. Product companies not paying attention will find themselves significantly handicapped in their ability to compete.

Interestingly, two of the five resource pools discussed in this chapter are related to partners: local partners and global partners. In other words, 40 percent of the sourcing success equation is composed of external delivery resources. In fact, embedded PS organizations are learning that the ability to leverage external partner resources is becoming almost as critical as managing internal resources when it comes to driving market success. And that thought leads us to our next chapter.

# Chapter 11

# Services Partner Strategy

I n the previous chapter, we overviewed several frameworks related to sourcing the delivery of services. Partners can be a critical component of a sourcing strategy. For that reason, I think it would be impossible to discuss successful services strategy within a product company without exploring the dynamics of partner strategy. The data shows us that partnering in the world of technology services has become a significant success lever. Yet, the data also tells us that a minority of services organizations maximize the positive impact of partner relationships. This chapter will explore why embedded services organizations often struggle in crafting their partner relationships and how to recast these partnership endeavors to improve success rates.

## PARTNER PRIMER

First, we better baseline our conversation on partner strategy by quickly defining what we mean by the term "partners." For services organizations within product companies, at least three types of partners come into play.

**Subcontractors:** These are partners that help the services organization deliver services engagements. The services project is booked by the product company and these partners provide resources to help deliver the engagement. These partners provide skills that complement or augment the resources of the services organization.

**Resellers:** These are partners that resell the products and services provided by the company. They most likely provide their own value-add services to help implement the products of the company. Their capabilities can overlap with the capabilities of the embedded services organization.

**Influencers:** These are partners that my not necessarily resell the products or services of the company, but they can have a significant influence on what products companies purchase. Think about large-system integrators, such as Accenture, that help companies decide what technologies to implement.

Product companies can create strategic tiers within these three categories. For example, specific partner programs may exist for "preferred" resellers or "strategic alliance" integrators. However, the three main categories are relatively universal across all product companies. The relationship between the services organization and these three types of partners varies.

Services organizations establish and embrace subcontractors because they help the services organization scale. In 2009, TPSA executed a survey titled "Partner Practices and Results." Forty technology companies participated. The survey responses clearly showed that a majority of service organizations are very comfortable leveraging partners to help deliver services engagements. In fact, 76 percent of the respondents to this 2009 survey stated they were "effective" or "very effective" at establishing partners for subcontract service delivery work.

The services organization, however, can find product resellers and product influencers potentially competitive because these entities may provide services that overlap with the services being offered by the product company. In fact, in that same 2009 survey, 70 percent of services organizations stated that system integrators were "ineffective" or "very ineffective" at helping their company sell new products. In other words, the services organizations did not place great value on the relationship the company had with system integrators. Despite these nuances, a common factor exists that influences the relationship with all three of these partner types: services-strategy profile.

## SERVICES STRATEGY PROFILE AND PARTNER STRATEGY

### Understanding Partner Needs

One of the greatest failure points in any relationship is the failure to understand the perspective of the other person. I feel this is especially true regarding partner relationships. Based on where product companies are in the product adoption life cycle, partners have very different requirements. Understanding the basic needs of the partner is the first step in crafting a successful partner relationship. Figure 11-1 maps the product adoption life cycle to the needs of partners. This figure identifies three distinct phases for partner needs over the product life cycle.

> **Prove the Market:** When new products and their markets are being developed, services partners need to be convinced there is a real and growing opportunity. Partners do not want to invest time and energy

to train employees on a technology unless a real chance exists to make money. Who can blame them? If they place the wrong bets, they may be out of business.

**Enable my Staff:** Once the product market is established, services partners will want help enabling resources to sell and deliver the product. The hotter the market, the more urgent this need will become. Services partners will want to position themselves to capture revenues while the capturing is good.

**Minimize Conflict:** Finally, as a product market matures, services partners will become nervous for two reasons. First, they will be rightly concerned about where to find the next market opportunity. Second, if the product provider becomes more services intensive, the anxiety will intensify in services partners as they become concerned the product vendor is now crowding partners out of the services opportunities.

## Meeting Partner Needs

Depending on the services-strategy profile a product company decides to pursue, the product company will want to pursue different tactics to meet partner needs. **A few scenarios are very important for product companies to consider. They represent inflection points in partner strategy. If they are mishandled, products may not get adopted, partners may get frustrated, or both.** Let's run through the product adoption life cycle and document these inflection point scenarios:

Figure 11-1  Partner Needs

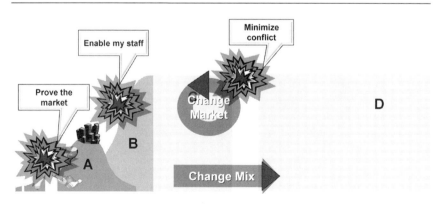

**Early Stage Product, Solution-Provider:** In this scenario, the product company has decided to source significant services capabilities directly to help drive the success of the new product. In this case, the solution provider is proving the market by creating successful customers. The solution provider is also creating proven services methodologies to support the product. As the market takes off, services partners will quickly want to understand how much of the services opportunity the solution provider is willing to cede to services partners. **Product resellers and product influencers will feel very threatened by a solution-provider profile unless the product company declares its intentions to transition to a more partner-friendly profile.**

**Early Stage Product, Product-Provider:** In this scenario, the product company does not want to source significant services capabilities. The objective is to get services partners to invest in the emerging market by training staff before the demand is proven. **To convince services partners to make this investment, product providers will need to show their commitment to creating the market.** This commitment can be demonstrated in several ways, including:

- Revealing marketing campaigns that will drive demand for the new product
- Sizing the estimated services market that will eventually surround the product market
- Subsidizing product training for the services partners
- Developing some level of initial services methodologies that services partners can use

In this scenario, the level of investment required by the product provider is directly correlated to the confidence the services partners have in the market opportunity. If a well-known product company is releasing a product predicted to be a wild success, the "prove it" requirement from the services partners is lessened.

**Hot Product, All Profiles:** When product sales are rapidly growing, all product companies, regardless of the services-strategy profile being pursued, must satisfy the same need from services partners: enablement. The more services partners are enabled to sell and deliver the product, the more market share will be captured.

**Maturing Product, Product Extender, Systems Provider:** The final scenario to be highlighted is perhaps the most difficult for a product company to navigate. This is when a product company pursues a change-mix strategy and decides to adopt a more services-intensive services-strategy profile. When this happens, existing services partner relationships must be reexamined. **The product company cannot pretend that the shift in services strategy will have no impact on existing partners. Existing partners will be starved for information on the intentions of the product company.** A simple example would be the day EMC decided to partner with Accenture to create a new EMC consulting capability. This move clearly sent a message to any existing EMC consulting partner that the landscape had changed. In press releases announcing the new EMC business unit, EMC executives stated they were not trying to become the next IBM Global Services.

So, there are four common scenarios where the needs of the services partners are very clear. Product companies make two common mistakes on their way to not meeting these partner needs. First, the product company does not internalize and empathize with these needs. The product company is too focused on making sure its own needs of securing customers and selling product are met. The partner conversations are focused too much on "look how great our product is" and not enough on "this is how you will make money with our product." Second, the product company begins thrashing around regarding what services-strategy profile to pursue. This thrashing sends mixed messages to services partners. One of the classic examples of this misstep occurred when Microsoft established Microsoft Consulting Services while remaining strongly committed to their services channel partners. The services messaging became confused and CEO Steve Ballmer had to reassure Microsoft partners that Microsoft was still the old partner-friendly product provider it had always been.

In summary, there are three golden rules product companies should consider when working to build an effective services partners ecosystem:

1. Understand where the product is in the adoption life cycle.

2. Understand what services partners need when a product is in this stage.

3. Be clear with partners what services-strategy profile you are pursuing.

Historically, some product companies are known to be adept at managing partner relationships and some are known to be abysmal at the process. For those product companies that were mediocre at building services partners, the negative impact on market success was sometimes minimal. At this point in time, however, I believe almost all product companies need to become at least competent in building effective services partner ecosystems—the economics have simply become too compelling to ignore.

## ECONOMICS OF PARTNER SUCCESS

We just discussed the process of aligning product maturity, partner needs, and services-strategy profile to create the right priorities for the services partner strategy. I think it would be beneficial to stop and discuss why these efforts are so important to the services organization. **In a nutshell, effective services-partner strategy has the potential to improve every key metric of a services business.**

Product companies often establish partnerships to create new market opportunities. However, as previously noted, 76 percent of service organizations in our 2009 Partner Practice Survey question the ability of system integrators to drive new market opportunities. In addition, 30 percent of those respondents feel that system integrators actually increase the cost of sales for the company. Finally, 49 percent of the respondents did not believe traditional channel partners are effective at driving new product opportunities. All of this data tells us that product companies often struggle to establish partnerships that truly drive incremental market opportunities. If that was the only reason to establish services partners, the motivation level would be low. Fortunately, services partnerships bring much more to the table than do new sales opportunities.

In Chapter 12, I will introduce tactics for tracking the maturity and effectiveness of a services organization. For project-based professional services, a set of metrics come into play for almost everyone. These metrics are listed in Table 11-1. The information comes from TPSA's metrics database.

Through our benchmarking work, we have a good sense of what the typical industry performance is for the metrics outlined in Table 11-1. Performance varies based on both the size of the PS organization and the services strategy profile the company is executing. We also know what the highest performing, or pace-setting PS organizations achieve on these metrics. I believe that if services partnering is driven to its full potential, PS organizations can outperform both industry averages and current pace setter results.

Through effective partnering, a PS organization can improve both labor multipliers and project margins. We have seen this correlation in actual raw project data aggregated from multiple companies for our project performance studies. In addition, delivery resources supplied by partners can assist in the ability to source engagements and scale the service business. Finally, services partners can and should become an effective channel for selling product and services offerings. This could reduce the overall cost of sales for the services organization. Putting all of these factors together, it is reasonable to believe effective services partnering could drive significant improvement in all these key metrics. Table 11-2 provides a snapshot of typical pace setter and potential performance of a PS organization for these key metrics. The last column of

Table 11-1  Critical PS Business Metrics

| Metric | Definition | Calculation |
|---|---|---|
| Billable Utilization Rate | The organization's ability to maximize its billable resources. | Total number of hours billed ÷ (2,080 X number of billable employees) |
| Growth Rate | The increase in services revenues from the previous year. | (Current year revenues ÷ Last year's revenues ) − 1 |
| Labor Multiplier | The average factor by which billable personnel can be charged over and above their fully loaded costs. Fully loaded costs = direct salary + direct fringe benefits + overhead + G&A + Margin. (A Labor multiplier of 1.0 indicates a breakeven point.) | Total dollar amount of personnel hours billed ÷ Fully loaded labor cost |
| Project Gross Margin | The difference between what customers pay for the services and what it costs the company to deliver those services. | Project revenue − Total costs to deliver the project |
| Sales Costs | The total costs for the selling efforts of each line of business. Total sales costs include salaries, expense accounts, and commissions for sales management, sales people, and sales support. | Total sales costs ÷ Total services revenue |
| Time to Source | The number of days it takes for resource to begin work after a signed statement of work (SOW) has been received from the customer. | Start date − SOW date |

potential performance represents the impact an effective services partner environment could have on this metric.

Is effective partnering important to a services organization? **What if a services organization could double its profitable growth rate and simultaneously reduce the time to source engagements by half?** That would be impressive—and that is the potential of partnering effectively.

## GETTING PARTNERING RIGHT: TRADITIONAL SUCCESS FACTORS

So there is economic gold in those partnering hills. Yet, services organizations struggle to mine that gold. Several well-written books exist on the topic

Table 11-2  Impact of Partnering

|  | TPSA Average | Pace Setter | Potential |
|---|---|---|---|
| Billable Utilization Rate | 65% | 75% | 85% |
| Growth Rate | 25% | 35% | 50% |
| Labor Multiplier | 1.42 | 1.80 | 2 |
| Project Gross Margin | 33% | 43% | 50% |
| Sales Costs | 7% | 5% | 4% |
| Time to Source (Business Days) | 10–15 | 5–9 | Less than 5 |

of building successful partnerships. One of my personal favorites is *Getting Partnering Right* by Rackham, Friedman, and Ruff. This book does an excellent job of summarizing the key success factors in building sound partner relationships. The authors argue that successful partnerships are built on three fundamentals:

1. A common vision

2. A clearly defined positive impact for each party

3. Intimacy between the partners that supports transparency and allows key information to flow back and forth

Within these three areas of vision, impact, and intimacy, the authors go on to articulate supporting success factors. For example, in the area of impact, most companies start partnership discussions because they believe the partnerships will lead to new market opportunities. This is a valid impact area, but Rackham et al have found that the probability of a partnership succeeding is higher when the partnership is grounded on reducing redundant efforts between the partners. Figure 11-2 summarizes these major and supporting success factors. The book elaborates on each of them.

These traditional and well-documented success factors in building partner relationships clearly apply to embedded services organizations. In addition, this work on effective partnering discusses three meta success factors I believe services leaders should be well aware of:

1. **Both parties changed** the way they did business to maximize the impact of the partnership.

2. The overall **pie got bigger** for both parties.

3. The partnership created a **competitive advantage** for both parties.

Figure 11-2  Traditional Success Factors in Partner Success

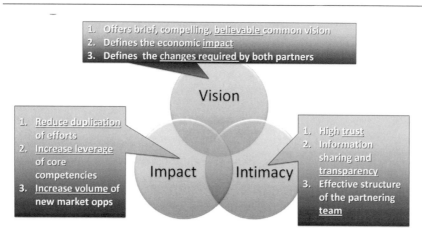

I had a conversation with Susan McKay, who at the time of this writing was responsible for managing service partner relationships for EMC's services alliances. Susan has also chaired a TPSA community of interest, composed of partner managers from multiple technology companies. She has seen first-hand the need for clearly defined benefits for partners and the need to provide as much transparency as possible. "When your partner is unclear how you are going to market, they get both nervous and confused. For partnerships to work, you have to be prepared to open your business processes to your strategic partners and modify those processes when required." In summary, we believe the traditional, well-documented factors that drive the creation of meaningful, effective partnerships are highly applicable to the creation of services partnership. Managing these factors are imperative if the services organization has any hope of leveraging services partners to improve the economics as discussed in the previous section. However, there are some nuances to services partnering services leaders must navigate.

## GETTING SERVICES PARTNERING RIGHT

### *Unavoidable Overlap*

When a product company establishes technology partners, the product company never chooses a partner that makes a competing product. Why would they do that? No, a product company chooses partners that have products that complement their customer solution. Services, unfortunately, is different. Even product providers, with their lean and mean PS, will have services capabilities that directly overlap with services partners. Your internal services group architects customer solutions? Well, your services partner would like that work. Your internal services group will help project manage complex integrations? Your services partners may have an army of certified project managers just waiting to engage. Because this overlap in services capabilities almost *always* exists between the product company and the services partners, there are few tactics the services organization should pursue to help reduce tensions.

## *Tactic #1: Define the Services Capture Rate*

The first tactic a services organization within a product company can use to help reduce tensions with service partners centers around the concept of opportunity capture. When a product company sells a product, a certain amount of services opportunity gets created. For complex, enterprise class products, the services opportunity may be worth three or four times the amount of the initial product sale. For simple products, the services opportunity may be worth a small percentage of the initial product sale. This relationship is referred to as the services opportunity multiplier. A visual representation of this concept is provided in Figure 11-3.

Once a product company accurately estimates this multiplier for a product offering, the product company can declare how much of the total services opportunity will be captured directly by the product company. The remaining services opportunity is left for the services partners. This slicing of the services pie is documented in Figure 11-4.

By defining how large the total service market is, and by clearly defining what percentage the product company intends to capture directly, tensions with service partners can be reduced. Figure 11-5 provides an example of how one product company documents and communicates its target PS capture rate across four different classes of product maturity. As the figure shows, this company expects to capture more of the total services opportunity for emerging products where the partner ecosystem is immature. The company also expects to capture more of the total services opportunity surrounding aging "legacy" products because the partner ecosystem will be waning and customers will still need assistance." I have done some very rough modeling on PS capture rates for software companies. I believe software companies can comfortably capture 25 percent of the total services opportunity without creating significant tension with the partner ecosystem—but I do not believe this area has been studied thoroughly. When capture rates exceed 25 percent, the product company is signaling a shift to a more aggressive services-strategy profile, and services partners have reason to be concerned.

Figure 11-3  The Services Multiplier

*Tactic #2 Where Partner Enablement Lives*

Another tactic product companies can use to improve the management of services partners is to make sure the services organization is given the responsibility for identifying, qualifying, and enabling services partners. This may sound like a no-brainer, but some product companies charter a separate partner organization to manage services partners. Unfortunately, this partner organization typically has no expertise in evaluating the delivery capabilities of a services partner. In addition, the partner organization will not have the skills and methodologies to help enable the services partner build competent delivery resources around company products. The services organization has all that!

TPSA has surveyed on various practices surrounding services partner management. In reality, the strong common practice is to have the services

Figure 11-4  Slicing the Services Opportunity

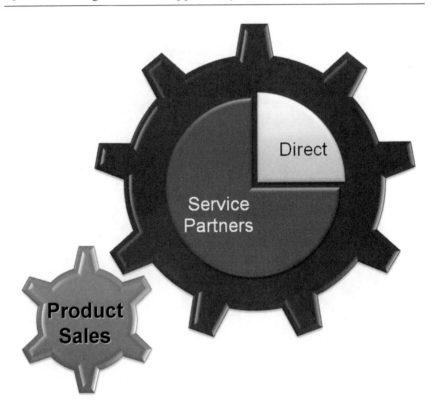

organization responsible for services partner enablement as shown in Figure 11-6. This chart comes from a survey we ran in 2009 that gathered input from 40 leading technology solution providers.

However, data from the same survey shows that the services organization is not always responsible for the selection of services partners and is documented in Figure 11-7. By putting another organization besides services in charge of selecting services partners, a company introduces unnecessary tension and risk.

### Tactic #3 Partner Certification and Evaluation

The final tactic I would like to suggest to improve the success of services partnerships involves ongoing certification and evaluation. You may believe that every product company that signs up services delivery partners surely must have programs in place to certify and evaluate those partners. After all, don't

Figure 11-5  The PS Capture Rate

they have a significant impact on the success of the end customer? In reality, our benchmarking shows that less than 40 percent of product companies have formal programs in place to certify services partners. In addition, less than 40 percent of product companies have formal programs to evaluate services partners on an ongoing basis. To add fuel to this fire, we did analysis on the

Figure 11-6  Who Is Responsible for the Enablement of Services Partners?

Figure 11-7  Who Is Responsible for Selecting Services Partners?

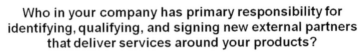

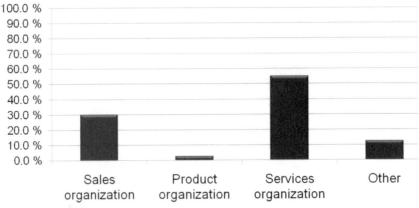

impact of having partner evaluation programs in place. One interesting correlation we found is documented in Figure 11-8. This graph shows that service organizations with formal partner evaluation programs in place were driving better margins when they used these partner resources.

## THE STATE OF SERVICES PARTNER MANAGEMENT

This chapter begins with the premise that successful partner management is becoming even more important to the overall success of a services organization. The chapter then introduces several frameworks management teams can use as they craft their services partner strategy. I would like to end this chapter with a snapshot of the current state of services partner management.

Referring back to the partner practices survey TPSA executed in 2009, there were several telling questions asked regarding how well the survey respondents felt their company was leveraging partner relationships. Through this survey, we captured the following data points:

- An overwhelming 70 percent of the respondents did not feel they were leveraging system integrators effectively as a channel for selling products.

- Only 12 percent of respondents felt partnering with system integrators actually decreased the cost of sales.

Figure 11-8 Impact of Partner Evaluation on Subcontracting Margins

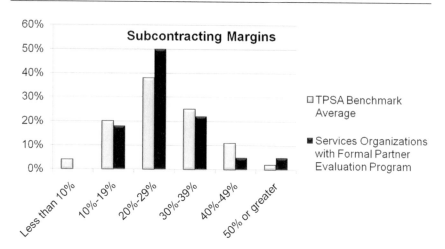

- Only 35 percent of respondents felt the involvement of partners improved the quality of the customer engagement.

Going back to our talent supply chain framework, I would argue that these data points highlight the fact that embedded service organizations are still struggling to gain the full potential impact of effective partnership. Remember the building blocks of the talent supply chain, below is an assessment of how PS organizations are managing the components of the chain.

1. **Offering Development:** Status: YELLOW. A clear majority of PS organizations fund formal services development activities. Product companies typically invest 2 to 3 percent of PS revenues back into services development activities. In addition, a majority of organizations have defined a formal services-development life cycle (SDLC). To be sure, structured services development is still a relatively young discipline in many product companies. However, the funding is there. In addition, academics are publishing very rich research on effective services-engineering processes and approaches.

2. **Talent Management:** Status: YELLOW. Most companies have mature HR processes to secure new talent from the industry. The friction point is that product companies are more optimized to hire product development talent than services delivery talent. In addition, product companies place greater emphasis on hard technical skills and pay too little attention to developing the software skills required during services delivery.

3. **Resource Management:** Status: YELLOW. You would think this area would be very mature, but it is not. Product companies are abysmal at developing and optimizing the skills they already have on board. Less than 35 percent of embedded services organizations have a formal skills evaluation process to help them track and develop the capabilities of staff. It takes over 20 business days (a calendar month) for most embedded PS organizations to get newly hired staff billable. And it takes over 15 days for them to source signed services engagements.

4. **Supplier Management:** Status: GREEN. Service organizations have become very adept at securing partners to help deliver service offerings. However, there is still room for improvement. Our benchmark data shows that less than half of embedded services organizations have formal partner evaluation and certification programs in place. In addition, embedded PS organizations continue to source over 80 percent of their delivery activities directly. Often with local delivery staff. In the following chapters, we will discuss why this approach is problematic in today's marketplace.

5. **Demand Management:** Status: RED. Finally, the most immature process area within embedded PS organizations (and perhaps all PS organizations) is demand management. PS organizations can define services offerings and the skills required to deliver them. However, if they have poor visibility from sales reps regarding what services will really book, it becomes difficult to staff the rights skills. This gap between forecast (what sales folks predict will be booked) and backlog (what is actually booked) can be significant. The wider the gap, the more challenged the services organization is to meeting it's sourcing and profit objectives.

In summary, product companies have mastered the ability to leverage the arms and legs of subcontractors during engagements. In other words, leveraging partners as a source of supply for specific skill sets. This is the area of supplier management. However, product companies are clearly struggling to leverage partners in the areas of demand management and offering quality. Figure 11-9 captures the current state of services partnership success.

When partner relationships are maximized, product companies should see positive impact in the areas of demand generation, offering development, as well as resource management. As a result, *all* the economic metrics previously outlined in Table 11-2 should be improved through the right partnerships. The industry is not yet there, and we are left with partner relationships that limp along under the premise of building new market opportunities that never materialize as hoped. I predict the future titans of technology solutions will excel in their ability to build and sustain meaningful services partnerships.

Figure 11-9 Leveraging Services Partners in the Talent Supply Chain

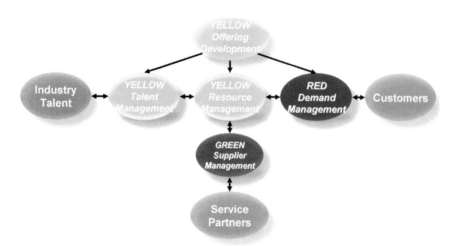

They will get there by viewing services partners as much more than cheap delivery arms and legs or entrees into new customer conversations.

Services partner management has indeed become a more important aspect of executing a services-strategy profile successfully. Yet, there is much more to keeping a PS organization on target in its pursuit to optimize a specific services-strategy profile. The next chapter introduces a framework management teams can use to monitor the overall maturity and health of any services business.

# Chapter 12

# The Services Dashboard

## TRACKING PROGRESS

This book has covered the journey product companies endure as they approach, enter, and hopefully exit alive a perilous place we call the services chasm. As services organizations navigate this journey with their product brethren, they need to know how they are doing. Is the performance of the services organization typical for other services organizations at the same location in the services chasm? This is the concept of benchmarking performance against like organizations. Closely related to benchmarking is ongoing reporting.

A common inquiry we receive from AFMSI, SSPA, and TPSA members is to provide guidance on how to establish a "services dashboard." A business dashboard is a graphical summary that allows managers to monitor the contribution and health of the departments in their organization. To gauge exactly how well an organization is performing overall, a dashboard captures and reports critical data points from each department within the organization, thus providing a "snapshot" of performance. **By having the right dashboard in place, a management team can better monitor the performance of the services organization and identify areas that need attention.**

Now, before we put a sample services dashboard on the table, we need to have a common understanding of benchmarking. *Benchmarking* is tied to *metrics* at the hip. If we do not have a common framework for metrics, then the concept of benchmarking performance and the format of any dashboard is almost meaningless. In fact, three key terms must *clearly* be defined before meaningful benchmarking and reporting can be accomplished:

- Results

- Metrics

- Practices

Before we define these key terms, let's explore why benchmarking and dashboards are so critical to the success of services managers.

## ENRON: NUMBERS VS. HUMAN PHYSICS

We are about to embark on a discussion of benchmarking that culminates in the mapping of a services business dashboard. On one level, this may seem like a very dry discussion. But I can assure you, it is not. My analogy is Enron. More specifically, the Enron story. On one level, Enron was simply a story of numbers. Fraudulent numbers, but numbers nonetheless. Enron executives were propping up revenue and profit numbers that simply were not real. But that is not why Enron, a case study in business failure, maintains such mind share. The real story of Enron is not one of numbers, but human physics. The human stories associated with the run up and collapse of Enron make the story so fascinating. Here are just a few: A relatively young reporter from *Fortune* magazine, Bethany McLean, was the first person to question Enron's business model and results. Pai, one of the key architects of Enron's business model, was able to exit the company unscathed and become the second largest land holder in the state of Colorado. And, the company energy traders were able to bring the state of California to its knees with power shortages. As an aside, I remember driving down El Camino Avenue in Sunnyvale when the traffic lights suddenly went dark because of a rolling blackout—I felt like I was driving in a third-world country with an unreliable power grid. Yet, I was in the heart of Silicon Valley! These are the stories that make Enron so fascinating—not the numbers. The same is true with the concept of benchmarking and reporting. It is not the numbers of benchmarking but the reasons we pursue benchmarking at all.

## THE HUMAN PHYSICS OF BENCHMARKING

In business there has always been the concept of "best practices." Managers want to compare their processes against best practices. They also want to compare their performance against "best in class" industry performance. But do managers and their companies pursue best practices simply to optimize the use of stockholder capital? Give me a break. **Managers, who are real people, pursue industry best practices because they have sticky, complex, business problems they have to solve or explain why they are not solved.**

"Why can't your PS consultants achieve the same high billable utilization rates that lawyers do?" Now that is an interesting question. Also, that is a question that is asked quite frequently by CFOs and COOs to services executives within technology product companies. The services executive has to have an intelligent response to that question. If the services executive cannot reply satisfactorily, he will either lose headcount or lose his job. Therein lies the spark required to make a manager say "Hey, we should benchmark our utilization against other embedded services organizations just like ours and see if they perform about the same."

What about a different type of question. "Should services organizations charge service partners to use services delivery methodologies developed by the services organization?" This is also an interesting question. On one hand, the company has invested real manpower into developing intellectual property that has market value. On the other hand, product companies are motivated to enable their services partners to competently implement products on behalf of the company. How do other similar companies monetize service methodologies? Is the services organization leaving money on the table by not charging partners for access to methodologies?

Crafting meaningful responses to these types of questions is where the conversation of best practices, best in class, and benchmarking is truly born. The Venn diagram shown in Figure 12-1 outlines the framework we use to navigate these complex discussions. This chapter will populate this diagram and explain why this framework serves services leaders so well when they are asked to answer difficult questions regarding the performance of their services business.

If you are about to embark on a journey to improve the performance of a services organization, it is extremely helpful to understand how good or bad current performance truly is. What if your services organization is already generating higher profits than any other competitor in the industry? What if your delivery staff is billing 10 percent more hours per week and your attrition rate is running very high at twice the industry average? These tidbits start your improvement initiatives in a different place than if you learn that your utilization rates and service margins actually lag industry averages.

In general, organizations like to benchmark both their practices and their results to better understand actual performance and the potential for improvement. **Results are quantitative performance data points a company can compare against relative industry and peer results. Practices are simple and complex business processes that help companies achieve target results.** Benchmarking is the first step in a continuous process to optimize services performance. The discipline of benchmarking practices and results provides three distinct business advantages:

1. **Prioritize goals and initiatives**. By understanding where current performance severely lags potential performance, management can identify and fund initiatives designed to close these specific gaps.

Figure 12-1  Objectives of Benchmarking

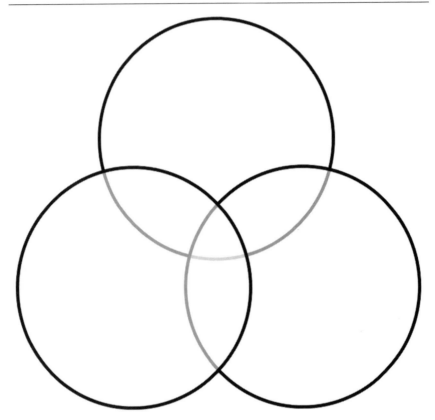

2.  **Monitor improvement**. Periodic benchmarking provides objective standards by which to measure performance improvement.

3.  **Understand impact.** Finally, the benefits of specific initiatives can be measured against the improvement made on specific results. What changes in practice actually drove improvements in business results? Understanding this correlation drives wiser investments.

Very good business reasons exist for services organization to clearly understand both current industry practices and current industry results. However, to fully leverage the benefits of benchmarking, a management team should have a common framework when referring to the concepts of industry practices, industry results, and benchmarking.

# CLEARER DEFINITIONS: RESULTS, METRICS, AND PRACTICES

To create a framework for effectively applying the concept of benchmarking, we need to establish a set of definitions. We start with the simple term "results." As mentioned, results are quantitative performance data points a company can compare against relative industry and peer results. The more tangible and objective a result is, the easier it is to compare against. For example, the Storage Performance Council (SPC) documents benchmark results for storage performance. The SPC web site states the organization provides *"information that is objective, relevant, and verifiable."* This is important if the benchmark is to be relevant to both storage product providers and storage consumers.

Another well-known example of results that can be used as benchmarks comes from the Transaction Processing Performance Council (TPC). This is a well-known nonprofit founded to define transaction processing and database benchmarks and to disseminate objective, verifiable TPC performance data to the industry. In the world of technology services, industry associations such as TPSA and SSPA play the role of aggregating industry results that can be used as benchmarks. We segment that quantitative date into two subcategories:

## *Business Results*

These are the results managers are ultimately attempting to achieve with their business. For example, increasing revenue growth, increasing project margins, or increasing customer satisfaction.

In the world of services, relevant business results include:

**Services Margins**

- *Description:* The profitability of services delivery activities.

- *Calculation:* Difference between what customers pay for the services and what it costs the company to deliver those services. Revenue – COS.

**Realization Rate**

- *Description:* The amount of revenue actually earned as a percentage of potential revenue represented by list prices.

- *Calculation:* Earned revenue (or dollars achieved for billable professionals) ÷ Revenue at list (or undiscounted list price ÷ Fees of work effort from earned revenue).

**Account Expansion**

- *Description:* The ability of a vendor to expand its account penetration and its volume of business within existing accounts.

- *Calculation:* Add-on revenue ÷ Dollar value of original proposal.

## Metrics

These are business activities a company can measure and benchmark themselves against other companies. For example, the percentage of revenue spent on services marketing. This is a metric that helps determine if the services organization is underinvesting or inefficient. However, how much money the services organization does or does not spend on marketing is not something the customer or CEO will consider a critical measurement of business success. To place a finer point on the distinction between results and metrics, how many services organizations list one of their top objectives as: to reduce spending on services marketing? That may be an objective of the services marketing department or the services finance director, but this is hardly a critical business result discussed in executive reviews.

In the world of services, relevant metrics include:

**Attachment Rate**

- *Description:* Percentage of product deals that involve billable service engagements.

- *Calculation:* Engagements involving services ÷ Total number of company engagements.

**Bid and Proposal Costs**

- *Description:* Total dollars spent on submitting a bid, including dollars spent on bid qualification, financial analysis, alliance and/or partner selection, feasibility analysis, proposal development, proposal submittal and best and final offer (BAFO).

- *Calculation:* Total dollars spent for submitting bids ÷ total contract value of bids submitted.

**Direct / Indirect Ratio**

- *Description:* Percentage of delivery resources that are subcontracted.

- *Calculation:* Total subcontracted hours ÷ Total billed hours.

**Of course, for benchmarking to be meaningful, companies must cal-
culate these business results and metrics in the same exact way.** The more
dissimilar such standards for calculating results and metrics become, the less
relevant are the comparisons and the less useful are the benchmarks. Also,
companies like to classify themselves as achieving best-in-class results. What
does that mean? Who is in the class being measured? And how is the term
"best" being defined? We have found the term "best in class" has become too
vague to be meaningful. We replace that concept with the term "pacesetters"
which will be described in more detail below.

## Practices

The next term that must be clearly defined is "practices." Businessdictionary
.com defines practices as the *methods, procedures, processes, and rules employed or
followed by a firm in the pursuit of its objectives.* To link practices to business results,
we say practices are simple and complex business processes that help companies achieve target business results. Example practices in a services organization include:

- Compensating services staff on customer satisfaction ratings

- Establishing an overlay sales force focused solely on selling services
  offerings

- Establishing a centralized project management office to review project
  proposals before they are sent to customers

As soon as the term "practice" is mentioned, the term "best practice" quickly
follows. Wikipedia defines a best practice as:

> An idea that asserts that there is a technique, method, process, activity,
> incentive or reward that is more effective at delivering a particular outcome
> than any other technique, method, process, etc. Best practices can also be
> defined as the most efficient (least amount of effort) and effective (best
> results) way of accomplishing a task, based on repeatable procedures that
> have proven themselves over time for large numbers of people.

In reality, it is often impossible to determine what the *best* practice truly is
for any given business activity. Why? Because companies can't or won't compare practices and practice costs across companies. This reality has led us to
create more practical categories regarding business practices that we will discuss later.

We have now clearly defined the terms "results," "metrics," and "practices."
However, before a services organization runs off to create a dashboard that

compares performance against industry practices and results, an approach should be developed for assessing the relevance of benchmark data to your organization. That is the topic of the next section.

## ASSESSING THE RELEVANCE OF PRACTICES AND RESULTS

Whenever companies review industry data, they must question how applicable the data is to their specific environment. To assess this relevance, there are three factors to consider.

### Sample Sizes

In general, the more companies surveyed when aggregating results and practices, the better. All things being equal, a larger sample size leads to increased precision when estimating the practices and results of the overall industry population. This can be seen in such statistical rules such as the law of large numbers. However, in the world of business, small sample sizes may be very relevant. For example, a company may simply want to understand the results of its three top competitors. This leads to the second factor of benchmarking: peer groups.

### Relevant Peer Groups

When comparing results and practices, companies need to make relevant comparisons. For example, we would not recommend Cisco professional services compare its financial performance against Indian firm Infosys. Even though both of these firms deliver technology professional services, they have fundamentally different business models and objectives. Cisco should compare itself to other product providers such as Juniper and Netapp. Peer groups that we believe are relevant when comparing services practices and results include:

1. **Services-Strategy Profile Peer Group:** Product providers should compare themselves against other product providers that are pursuing the same strategy for their services organizations. For example, the billable utilization rates of delivery staff in product providers are very different than the billable utilization rates in solution providers. For very good reasons.

2. **Size of the Services Organization Peer Group:** Large services organizations generate different metrics and can support different practices than can small services organizations.

3. **Same Industry Peer Group:** Finally, nuances exist within industries. For example, some services practices vary between hardware and software companies.

These peers groups appear in the above order for a reason. Our data shows the most relevant peer group in services benchmarking is indeed those with the same services-strategy profile, followed by size. In fact, the pattern recognition of services practices across industries in amazing when the data is categorized by services-strategy profile and size.

## Shape of the Results

Finally, after understanding the size of the dataset being examined and the relevance of the companies surveyed, a company must consider the shape of the results. **The concept of an industry average or peer group average can be very misleading. Averages can hide the true behavior of the industry.** Data points can be spread widely creating a large standard deviation. In other words, industry results are spread over a very large range. In other instances, instead of creating nice even bell curves, datasets can create truncated curves weighted heavily to one side. A classic example of a truncated curve is the data concerning subcontracting within embedded PS organizations. On average, the embedded PS organizations benchmarked by TPSA subcontract less than 20 percent of their delivery. However, the curve is truncated with a long tail to the right as shown in Figure 12-2. What this shows is that some PS organizations are very aggressive in their subcontracting while a majority are very conservative. Simply looking at the average of "less than 20 percent" does not tell the complete story.

By considering how many companies were benchmarked, how relevant those companies are to your company, and the shape of the results, companies can begin to apply results and practices in a meaningful way. In addition, by understanding these three dynamics of the benchmark data, the services management team is in a much stronger position to defend any recommendations made to executive management from benchmark comparisons. The next section discusses tactics for making meaningful comparisons.

## RESULTS ZONES: ASSESSING RESULTS DATA

First, services organizations can start by comparing results and metrics. Once again, results and metrics are numerical data points. There is typically an expected range for the results. For example, the results for billable utilization rates may range from 40 to 100 percent and billable rates may range from $50 per hour to $400 per hour, and so on. A clear order exists of what constitutes

Figure 12-2  Subcontracting in Embedded PS

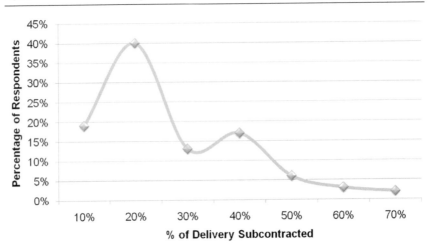

good or better performance. For example, higher billable rates are always desirable if they can be achieved.

So, working with numerical results data, it is helpful to think in terms of red, yellow, or green performance:

> **Severely Lagging:** If your services organization is red on a specific result compared to the range of results reported from the relevant peer group, it would mean the result for your firm is obviously lower than the average for peer organizations. For example, billable utilization of 40 percent would obviously lag a peer average of 65 percent. What exactly determines whether a result should be rated red? The answer depends on the nature of the results data. For a result translated into a standard normal curve, any specific company result that is more than one standard deviation below the mean for the peer group would be considered red. The bottom line is any reasonable person should be able to look at the peer results and your results and agree your results are not aligned with peer results! By identifying red results, a services organization can clearly understand where performance improvements are most likely to be found.

> **Lagging:** If your services organization is yellow on a specific result, it would mean the result is a little behind peer group performance. In terms of a standard normal curve, any company result that is below the mean but within one standard deviation below would most likely classify as a yellow, or lagging, result. If no results are severely lagging, a services organization would next turn its attention to improving lagging results.

**On target:** Finally, results can be classified as green or on target. Green results reflect the fact that the services organization is performing at or above the level of peers on this result.

Figure 12-3 maps severely lagging, lagging, and on target results on a standard normal curve.

When viewing the results zones, everything that is average or above average can be considered on target. Exceptionally outstanding results are classified as "pacesetter results." When we benchmark, we define pacesetter results as those in the top 25 percent of the results sample. However, a lot of the real value regarding the benchmarking of results lies on the left-hand side of the bell curve. The reason for this is simple: The big bang for the buck in benchmarking is in understanding underperformance, not overperformance. Although benchmarking does provide the opportunity to crow about on-target results, there is relatively little business value in itemizing all the things you are already doing well. What is the action plan there? Keep doing everything the same? The business value in benchmarking is clearly identifying the results that are subpar. This is where the opportunity for improvement most likely exists. And this leads to the next section: how to apply practice data.

## LINKING PRACTICES TO RESULTS

At the beginning of this chapter, I outlined why companies are motivated to benchmark their performance. Now, the discussion arrives at what should be the fundamental reason any organization benchmarks: to understand what practices drive better results. In other words, what services practices really do improve financial performance?

To understand practices effectively, we must segment them into meaningful categories, much like we did with results. However, since practices are either pursued or not pursued, practice data does not have a numerical relationship

Figure 12-3  Results Zones

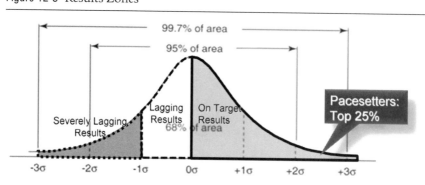

as with results. This means that practices do not lend themselves to be analyzed across a normal bell curve. To address this, we segment practices into five categories.

## Common Practice

*The common practice represents what a clear majority of companies are doing regarding a specific business practice.* For example, 97 percent of product companies compensate their product sales representatives to sell any professional service offerings the company may have. Is this the best practice for a product company? That answer is complicated. However, this is clearly a common practice. Management teams often need to understand the industry common practice. In this example, it is helpful when creating a competitive compensation package to understand the industry common practice regarding the compensation of product sales representatives for selling professional services.

## Pacesetter Practice

We have created a category called the pacesetter practices. *A pacesetter practice is one that consistently presents itself in the highest financial performing services organizations.* In other words, what practices are high-performing services organizations most likely to have in place? Once again, these may not be documented best practices and they may not be the most common practices in the industry, but high-performing services organizations are likely to have the practice in place. For example, we know that, compared to all PS organizations, high-performing PS organizations are more likely to manage their delivery resource pools globally rather than locally.

## Required Practice

The overlap of common practices and pacesetter practices represents a practice that a majority of the industry pursues *and* is implemented by a majority of the highest performing services organizations. Practices that fall in this overlap area are called *"required practices." In other words, these practices are most likely table stakes for successful services organizations.*

## Reasonable Practice

*A reasonable practice is one that multiple companies have implemented successfully, and it has created business benefits.* Perhaps it cannot be defended as the clear cut best practice. Also, it may not be the common practice in the industry. However, it is a defined practice that has been implemented by some companies. And it has created some known benefits. For example, the practice of accurately tracking and budgeting the amount of time services-delivery staff spend on presales activities is a reasonable practice for PS organizations. This practice creates known benefits and is reasonable to implement.

### Recommended Practice

Finally, the overlap occurs between reasonable practices and pacesetter practices. Practices that fall in this overlap area are called *"recommended practices." These are practices that are not overly difficult to implement within a services organization and are already found in a majority of the highest performing services organization.*

These five practice types can be segmented into practice zones using a Venn diagram as shown in Figure 12-4.

The term "best practice" does not appear in Figure 12-4. As stated earlier, best practices are defined as the most efficient (least amount of effort) and effective (best results) way of accomplishing a task, based on repeatable procedures that have proven themselves over time for large numbers of people. Best practices most likely would be found within pacesetter practices but could be found anywhere on the diagram. The litmus test is that the practice has been proven to be the most efficient and effective way to execute a services practice. Once again, this proof is often unavailable, but if a best practice has been identified clearly, it should be pursued.

There is one more type of practice not shown in Figure 12-4: a "differentiated practice." **A differentiated practice is an approach employed by an organization that is unique (not a common practice) and creates improved business results.** We say business results because the practice may not drive financial improvement but may drive other benefits such as improved product adoption, improved customer satisfaction, and so on.

These practice zones create a clear priority for the order an organization should attempt to master industry practices:

1. **Required Practices:** First, understand and implement practices that are common in the industry and are common in high-performing services organization.

2. **Recommended Practices:** Next, understand and implement practices that are reasonable to implement and are common in high-performing services organizations.

Figure 12-4  Practice Zones

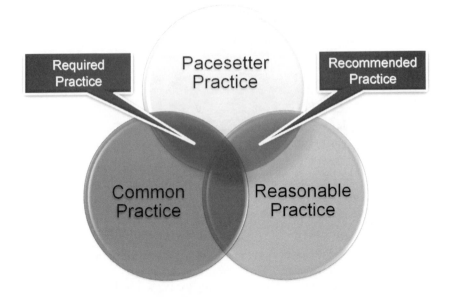

3. **Best Practices:** Third, understand if there are any clearly defined best practices that were not already covered by the required and recommended practices implemented.

4. **Differentiated Practices:** Finally, strategize on ways the services organization could innovate existing practices to create unique advantages in the marketplace.

This natural order of urgency for adopting practices is documented in Figure 12-5. First, there should be a priority on practices that are common in the industry and common within high-performing pacesetters. These practices are table stakes. From there, practices that are pursued by pacesetters and are not too burdensome to implement should be considered. If well-documented and well-defended industry best practices are not already flagged in the required or recommended categories, they should be considered. Finally, with basic optimization in place through the adoption of proven practices, a services organization can become more creative and seek to design new and inventive services practices. These differentiated practices have the potential to create unique competitive advantage. However, the low hanging fruit for a majority of services organizations will be to first implement practices that are proven to boost performance (required, recommended, and best practices).

Figure 12-5    Practice Priorities

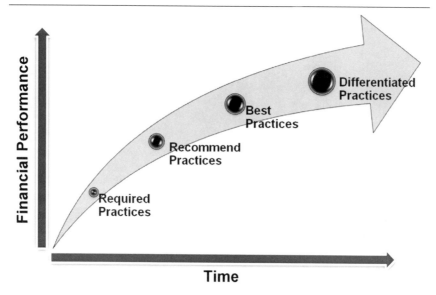

We close this section on practices with one final caution: **The fact that a practice is a *common practice* does not mean it should be a *recommended practice*.** In other words, just because a practice is found in many service organizations, it does not mean the practice should necessarily be preferred. For example, at this point in time, the management of strategic service partners for product companies is commonly the responsibility of a partner or "channel" organization. However, we see an emerging pacesetter practice where strategic services partner management is migrated to the services organization. In short, the minority practice could well be (and often is) the recommended practice, not the common or majority practice

## STEPPING STONES TO SERVICES SUCCESS

By benchmarking current practices against known *required* and *recommended practices*, a services organization can baseline its maturity. In our benchmarking process, we provide a summary rating to the services organization that rates the performance on numerous results, metrics, and practices. The data is aggregated and summarizes total performance into one of four grids. Figure 12-6, Assessing Results and Practices, represents a services organization that found its results and metrics on target (though not pacesetting) and its practices relatively mature. In this specific example, the organization found it had already implemented a majority of the required and recommended practices.

Figure 12-6  Assessing Results and Practices

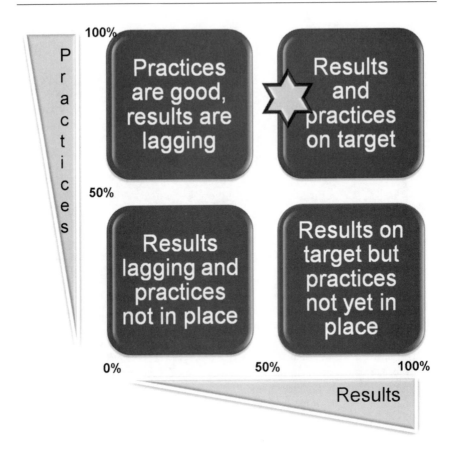

However there were still some recommended practices the organization had not yet implemented that could help improve results further. An effective benchmarking process should help a services organization answer three fundamental questions:

1.  Are my results reasonable compared to peer services organizations?

2.  Are my practices similar compared to peer services organizations?

3.  What required and recommended practices can we focus on to improve results?

With the answers to these questions, a services organization can begin the process of improving performance. After benchmarking, the management team should prioritize initiatives to improve existing practices. Top priorities are converted to specific plans. Those plans should identify what practices are being improved and what results or metrics will be used to validate improvement. Finally, the organization executes the improvement plans. Figure 12-7 documents this four step process.

## THE SERVICES DASHBOARD

With a very thorough taxonomy for evaluating business results, metrics, and practices, we can now assemble a meaningful dashboard that services managers can use to track and report on the health of their business.

### *Attributes of a Good Dashboard*

There is an entire industry composed of both software vendors and consultancies that support the creation of business dashboards. These vendors and consultants cite common attributes for an effective dashboard:

- An intuitive, easy-to-understand graphical display is presented.

- A logical structure to the information is presented.

- Little or no user training is required to interpret the dashboard.

- Regular and frequent updates of dashboard information are available for accuracy and relevance to current conditions.

- A consolidated source of information from multiple sources, departments, or markets can be viewed simultaneously.

Figure 12-7  Stepping Stones to Services Success

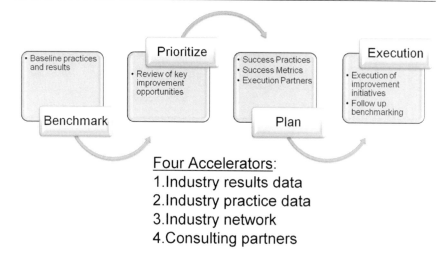

With these design principles in mind, the leaders from all of our associations have worked with both member companies and leading industry consultants to craft a baseline services dashboard that can be used for almost any line of technology services (support, professional services, managed services, etc.).

## Categories

We reviewed the data being gathered by the benchmark instruments of AFMSI, SSPA, and TPSA. We also reviewed those instruments with leading technology companies from our membership to understand what information they are were tracking for their services business. Finally, we reached out to firms providing consulting on how to optimize services strategy and operations to gain their opinions on what data should be tracked in a services dashboard. Through all of that discussion and analysis, we were able to define 10 universal categories where services businesses need to baseline their performance. The categories are outlined in Table 12-1.

Table 12-1  Categories for the Services Dashboard

| Category | Relevancy | Example Result, Metric, or Practice |
|---|---|---|
| **Business Performance** | Is the services organization delivering key business results such as target revenues and profits? | • Services revenues<br>• Services bookings<br>• Project margins |
| **Customer Experience** | Is the services organization delivering an acceptable customer experience? | • Customer satisfaction results<br>• Customer satisfaction compensation practices |
| **Services Delivery** | Is the services organization delivering services offerings efficiently and effectively? | • Billable utilization rates<br>• Productive utilization rates<br>• Project completion ratios |
| **Services Operations** | How mature and cost effective is the infrastructure supporting the services organization? | • Cost of G&A as percent of services revenues<br>• Ability to track resource availability<br>• Time to source services engagements |
| **Partner Management** | Does the services organization have a mature and effective | • Percent of services delivery subcontracted |

Table 12-1  (continued)

| Category | Relevancy | Example Result, Metric, or Practice |
|---|---|---|
| | capability to evaluate and enable services-delivery partners? | • Services partner margins<br>• Time to enable services partners |
| **Services Engineering** | How mature and cost effective is the capability to design and deploy new services offerings? | • Time to market for new offerings<br>• Cost of services development as percent of services revenues<br>• Percent of services engagements that receive formal project reviews |
| **Services Marketing** | Does the services organization have the ability to enable sales channels to sell services, help drive demand, and increase customer awareness? | • Cost of marketing as percent of services revenues<br>• Percent marketing dollars spent on demand generation |
| **Services Sales** | Is the services organization effective at selling services? | • Discount rates<br>• Realization rates<br>• Cost of services sales as percent of services revenues<br>• Hit rates<br>• Attach rates |
| **Product Development Impact** | Does the services organization effectively influence the development process for new product offerings? | • Defined process for engaging services into the product development life cycle<br>• Defines process for information from the services knowledge to influence product features |
| **Economic Impact** | Does the services organization have the ability to calculate its influence on key metrics such as total account profitability or product renewal rates? | • Total account profitability with and without services engagement<br>• Product renewal rates with and without services engagement |

Using these 10 categories, you can map almost any result, metric, or practice related to managing a services business. But the elegant aspect of these categories is how you can map them visually.

### Graphical Representation

So finally we are here, ready to gaze at a services dashboard. To ease into it, let's start with the core gauges of the dashboard. These gauges report on how well the overall services engine is running and on the health of the core components of the engine. Figure 12-8 shows the key areas represented on the core dashboard.

The outer five gauges represent the life cycle of the services experience. First the service is sold to the customer by Services Sales. Services Delivery is then responsible for delivering what was sold. Services Operations is responsible for scaling delivery capabilities. Services Engineering is developing and optimizing offerings. Services Marketing is creating demand, which leads right back

**Figure 12-8**  Core Guages on the Services Dashboard

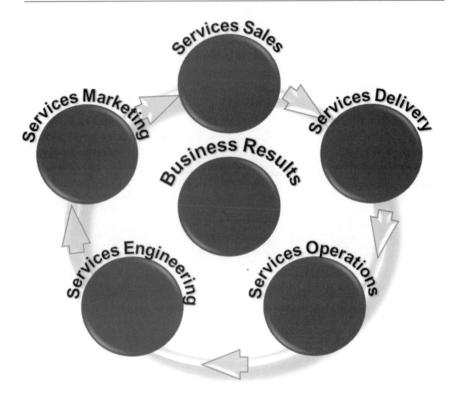

Figure 12-9  Core Services Dashboard

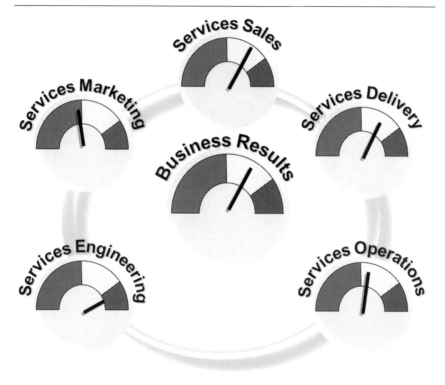

to selling services. Figure 12-9 provides an example dashboard for these six gauges.

We can now layer on the four categories from Table 12-1 not yet represented on the dashboard. These missing categories represent how the services organization extends both its influence and impact out beyond its core business of delivering services. The four areas of influence are customer experience, partner management, product development, and economic impact. These influences are mapped onto Figure 12-10.

The complete services dashboard is shown in Figure 12-11. The placement of the dials in relevant. Customer experience occurs at the intersection of Services Sales and Services Delivery activities. Services Operations and Services Delivery both touch services delivery partners. Services Marketing and Services Engineering should be partnering to influence the features in new product releases. Finally, economic impact metrics, such as the influence of services on product sales, are an extension of core services business results such as project margins.

Figure 12-10 Extended Guages for the Services Dashboard

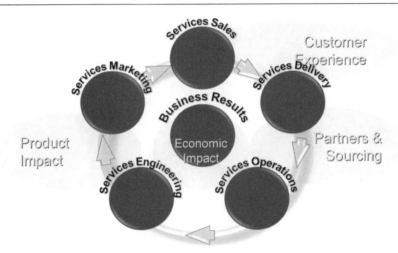

At first glance, it can be overwhelming, but every dial on the dashboard is mapped to key data points that reveal the effectiveness and health of the services organization.

## CLOSING THOUGHTS

A successful journey to create a dashboard that monitors the health of a services organization starts with the concepts of results, metrics, and practices. Everyone in business is familiar with the concept of pursuing best practices. However, the effective application of benchmarking is not common to all organizations. This gap between concept and application exists, at least in part, because management teams do not share a common framework for applying practices and results data. To overcome this gap, we strongly recommend services organizations pursue the following success factors when crafting their services dashboard:

1.  Embrace a common taxonomy for interpreting industry results, metrics, and practices.

2.  Segment common practices from pacesetter practices.

3.  Understand that common practices are not necessarily best or even recommended practices.

4.  Establish relevant peer groups when evaluating industry data for both practices and results.

Figure 12-11  The Extended Services Dashboard

5.  Approach benchmarking and the creation of a services dashboard as the beginning of a journey to improve services performance.

Speaking of journeys, we are getting very close to the end of ours. There is only one more topic I want to cover before closing this tomb. It concerns the industry trends that will force the creation of new services-strategy profiles.

# Chapter 13

# Emerging Profiles

W e are reaching the end of our journey on how to set services strategy to maximize product success. I hope you have found the frameworks introduced in this book helpful. I believe these insights will serve the technology services industry very well as more and more product companies realize services strategy can no longer be an afterthought. However, the business world is not a static place. The goal line is constantly shifting to a new location—always just a little further down the field. In this chapter, I want to explore how the role of services within product companies may migrate beyond the four profiles currently in play and defined in this book. This chapter is designed to motivate, not demoralize, business leaders. But I won't make any promises.

## MARGIN MAPS: THE CURRENT STATE

If you are in the process of shifting your services-strategy profile, you will undoubtedly be forced to review the overall economics of your company. In other words, you will reexamine exactly where the margin dollars will be coming from in your new product and service revenue mix. As you start that modeling process, you do not have to start with a blank slate. As documented in the previous chapters, we have a very good sense of the amount of revenue coming both from product and services within these common services-strategy profiles. In addition, we have very good data regarding the actual margins generated by these business lines. Putting these two variables together, percentage of revenue and margin, we can create a graph that maps the expected strike zone for each business activity. Let's build it out.

First of all, let's map the revenue and margins that product companies achieve from hardware and software. For these two revenue streams, the theoretical strike zones, ignoring services-strategy profile, are quite large. Figure 13-1 maps the potential for these two areas. What the picture shows is that software revenues can range from 2 to 90 percent or total company revenues in a product company. A software product provider like salesforce.com or Autodesk will have a vast majority of their revenue coming from software. However, a hardware company newly investing in software may have a very

Figure 13-1  Strike Zone for Hardware and Software Revenues

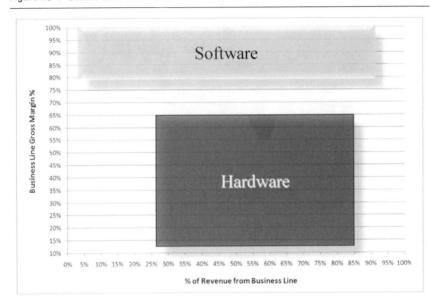

small percentage of revenue coming from software. Software margins, depending on how they are calculated, can run from 80 to 99 percent.

Hardware companies can typically achieve 25 to 85 percent of their revenue from hardware products. Margins, however, vary widely. Cisco can achieve 65 percent on its hardware products but PC manufacturers such as Dell can find themselves barely in the double digits. The range for hardware margins mapped is 12 to 65 percent.

If you were pursuing a product-extender strategy, your target strike zone within these theoretical bumpers would be much tighter as documented in Figure 13-2.

Now that you are getting the hang of the map, we can layer on the remaining business lines. Figure 13-3 shows a margin map documenting the theoretical strike zones for hardware, hardware support, software, and software support. This map paints a clear picture of why software companies typically generate higher operating incomes than do hardware companies. The margin structure is much higher for software and software support than for hardware and hardware support.

Finally, we can complete the margin map by layering on the strike zone for project-based professional services as shown in Figure 13-4. As we know from

Figure 13-2  Product-Extender Strike Zones

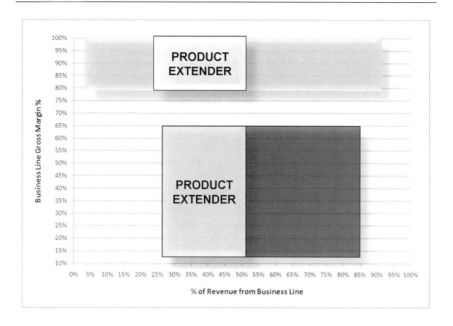

Figure 13-3  Adding Support Strike Zones

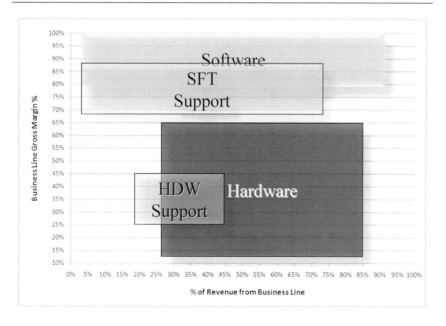

Figure 13-4  PS Strike Zone

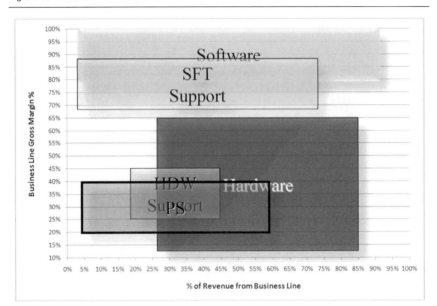

the previous chapters, PS revenues can run from 5 percent for a product provider to well over 50 percent for a solution provider. We benchmark this service line extensively, and margins typically range from 20 percent (a breakeven business model) to double that at 40 percent.

The completed margin map shown in Figure 13-4 provides the boundaries for the current business models being executed in the technology industry today. Yes, some companies may achieve results slightly out of these boundaries, but these are reasonable boundaries for business planning purposes today. Where your dart lands on this map for each business line should have a lot to do with the services-strategy profile you are working to execute.

What I want you to think about now is not this year's business plan, or even next year's business plan, but the business plan you will be executing 5 years from now. How will you make your money in the future? **You need to be aware that this margin map is shifting.**

## EVAPORATING MARGINS

In Chapter 1, I described the failure pattern product companies follow when product markets mature. I also highlighted new trends, such as cloud computing, that are putting even more pressure on successfully aligning product-services strategy. Another way to internalize the mounting pressure on product companies to change their services-strategy profile relates to the margin map. As the previous map demonstrates, the three greatest potential sources for margin dollars within a technology product company are obvious:

- Software margins
- Software maintenance margins
- Hardware margins

Unfortunately, all three of these margin wells are under severe duress.

## Compressing Hardware Margins

Cisco and Intel are two of the leading hardware vendors on the planet. They are both known for driving high-margin, highly profitable business models. However, even these industry stalwarts are not immune to reduced product margins. Figure 13-5 shows the trend for average product margins at these two companies as reported in their annual reports. At one level, the decreases do not seem very dramatic. However, if these two companies were able to maintain their higher product margins in 2008, they would have generated almost $3 billion in additional product margin dollars. I'm sure that money could have come in handy. To offset this loss and maintain the same operating profit, both companies would have had to reduce expenses somewhere in the business model. This trend of fewer hardware margin dollars is ubiquitous in the tech industry, from chips to routers to servers to PCs.

Figure 13-5  Cisco and Intel Product Margins

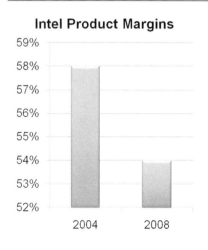
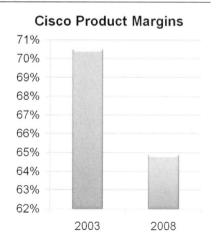

### Compressing Software Maintenance Margins

It is no industry secret that software maintenance is an important source of margin dollars for technology companies. However, this lucrative margin stream is under immense pressure. Our industry association, the SSPA, has been working with members for the past 4 years in developing tactics to help defend this service line by connecting maintenance activities to direct business value for customers. Despite these efforts, the pressure mounts. A recent *Wall Street Journal* article titled "Rethinking Software Support" captures the dynamics well:

> *Oracle Corp.'s lucrative business selling maintenance contracts could come under pressure if companies turn to lower-cost alternatives as the recession drags on.*
>
> *Consider Santa Fe Natural Tobacco Co. The small cigarette maker, which is a unit of Reynolds American Inc., recently switched its service contract for Oracle human resources software to Rimini Street Inc., a software support company that says it charges half of what Oracle does.*
>
> *"We were paying higher fees," Rusty Gaston, Santa Fe's chief information officer, said of the Oracle contract. "And getting no more for it."*
>
> *How many of Oracle's customers follow suit is an open question for the Redwood City, Calif.-based company, which garnered nearly half of its $22.4 billion in sales last fiscal year from highly profitable maintenance and support contracts.[1]*

Can companies such as Oracle, SAP, IBM, and even EMC and HP imagine a world where customers are no longer automatically renewing high-margin support contracts? These companies may have to not only imagine such a world, but learn to thrive in it.

### Evaporating Software License Margins

Perhaps the most disconcerting trend surrounding margin dollars centers on the software license. When salesforce.com first came to market, they trumpeted the death of the traditional software license where a company pays large upfront fees for the right to license a software package. However, all salesforce.com really did is shift from a large, up-front and on-site software distribution

---

[1] Rethinking Software Support by Jessica Hodgson, March 12, 2009, *The Wall Street Journal.*

model to a centralized, pay-as-you go model. The customers no longer had to outlay large sums of capital at the beginning of a software contact. They could spread the payments over months and months. But they still had to pay to use the software. What if customers stopped paying for software altogether?

This terrifying scenario of free software is already a reality. We all use Google applications—most likely daily. For me, it has become one of the most powerful software applications I leverage to conduct my work. Yet, I don't pay a dime for the privilege. Every week I blog on thomaslah.wordpress.com. The application provides me incredibly detailed information on my blog traffic, including how many readers I have, where they came from, what search terms they used to find my site, and what they clicked when they were there. I don't pay a dime for the service.

Are the two examples of Google and blogging too consumer oriented? Does this trend of free software apply to real business applications? I would argue it does. Would you consider systems management software a core business application? This is the software that provides the following capabilities to an IT department or manager:

- Inventory of software deployed on the company network
- Map of the network environment
- Inventory of all machines on the company network
- Network performance monitoring and license monitoring
- Asset reporting and inventory reporting
- Software to track IT Helpdesk tickets

Now, what if you could install software that does all that for your medium-size business for free? As of the writing of this chapter, you can. A company named Spiceworks (www.spiceworks.com) provides network management software to small and medium-size businesses (SMB)—at no cost. It is an ad-based revenue model, much like Google's. I've spoken to Spicework's head of marketing. He said they don't even consider themselves a software company, but a media company. Enterprise software providers such as CA, HP, and IBM are working hard to move their applications downstream into the fast-growing market segment of SMB. How do they compete with free?

These trends of evaporating margin dollars place immense pressure on the traditional profiles of technology product companies. So what could the future look like if these trends are unrelenting? Before I paint that terrifying picture, I need to provide a simple framework that will allow us to think about current vs. future margin streams.

## SERVICE TYPES

There is body of academic work out of Germany that focuses on classifying types of services by their characteristics. One of the premises of the work is that to successfully engineer services offerings, you should understand their unique characteristics. For more information on this work, read the academic article "Services Engineering: State of the Art and Future Trends" by Klaus-Peter Fahnrich and Thomas Meiren.[2] **The concept of classifying types of services has great potential for the technology industry.** The power of viewing service offerings by type allows companies to begin breaking down the artificial boundaries that companies use to classify services as a "support offering" or "professional services offering." Instead, the management team can apply an objective eye to a type of services—not who in the company provides the service. In addition, **by understanding the subtle yet critical differences in service types, product companies can more readily identify where they have capability gaps.** In this section, I will introduce six distinct classes of services that technology companies can provide. It may feel like I am dragging you through the glass, but trust me—the pain is worth the gain.

### *Eight Service Attributes*

To classify services into different types, you need a set of attributes that can be applied to distinguish the differences in the services. At least eight attributes must be considered when comparing types of services:

- **Location:** Does the service need to be delivered directly on site, or can the service be delivered remotely?

- **Customer Intimacy:** To successfully deliver the service, how much does the services provider need to understand concerning the uniqueness of the customer's environment?

- **Time to Deliver:** How long does it take to deliver the service? Less than an hour? Weeks?

- **Variance in Deliverables:** Are the final deliverables the same from customer to customer or are they completely custom?

- **Delivery Skills:** What level of skills is required to deliver the service offering? Skills that can be taught in a two-week training course or skills that take years to develop?

---

[2] *Advances in Services Innovations.* 2007. Services Engineering: State of the Art and Future Trends by Klaus-Peter Fahnrich and Thomas Meiren. New York: Springer Belin Heidelberg.

- **Technology Interaction:** Does the delivery of the service require intense interaction with technology or perhaps no interaction with technology?

- **One to What?** Is this service designed to be delivered in a one-to-many fashion (training course with 40 attendees) or in a one-to-one fashion (customer analysis project for a specific customer)?

- **Pricing Model:** Is the service sold on a time-and-materials basis, fixed price, or does the customer pay per transaction?

These eight attributes are a solid starting point when classifying service types because they immediately tease out critical differences in service offerings. On one extreme of these attributes, you have very customized services requiring an on-site customer presence and specialized delivery staff. On the opposite end of the spectrum, you have highly automated and standardized services. Figure 13-6 shows these extreme settings. Column #1, labeled "Custom," represents services that must be delivered in a very intimate, custom manner. Column #3, labeled "Standard," represents services that can be automated and rapidly scaled.

Another way to visualize the difference between highly custom and highly standard offerings is to take these attributes and map them to a spider graph. Figure 13-7 applies a rating of 1 when the service attribute is highly customized and a rating of 3 when the attribute is highly standardized.

It is important for product companies to understand the differences in these service types. More specifically, it is important for product companies to understand that these differences in services attributes create more than just two big buckets of "custom" vs. "standard" offerings.

Figure 13-6  Service Attributes Table

| | Attribute | Custom 1 | 2 | Standard 3 |
|---|---|---|---|---|
| 1 | Location | On site | Blend | Off site |
| 2 | Customer Intimacy | High | Med | Low |
| 3 | Time to Execute | Week | Hours | Seconds |
| 4 | Variance in Deliverables | High | Moderate | Low |
| 5 | Delivery Skills | Complex | Moderate | Simple |
| 6 | Technology Interaction | Complex | Moderate | Simple |
| 7 | One to What? | One | Few | Many |
| 8 | Pricing | Time and Materials | Fixed | Transaction |

Figure 13-7  Service Attributes Graph

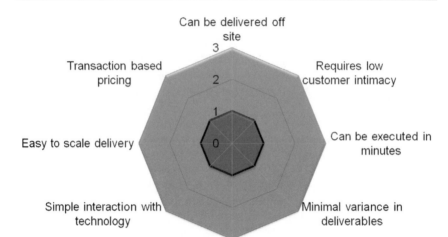

## Six Service Types

Using the eight attributes, we can easily define six unique service types that product companies may have to grapple with as their products mature. Each service type will be given a letter for identification.

## Service Type A

The first type of service would be one that falls into the highly automated category previously defined. This type of service has the following attributes:

- The service can be delivered away from the customer's location.

- The service *does not* require a high degree of understanding of the customer's unique environment.

- The time to execute the service is tracked in minutes (or even seconds). Think of calling in to register your new computer.

- The deliverable is the same from customer to customer.

- Because the service is repetitive in nature, the skills required to deliver it are not complex.

- The interaction with technology is simple and repetitive.

- The service is designed to be delivered one to many. For example, one customer service representative serving many customers throughout one eight-hour shift.

When a company offers this type of service, the path to services success is relatively straight forward: Automate. Automate every aspect of the service experience that is practical. The following table summarizes Service Type A.

| A | Highly Automated | | | |
|---|---|---|---|---|
| 1 | Location | On site | Blend | Off site |
| 2 | Customer Intimacy | High | Med | Low |
| 3 | Time to Execute | > Week | Hours | Minutes |
| 4 | Variance in Deliverables | High | Moderate | Low |
| 5 | Delivery Skills | Complex | Moderate | Simple |
| 6 | Technology Interaction | Complex | Moderate | Simple |
| 7 | One to What? | One | Few | Many |
| 8 | Pricing Model | Time & Materials | Fixed | Transaction |

## Service Type B

The second type of service looks almost exactly like Service Type A, but this service must be executed at a specific location. This service would be one that has the following attributes:

- *The service must be delivered at a specific location. Think of customer's checking out of a store.*

- It does not require a high degree of understanding of the customer's unique environment.

- The time to execute the service is tracked in minutes (or even seconds). Think of calling in to register your new computer.

- The deliverable is the same from customer to customer.

- The skills required to deliver the service remain relatively simple.

- The interaction with technology is simple and repetitive.

- The service is designed to be delivered one to many. For example, one customer service representative serving many customers throughout one eight-hour shift.

When a company offers this type of service, the path to services success is a combination of automation and self-service. The following table summarizes Service Type B.

| B | Self-Serve | | | |
|---|---|---|---|---|
| 1 | Location | On site | Blend | Off site |
| 2 | Customer Intimacy | High | Med | Low |
| 3 | Time to Execute | > Week | Hours | Minutes |
| 4 | Variance in Deliverables | High | Moderate | Low |
| 5 | Delivery Skills | Complex | Moderate | Simple |
| 6 | Technology Interaction | Complex | Moderate | Simple |
| 7 | One to What? | One | Few | Many |
| 8 | Pricing Model | Time & Materials | Fixed | Transaction |

## Service Type C

The third type of service must be delivered at a specific location, as does Service Type B. However, this service also involves a higher degree of customer intimacy. Also, the deliverables may vary somewhat from customer to customer. However, delivery staff are ultimately executing a finite set of activities, and they may be interfacing with multiple customers within one day. Think of the classic field service position with a product company. This service has following attributes:

- The service must be delivered at a specific location. Think of customer's checking out of a store.

- *It requires a* **high degree** *of understanding of the customer's unique environment.*

- *The time to execute the service is tracked in hours.*

- *The deliverable may vary slightly from customer to customer.*

- *The skills to deliver the service have moved from simple to moderate.*

- *The interaction with technology ranges from simple to moderate.*

- The service is designed to be delivered one to many. For example, a field services technician may visit multiple customers on one day.

When a company offers this type of service, the path to services success is a combination of automation and training the delivery staff well. The following table summarizes Service Type C.

| C | Train Well | | | |
|---|---|---|---|---|
| 1 | Location | On site | Blend | Off site |
| 2 | Customer Intimacy | High | Med | Low |
| 3 | Time to Execute | > Week | Hours | Minutes |
| 4 | Variance in Deliverables | High | Moderate | Low |
| 5 | Delivery Skills | Complex | Moderate | Simple |
| 6 | Technology Interaction | Complex | Moderate | Simple |
| 7 | One to What? | One | Few | Many |
| 8 | Pricing Model | Time & Materials | Fixed | Transaction |

Graphically, the differences between the attributes of Service Type A and Service Type C are shown in Figure 13-8.

## Service Type D

The fourth type of service, again, must be delivered at a specific location, as with Service Types B and C. This service also involves a higher degree of customer intimacy. The deliverables may vary somewhat from customer to

Figure13-8  Service Type A vs. Service Type C

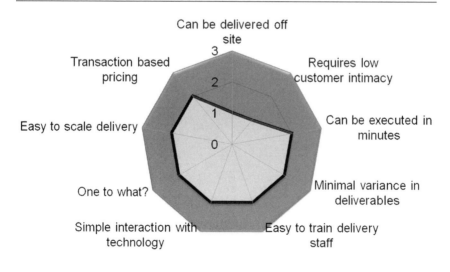

customer. The difference from the previous service type is that this service may take longer to deliver. Instead of a field service technician servicing many customers in one day, this may be a PS consultant delivering a package that takes anywhere from a half day to three days on the customer site. This service has following attributes:

- The service must be delivered at a specific location. Think of customer's checking out of a store.

- It requires a high degree of understanding of the customer's unique environment.

- The time to execute the service is tracked in hours.

- The deliverable may vary slightly from customer to customer.

- Skills required to deliver this service are moderate to complex.

- *The interaction with technology ranges from moderate to complex.*

- *The service is designed to be delivered one to one. For example, a PS consultant may deliver a packaged service to one customer over one or two days.*

When a company offers this type of service, the path to services success is defining clear deliverables and developing tools to accelerate delivery. The following table summarizes Service Type D.

| D | Standardize Deliverables | | | |
|---|---|---|---|---|
| 1 | Location | On site | Blend | Off site |
| 2 | Customer Intimacy | High | Med | Low |
| 3 | Time to Execute | > Week | Hours | Minutes |
| 4 | Variance in Deliverables | High | Moderate | Low |
| 5 | Delivery Skills | Complex | Moderate | Simple |
| 6 | Technology Interaction | Complex | Moderate | Simple |
| 7 | One to What? | One | Few | Many |
| 8 | Pricing Model | Time & Materials | Fixed | Transaction |

## Service Type E

The fifth type of service, unlike the previous three, can be delivered off site—away from the customer. However, unlike Service Type A, which is also delivered remotely, this service involves more customer and technical complexity. Also, the deliverable may vary widely from customer to customer. Think offshore software development. This service has the following attributes:

- *The service can be delivered remotely.*

- It requires a moderate to high degree of understanding of the customer's unique environment.

- *The time to execute may take hours or weeks.*

- *The deliverable may vary greatly from customer to customer.*

- *Delivery skills range from moderate to complex.*

- *The interaction with technology ranges from moderate to complex.*

- *The service is designed to be delivered one to few or one to many.* For example, a resource that provides unique technical expertise for multiple active customer engagements. This resource may be located centrally and leveraged by several on-site engagement teams.

When a company offers this type of service, the path to services success is defining a clear set of skills required to support the services capability. The following table summarizes Service Type E.

| E | Standardize Skills | | | |
|---|--------------------|---|---|---|
| 1 | Location | On site | Blend | Off site |
| 2 | Customer Intimacy | High | Med | Low |
| 3 | Time to Execute | > Week | Hours | Minutes |
| 4 | Variance in Deliverables | High | Moderate | Low |
| 5 | Delivery Skills | Complex | Moderate | Simple |
| 6 | Technology Interaction | Complex | Moderate | Simple |
| 7 | One to What? | One | Few | Many |
| 8 | Pricing Model | Time & Materials | Fixed | Transaction |

## Service Type F

The sixth and final type of service is the polar opposite of Service Type A and is the "highly custom" example previously described. Service Type F requires high-touch, high-customer intimacy and results in very customer-specific deliverables. Think traditional management consulting. This service has following attributes:

- *The service must be delivered directly with the customer.*

- It requires a *high* degree of understanding of the customer's unique environment.

- The time to execute is usually measured in weeks.

- The deliverable varies from customer to customer.

- The skills required to deliver the service are *complex*.

- The interaction with technology ranges from moderate to complex.

- The service is designed to be delivered one to one. For example, a resource that provides unique technical expertise for multiple active customer engagements. This resource may be located centrally and leveraged by several on-site engagement teams.

When a company offers this type of service, the path to services success is skills development. Delivery resources must be groomed through a combination of training and engagement experience before they are competent to deliver these types of offerings. The following table summarizes Service Type F.

| F | Develop Well | | | |
|---|---|---|---|---|
| 1 | Location | On site | Blend | Off site |
| 2 | Customer Intimacy | High | Med | Low |
| 3 | Time to Execute | > Week | Hours | Minutes |
| 4 | Variance in Deliverables | High | Moderate | Low |
| 5 | Delivery Skills | Complex | Moderate | Simple |
| 6 | Technology Interaction | Complex | Moderate | Simple |
| 7 | One to What? | One | Few | Many |
| 8 | Pricing Model | Time & Materials | Fixed | Transaction |

Now that we have a framework that makes it easy to understand six distinct types of services a product company may offer, we can marry to our margin map to glimpse the future of the technology industry.

## EMERGING PROFILE EXAMPLE

This book maps real industry data and documents the services-strategy profiles currently being pursued in the industry. Essentially each one of these services-strategy profiles represents a strike zone on the margin map introduced at the beginning of this chapter. A software company executing a product-extender profile will get so much money from license sales, maintenance contracts, and project-based services like PS. The margin range that companies typically achieve on these three revenue streams is known through our industry benchmarking. Understanding the margin dollar potential of a software product extender becomes a simple math exercise. In fact, there is not a great deal of mystery regarding the margin potential of hardware and software companies executing the current services-strategy profiles. The two questions that determine profitability of a specific company are simple:

1. How hot is the product?

2. Is the management team executing well enough to hit the upper margin boundaries for each revenue stream?

So for companies that master the concepts in this book and maximize their product and services margin streams, it becomes easy to see themselves maximizing the margin potential of their business. However, this last chapter is not about the current state—it is about navigating the future.

## Product Extender: Current Margin Map

To take a look into the future of services-strategy profiles, we can start with the current state. To create a realistic example, I am going to use the revenue and margin data from a real multi-billion-dollar hardware company. The exact breakdown of the revenue mix and gross margins achieved on each business are educated assumptions.

In a recent quarter, this hardware company achieved slightly over $3 billion in revenue and over $1.6 billion in margin dollars. Like many hardware companies, their product portfolio has branched into software that complements their hardware products. Software (SFT) now represents 12 percent of total company revenues. All services activities now represent 43 percent of total company revenues. As a classic product extender, this company has also been slightly expanding its professional services capabilities. I am estimating PS now represents 10 percent of total revenues. The estimated revenue mix and margin mix for the current business is documented in Table 13-1. The graphical version of this company's margin map is documented in Figure 13-9.

## The Margin Map in 3 Years

Now, let's hypothesize what the margin map for this hardware company could look like 3 years down the road. Based on the data points we track surrounding the technology services industry, it would be safe to make the following assumptions regarding trends that will impact the margin map of this hardware company:

• Hardware revenues and margins for legacy products will decline as markets mature and commoditize.

Table 13-1   Revenue and Margin Mix

| Total Quarterly Revenue | | % of Total Revenue | Gross Margin | Margin Dollars |
|---|---|---|---|---|
| $3,150,762 | HDW | 45% | 40% | $   567,137 |
| | SFT | 12% | 98% | $   370,530 |
| | HDW Maint. | 18% | 38% | $   215,512 |
| | SFT Maint. | 15% | 89% | $   420,627 |
| | PS | 10% | 30% | $     94,523 |
| | New Service Transactions | 0% | 0% | $         – |
| | SUM | 100% | | $1,668,328 |
| | SVCS SUM | 43% | | $   730,662 |

Figure 13-9   The Current Margin Map

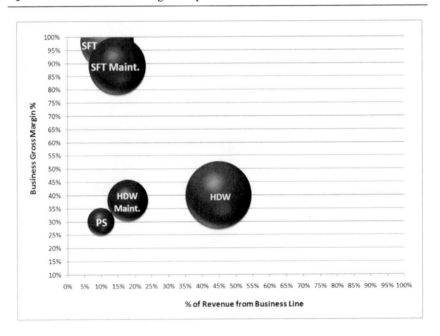

- Hardware maintenance revenues and margins will decline as hardware sales decline.

- Software revenues and software maintenance revenues will increase as the company continues to invest in new software opportunities.

- PS revenues and margins will increase as the company continues to optimize this revenue stream.

Applying these trends to the current margin map, we can generate an updated version of what the margin map may look like 3 years down the road. The data is shown in Table 13-2 and Figure 13-10. Keeping the company at the same level of revenues, you can see the impact of the above trends. Services remains 43 percent of total company revenues, but total margin dollars increased because more revenue is coming from lucrative software and PS improved their project margins. In essence, the shift in the margin map is not bad for this hardware company.

## The Margin Map in 6 Years

Now, let's hypothesize what the margin map for this hardware company could look like 6 years down the road. Continuing to play out current trends we see

Table 13-2  Revenue and Margin Mix 3 Years in the Future

| Total Quarterly Revenue | | % of Total Revenue | Gross Margin | Margin Dollars |
|---|---|---|---|---|
| $3,150,762 | HDW | 39% | 35% | $ 430,079 |
| | SFT | 18% | 98% | $ 555,794 |
| | HDW Maint. | 15% | 30% | $ 141,784 |
| | SFT Maint. | 15% | 89% | $ 420,627 |
| | PS | 13% | 38% | $ 155,648 |
| | New Service Transactions | 0% | 0% | $   – |
| | SUM | 100% | | $1,703,932 |
| | SVCS SUM | 43% | | $ 718,059 |

Figure 13-10  Margin Map 3 Years in the Future

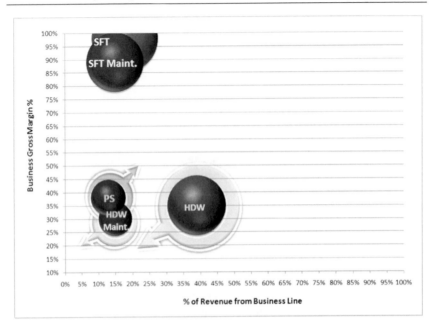

in the industry, it would be fair to make the following assumptions regarding trends that will impact the margin map of this hardware company:

- Hardware revenues and margins for legacy products continue to decline.

- Margins for new hardware offerings are not as high as they were for previous new hardware offerings.

- Hardware maintenance revenues and margins continue to decline.

- Software maintenance revenues and margins decline as customers begin pushing on this expense.

- PS margins flatten.

Applying these trends to the current margin map, we can generate an updated version of what the margin map may look like 6 years down the road. The data is shown in Table 13-3 and Figure 13-11. Again, we keep the company at the same revenue level.

To simply keep revenue and margin neutral (generate the same amount of revenue and margin dollars), this hardware company will need to make some

Table 13-3  Revenue and Margin Mix 6 Years in the Future

| Total Quarterly Revenue | | % of Total Revenue | Gross Margin | Margin Dollars |
|---|---|---|---|---|
| $3,150,762 | HDW | 20% | 20% | $ 126,030 |
| | SFT | 20% | 85% | $ 535,630 |
| | HDW Maint. | 5% | 30% | $ 47,261 |
| | SFT Maint. | 12% | 60% | $ 226,855 |
| | PS | 13% | 38% | $ 155,648 |
| | New Service Transactions | 30% | 63% | $ 595,494 |
| | SUM | 100% | | $1,686,918 |
| | SVCS SUM | 60% | | $1,025,258 |

dramatic changes to its business. First, legacy hardware and hardware mainte-nance now only represent 25 percent of total company revenues. Pressure on software maintenance has prevented software from plugging this gap in lost revenue dollars. What actually plugs the margin hole becomes a place holder titled "new service transactions." This new category is composed of new service

Figure 13-11  Margin Map 6 Years in the Future

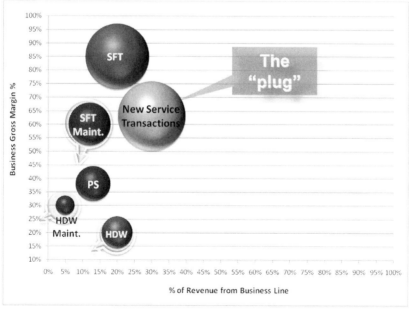

offerings. The 30 percent in revenue and 63 percent gross margin for these new service transactions was achieved by reverse engineering. The hardware company needs to achieve those targets if it is to stay revenue and margin neutral.

### Plugging the Margin Hole

So in the above example, we take a multibillion dollar hardware company and watch its revenue mix transform until the company suddenly needs a whole host of new service offerings that are generating some pretty healthy margins. What will be in this black box ominously named "new service transactions"? One way to wrestle this unknown to the ground is to think in terms of the six service types defined earlier in the chapter. This black box titled "new service transactions" will be composed of service types not typically offered by hardware and software companies in today's technology marketplace. Our example hardware company most likely offers three of the service types we have defined: Type C, Type E, and Type F field services.

## Type C Field Services

These are the on-site, break-fix services traditionally provided by hardware companies.

| C | Train Well | | | |
|---|---|---|---|---|
| 1 | Location | On site | Blend | Off site |
| 2 | Customer Intimacy | High | Med | Low |
| 3 | Time to Execute | > Week | Hours | Minutes |
| 4 | Variance in Deliverables | High | Moderate | Low |
| 5 | Delivery Skills | Complex | Moderate | Simple |
| 6 | Technology Interaction | Complex | Moderate | Simple |
| 7 | One to What? | One | Few | Many |
| 8 | Pricing Model | Time & Materials | Fixed | Transaction |

## Type E Support Services

These are the off-site support services typically offered by a hardware or software company.

| E | Standardize Skills | | | |
|---|---|---|---|---|
| 1 | Location | On site | Blend | Off site |
| 2 | Customer Intimacy | High | Med | Low |
| 3 | Time to Execute | > Week | Hours | Minutes |
| 4 | Variance in Deliverables | High | Moderate | Low |
| 5 | Delivery Skills | Complex | Moderate | Simple |
| 6 | Technology Interaction | Complex | Moderate | Simple |
| 7 | One to What? | One | Few | Many |
| 8 | Pricing Model | Time & Materials | Fixed | Transaction |

## Type F Professional and Consulting Services

These are the project-based, high-skill, high-touch services that product companies have been dabbling in for almost two decades now.

| F | Develop Well | | | |
|---|---|---|---|---|
| 1 | Location | On site | Blend | Off site |
| 2 | Customer Intimacy | High | Med | Low |
| 3 | Time to Execute | > Week | Hours | Minutes |
| 4 | Variance in Deliverables | High | Moderate | Low |
| 5 | Delivery Skills | Complex | Moderate | Simple |
| 6 | Technology Interaction | Complex | Moderate | Simple |
| 7 | One to What? | One | Few | Many |
| 8 | Pricing Model | Time & Materials | Fixed | Transaction |

As the company works to optimize its services margins, it will layer in a new service type:

## Type D Packaged Services

These are the repeatable, higher margin offerings product companies have been pursuing for several years.

| D | Standardize Deliverables | | | |
|---|---|---|---|---|
| 1 | Location | On site | Blend | Off site |
| 2 | Customer Intimacy | High | Med | Low |
| 3 | Time to Execute | > Week | Hours | Minutes |
| 4 | Variance in Deliverables | High | Moderate | Low |
| 5 | Delivery Skills | Complex | Moderate | Simple |
| 6 | Technology Interaction | Complex | Moderate | Simple |
| 7 | One to What? | One | Few | Many |
| 8 | Pricing Model | Time & Materials | Fixed | Transaction |

However, service types C, D, E, and F will not cover the revenue and margin bet for the product company of the future. I feel product companies will find themselves applying technology and service science to automate service transactions that previously were delivered in a custom, high-touch manner. In other words, services currently being delivered in a C, D, E, or F manner will be migrated to service types A and B, where customers can self-serve. Marrying the margin map of the future with our six service types, we may hypothesize what types of services will compare each services-related bubble on the margin map as shown in Figure 13-12.

Figure 13-12  Service Types on the Margin Map

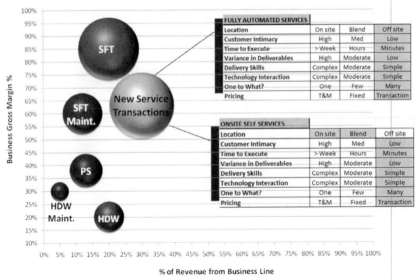

As can be seen, traditional software maintenance is delivered as a Type E service. Hardware maintenance now has a blend of on-site (C), off-site (E), and packaged (D) offerings. Professional services is leveraging both traditional custom engagements (F) and newly developed packages (D). The foreboding transactions bubble is composed of new packages (D), new off-site services (E), new self-serve offerings (B), and new totally automated services (A).

## *The Exploding Services Offering*

A final way to contemplate this transition in both the margin map of product companies and the types of services product companies offer is to think about "exploding services." When a product company first works to solve a complex problem for a customer, the experience may indeed be very custom—a classic Type A service engagement. However, as the technology and the marketplace matures, a product company must explode its service capabilities outward so that a custom offering can eventually have attributes of more standardized service types, such as Types C, D, and E. As the technology marketplace embraces new concepts like cloud and utility computing, technology providers will now need to explode their service capabilities to the far edges of the service attributes graph. For some product providers, these are new boundaries never before explored. Figure 13-13 documents the concept of the exploding service offering. The secret of service success for technology companies: Throw the initial service dart at the center of the graph, get market traction, and then explode service capabilities to deliver the service in a more standard, scalable, fashion.

## PLANNING FOR SUCCESS

There are two frameworks introduced in this chapter that have the potential to serve product companies very well in the future:

- Margins Maps
- Service Types

Once again, the current margin map for hardware and software companies is relatively well documented and well understood if not always well executed. *The challenge at hand is for product companies to optimize new margin maps that contain service types they have never offered before.*

At the beginning of this book, I stated the main premise:

> **Effectively aligning a company's services strategy to the overall company strategy will become the defining discipline**

Figure 13-13  The Exploding Services Offering

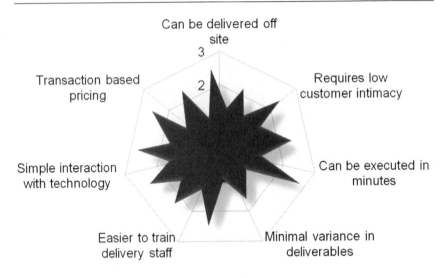

**in any product company's success.**

Hopefully, this book has documented a set of frameworks that product companies can use to create constructive, functional dialogues surrounding services-strategy decisions. If nothing else, I hope this book has opened the eyes of both product and service leaders alike. There is indeed an economic tsunami approaching. This is no sand castle crasher. This wave is huge. That sucking sound you hear is your traditional revenue and margin streams being swallowed into the ocean. What you sense now is that awkward calm that settles in, just before the crash. And the wave is coming. It is massive. It starts with an "s" and ends with an "s." I strongly recommend you brace yourself.

# Service Visions

In August of 1008, I started a weekly blog titled "Services Visions." The objective of this blog is to help frame the issues and challenges facing technology services organizations. You can follow the blog by visiting:

> http://thomaslah.wordpress.com/

In the meantime, my partner in services research, Bo DiMuccio, has also started blogging on the data trends we see in the industry. His insightful blog can be viewed by visiting:

> http://bdimuccio.wordpress.com/

At the writing of this appendix, I have posted 65 blog entries. I have covered topics ranging from how to calculate billable utilization to the ramifications of the merger of Sun Microsystems and Oracle. Of these 65 entries, three have received considerably more traffic than all the other entries. I thought it would be interesting to repurpose them here for your reference.

## CALCULATING UTILIZATION

*By Thomas Lah*

> http://thomaslah.wordpress.com/2008/12/01/calculating-utilization/

When business slows, PS organizations begin scrutinizing billable utilization with renewed vigor. PS management is under increased pressure to justify both billable utilization rates and how nonbillable time is being spent. Clearly, the concept of utilization is one of the key building blocks of any profitable professional services organization and billable utilization is a key indicator of staff productivity. However, professionals in the industry continue to debate the appropriate way to calculate and report this fundamental metric. What number should be used when determining the total available hours for each consultant? Should the total available hours be modified from country to country to accommodate variances in holidays, vacation, and work week policies? If there is no standard way to calculate utilization, how can geographies compare productivity?

As an industry association, TPSA will never completely put to rest the debate surrounding utilization calculation. However, TPSA does provide a recommended practice for the most effective way to calculate utilization across multiple geographies.

First, we need to provide the key definitions that are used when calculating and discussing the concept of utilization:

## Total Available Hours

> Standard number of working hours available during a time period before vacations, holidays, or personal time off.

The question of what baseline number should be used here is the greatest source of debate regarding calculating utilization. The most prevalent number used in the industry for total available hours available in a year is 2,080. This number is calculated by taking the 52 weeks of the year and multiplying them by a standard 40-hour work week. The next most standard number adopted by companies is 2,000. However, some TPSA members establish a unique number of available hours number for each country.

## Billable Utilization Rate

> Total number of hours billed during the period ÷ Total available hours for the period.

Once a company agrees on the denominator of available hours, it should be relatively easy to calculate billable utilization rate—providing the company accurately records billable hours for each consultant. The challenge with this calculation concerns customer activity that is billed vs. unbilled. For example, if a consultant performs work for a customer but is not able to charge the customer for that time, it should not be added to the numerator of this calculation.

*Productive Utilization Rate*

> Total number of hours billed + Total number of unbilled customer project hours + Total number of hours allocated to approved projects + Total number of hours in training/ total available hours.

Just because a delivery consultant does not bill an hour does not mean the time was misspent. Productive utilization rate tracks the percentage of time the consultant spends on approved initiatives and activities that do have value to the company.

Now that we have a common set of terms, I will outline four practices TPSA recommends regarding utilization calculation practices:

## Number 1: Create a Common Baseline Number Across All Geographies

By basing all utilization calculations throughout the world on a common denominator, it becomes exponentially easier for the management team to easily understand the differences in geographic performance. Also, by establishing a common denominator, all finance and service operations staff will benefit from using the same exact process to calculate billable utilization. As previously mentioned in this article, the most common number in the industry to use for available hours is 2,080.

TPSA acknowledges that some organizations, based on geographic location of billable resources, seniority of consulting staff, and so on, will never have 2,080 billable hours available. For these organizations, the achievable target billable utilization rates will be lower by definition. Understanding the realistic achievable billable utilization target for your PS organization is an important step in modeling the business.

## Number 2: Create Common Categories

Secondly, TPSA recommends the PS organization establishes common categories for delivery consultants to track their time. Recommended categories for delivery staff to track their time include:

- **Billable Time:** Hours tracked against a customer project and billed to an external customer.

- **Nonbillable Customer Project:** This would be activity performed for a customer but not billed. It is critical the PS organization tracks and quantifies this "sales cost offset" activity to ascertain the financial impact of such activity on PS financial performance and company financial performance.

- **Training and Certification:** Hours spent attending formal skills development training.

- **Internal Project:** Hours spent on approved internal projects such as solution development or product enhancement and fixing. Even if there is cost relief from another department for the use of the PS resource, the hours should be tracked in this category. The PS management team must understand how much time delivery staff are spending with customers as opposed to supporting internal initiatives.

- **Holiday:** Hours off for company holidays.

- **Vacation:** Hours off for personal vacation accrued.

- **Other:** Any hours spent that cannot be categorized in one of the five previous categories.

## Number 3: Set Billable Utilization Threshold per Geography

TPSA recommends global PS organizations establish specific billable utilization targets on a country or regional basis. This acknowledges the reality that economic and cultural variances will impact achievable billable utilization.

## Number 4: Track Productive Utilization

Finally, TPSA recommends embedded PS organizations that support a product portfolio track both billable utilization rate and productive utilization rate. This comparison is critical during periods of new product release when billable utilization may fall due to support activities surrounding product rollout. However, productive utilization rate, if tracked, may actually spike higher as delivery staff find themselves working overtime to support a large product push.

## Example: Calculating Utilization

All of the concepts listed in this section are brought together in the image for this entry: *Utilization Targets by Geography*. In this table, you can see that the United States, Germany, and Japan have each been given different billable utilization targets. Also, Germany is modeled to experience higher holiday and vacation time while Japan is modeled to experience a greater amount of hours spent on nonbillable customer project activities.

Once again, TPSA will never remove all of the debate surrounding how billable utilization is calculated. However, by following these recommended practices, PS management can present a consistent methodology to help executive management understand billable utilization dynamics across multiple geographies.

## BILLABLE VS. NONBILLABLE
*By Thomas Lah*

http://thomaslah.wordpress.com/2008/08/18/billable-vs-non-billable/

At least twice a month I get into a discussion related to billable vs. nonbillable headcount. PS organizations are always concerned that the number of nonbillable staff is too high. This is a valid concern–too much overhead and profitability suffers. But how much is too much? *What percentage of your PS headcount can you afford to be nonbillable?*

Two years ago I spoke at an AFSMI conference on the topic of PS business models. After the session, an audience member approached me on this topic of billable vs. nonbillable headcount. The gentleman said "90 percent of our PS headcount has to be billable–otherwise I just don't think we can make money in this business." Is that true? Should PS organizations drive to a 90/10 model where 90 percent of all headcount is in a billable role?

Figure A-1  Utilization by Geography

| | Billable | Non-Billable | | | | | | | TOTAL Available Hours | Billable Utilization |
|---|---|---|---|---|---|---|---|---|---|---|
| | | Pre-Sales | Customer Project | Internal Project | Training | Admin | Holiday | Vacation | | |
| Japan | 1250 | 100 | 194 | 140 | 100 | 80 | 96 | 120 | 2080 | 60% |
| Germany | 1350 | 40 | 60 | 60 | 110 | 80 | 180 | 200 | 2080 | 65% |
| US | 1435 | 100 | 69 | 100 | 80 | 80 | 96 | 120 | 2080 | 69% |

If PS organizations create business organizations where almost everyone must be billable, critical activities will suffer. For example, if everyone is out delivering engagements, who is responsible for the following activities:

- **Services Marketing:** Developing service positioning and executing demand generation campaigns

- **Services Engineering:** Capturing lessons learned and improving delivery methodologies

- **Service Operations:** Process development and process improvement to optimize resources productivity

The argument can be made that all of the above activities are the responsibility of every consultant and practice manager in the PS organization. But without specific resources dedicated to the above nonbillable activities, they quickly become low priority to the business of delivering customer engagements. To counter this, PS organizations do indeed create nonbillable positions focused on the health and improvement of the organization. But back to the original question: What ratio makes sense for billable to nonbillable resources? That leads us to the image for this entry.

In November of 2007, TPSA hosted its fall summit. The theme was *Human Capital Management*. In the opening keynote session, we discussed this topic of billable and nonbillable resources. We polled the audience of over 150 PS leaders with the following question:

What percentage of your total PS headcount is billable?

1. 60%

2. 70%

3. 80%

4. 90%

The results of the pole are shown in Figure A-2.

**This simple data point demonstrates that 90/10 is not a rule in the industry.** A majority of PS organizations that reach a critical mass do not have 90 percent of their headcount dedicated to billable resources. In fact, 42 percent of the audience responded that 30 percent of their headcount was nonbillable. The data point also demonstrates quite a spectrum in the industry. What ratio makes sense for your PS organization? The size of the PS business, the nature of services offerings, and the charter of PS organization will all influence this answer. But that is the point—there is no one pat answer to this question of billable vs. nonbillable headcount.

Figure A-2  Percentage of total headcount Billable vs. Non-Billable as Indicated in 2007 TPSA Poll

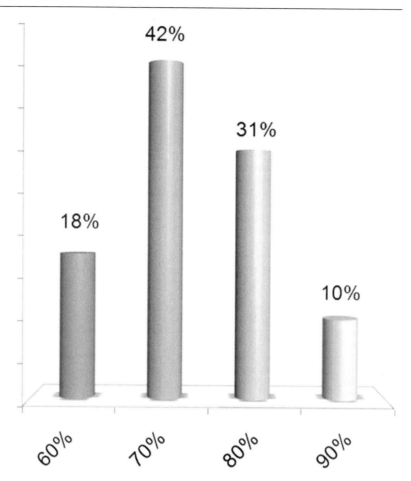

## PACKAGING PROFESSIONAL SERVICES

*By Thomas Lah*

http://thomaslah.wordpress.com/2008/08/11/packaging-ps/

Over the summer, I read an interesting article where PS firm Deloitte announced a new online service titled Deloitte Digital. The tagline for the service is "Professional Services Online." The initial article I read on *Business Spectator* contained the following quote:

*Deloitte Digital Chief Executive Peter Williams said the online tools are easily accessible and complement Deloitte's traditional face-to-face service delivery. Offering out services online will appeal to both our top-end clients and the middle market, as well as smaller businesses who will now gain access to Deloitte thinking."*

This concept of packaging and productizing PS offerings is not new. For a keynote at the 2008 TPSA Spring Summit, I had searched Google on the term "packaged services." IBM, HP, SAP, and Oracle all had tens of thousands of entries related to offering packaged or productized services.

The desire to productize professional services is driven by the need to take out the variability that makes custom PS engagements so expensive. If a PS firm can codify the value of working with consultants into a highly repeatable experience, with well-defined deliverables, the service experience begins to take on the attributes of a product. This is important because products can be scaled. This concept of increasing leverage by productizing professional services is captured in Figure A-3.

The image in this figure captures the reality that products can be created and sold in a one-to-many fashion, which increases their ability to be scaled. Custom, on-site professional services are a one-to-one experience, which makes scalability very hard. Productized professional services help a PS organization move its portfolio up the slope of scalability. But is this a good thing?

If a PS firm can productize its offerings, the company can cost effectively reach markets that were unattractive before. Go back to the article referenced at the opening of this entry. With Digital Deloitte, the firm can now service small and medium-size customers in a way that previously was impossible. And Deloitte feels the value-added tools that codify Deloitte expertise will be appealing to large companies as well. Going back to the first post of this blog, Three Forces Driving Labor Margin, I argued that reducing delivery costs and increasing productivity were exactly the pressure points PS firms needed to address in this decade.

But how far can PS firms take this approach? Chris Dowse, the CEO of Neochange, commented on my first blog entry. Chris worries that solely focusing on productivity and cost reduction could create a "race to the bottom" for PS organizations. I agree with Chris—only focusing on cost reduction would be the kiss of death of any services organization. But are packages themselves a bad idea? Is Deloitte simply devaluing its more intimate, custom offerings by launching Deloitte Digital? Can custom and packaged PS offerings coexist under one brand?

I am a firm believer that packaged and custom PS offerings must coexist within profitable technology PS organizations. Nicolas Steib, global head of

Figure A-3   Increasing Leverage by Productizing Professional Services

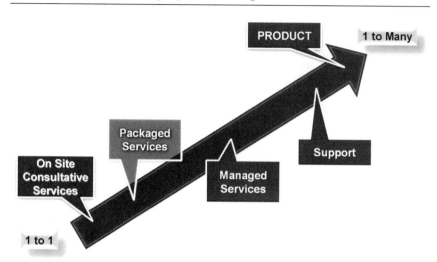

Field Services at SAP, spoke at our Spring 2008 summit. He presented analysis his group has been doing on the long tail of SAP's service portfolio. At the end of the tail are lots of one-off, custom engagements that are never repeated for multiple SAP customers. SAP is convinced they must reduce the requirements for so many custom experiences by creating service packages or enhancing the product to avoid the need for the customization. I do not believe every custom PS engagement can be avoided, but I do believe a healthy mix of packaged offerings with custom offerings should be the target of every PS organization. **Packages represent scalability. They open new markets. They force a discipline of capture and reuse. And, perhaps most importantly, packages help reduce engagement risk for the customer.**

Deloitte is a classic consulting firm—built on the premise that you pay a premium price for premium expertise. And if the Deloitte's of the world are aggressively packaging their expertise into digital offerings, I am not sure how other firms can ignore the approach

# Critical Success Factors in Sourcing Strategies

Randy T. Mysliviec is a seasoned services executive with stints at IBM and Convergys, and he currently serves as the CEO and founder of RTM Consulting. I asked Randy to provide this appendix on critical success factors surrounding the sourcing of services staff. As mentioned in the text, product companies are being forced to rethink their approach to delivering technology services. This article outlines key points to consider when a services organization decides to alter and optimize its approach to sourcing.

## EXCERPTS FROM "ESSENTIALS OF GLOBAL RESOURCE MANAGEMENT IN TECHNOLOGY PROFESSIONAL SERVICES"

*By Randy T. Mysliviec, CEO and Founder, RTM Consulting*

*Global resource management (GRM) is about the process of getting the right person in the right place at the right time to effectively and efficiently fulfill a service need.*

Too many companies want to separate the issues of managing utilization from the management choices of organization, operations, measurement, talent management, etc. TPS organizations that are effective at GRM treat the matter holistically. This appendix will focus on how to deal with the matter holistically and some of the key considerations and implications involved. There are essentially four important attributes of successful GRM approaches we will focus on:

1. **Building Necessary Infrastructure:** Effective GRM is highly dependent on building a foundation of necessary infrastructure and the processes required to manage skills inventories, skills usage, skills building, resource allocation, project and change management, and measurement input for financial, quality, and operational management purposes.

2. **Effective Resource Pool Management:** Effective management and execution of the aforementioned processes requires discipline and organizational commitment to the investment and execution necessary to implement GRM processes.

3. **Definition of Core Solution Offerings:** To facilitate more product-like attributes of labor requirements means driving more packaged service sales. Effective services management leading to better definition of core solutions offerings is critical to effective GRM.

4. **Measuring and Monitoring:** The above infrastructure and process definitions require appropriate and supporting measures necessary to monitor effective execution such as utilization, quality metrics, project effectiveness, costs, and certainly revenue and profits.

## INFRASTRUCTURE

Starting with **Infrastructure,** we follow with some dialogue of issues and critical infrastructure and processes necessary to implement effective GRM.

### Forecasting

Forecasting is knowing what future demand looks like in order to drive investment decisions (long and short term). These essential elements impact *all* aspects of what we do in TPS, not just GRM—how many people to hire and when, how much to invest in training, services management, tools, and so on. The forecasting process, irrespective of a company's organizational construct, must facilitate the most precise estimate of need, by person and skill, by month, to span the necessary hiring horizon. Normally some what-if methodology is used to provide sensitivity analysis to your projections and ultimately a capacity resource plan to guide your investment decisions. Effective interlock of the resource management team and sales is imperative for effective forecasting and capacity planning.

### Recruiting

There are many ways we have traditionally accomplished acquisition of people—recruiting firms, hiring fairs, web boards, and so on. Today's environment requires less-expensive and more-responsive approaches to acquiring the right people to arrive at the right place at the right time. This time line must also allow for proper on-boarding and training of new personnel. A proven technique is the adoption of a "warm pool" recruiting program, driven by a continuous recruiting process vs. the start and stop method deployed by most firms today. The warm pool approach invests in appropriate methods to create "warm" candidates in a pool, that are recruited into permanent roles in a just-in-time hiring system to meet specific job or project needs.

## BUILDING A BENCH

A somewhat controversial but important subject related to recruiting is investment in a "bench" of resources. The bench is a critical element of driving a GRM system that enables the "right time" element of GRM. For too long companies have viewed building a bench unnecessary, defaulting to hiring only when we have a contract in hand. Contemporary thinking on investment in a bench is changing, and must change. Reality is that the lost opportunity cost of losing a deal because you could not serve it quickly enough, or failing to find needed resource in time to serve a committed project can more than offset the cost of funding the bench. An added bonus of the bench is having available resource to support active business capture needs, and avoiding disruption of resources already committed to client funded projects.

### Talent Management and Retention

There are many aspects of talent management and retention (e.g., training, career management, job rotations, compensation, and morale management). To properly describe all aspects of talent management could be subject of an entire book. Critical factors we will describe are:

Figure B-1  Warm Pool Recruiting

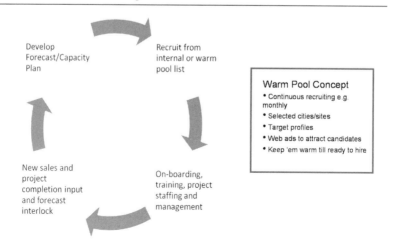

- **Training:** programs for rapid and cost-effective skills building must be in place. These programs should focus on low-cost global delivery of training, preferably interactive web-based learning systems. There are many companies that provide advice and/or assistance for this need, however, for large employee populations, you may find it will be cost effective to build internal capabilities to deliver training. Software tools for managing training environments and delivery of web-based training are readily available from a variety of suppliers. Cross-training employees in multiple offers or disciplines will pay dividends in improved utilization. Cross-training needs to be balanced with the need for marketplace value placed on specialization. Employee certification is a proven way to manage effectiveness of training and ensure better quality service delivery.

- **Career Management**: High achievers are very marketable, looking for rapid career progression. Your firm should provide appropriate career progression steps supporting this need in an affordable manner. A good way to show career progression is through the creation and publication of a career map or ladder. The career map or ladder is then used in ongoing employee development planning and discussions.

- **Job Rotations:** PS employees commonly like to learn new things, take on new challenges. Making rotations a part of your culture will reinforce building a more responsive and adaptable workforce.

- **Compensation:** Compensation should be considered a very important element of GRM as it relates to impacts on recruiting and retention.

- **Choices for Sourcing** Labor: Frequently discussed as an element of strategic sourcing, this highly complex topic could drive a book on its own. Two choices discussed here: first, where to source employees, and second, where to source temporary labor.

For employees and work that is typically more static (e.g., less travel required), common low-cost sites today are India, South America, China, and the Philippines. Domestically, rural communities are also a source of lower cost labor. More and more, companies are finding that mobility of people from these sites is more affordable and possible. This opens up the use of offshore and near shore resources to less static work, such as systems integration projects.

China has emerged as a front runner in new growth of technology workers with even Indian firms putting more of their growth strategy into China. Intellectual property issues still constrain China ventures, although the Chinese government is moving slowly toward providing more protection. Companies are also finding ways to do lower value work or using technology itself to protect intellectual property in a variety of ways. Aside from China, an important trend is use of Eastern European labor to service the EMEA region, as an alternative to generally more expensive labor from western European countries. The Middle East remains a challenging area due to ongoing political strife that constrains choices of people including nationality, gender, and religion. Effective operations in the Middle East are possible although thorough planning and knowledge of local customs and laws is a necessity. Probably the biggest growth area we will see has already begun in other third-world countries such as Vietnam and Cambodia, where labor costs offer substantial advantages even given the investments required to start up in these regions.

Keeping these factors in mind, some important aspects of choosing where to locate labor pools include:

- Proximity to where the work will need to occur
- Type of work to be done
- Labor cost
- Availability of skilled resources in local markets
- Local government labor laws and regulations
- Travel and visa issues
- Cultures and languages
- Other financial/legal issues (e.g., taxation, impact on corporate structure, currency exchange, economic policy and stability, intellectual property protection)
- Employee safety and country stability issues

For suggestions on sourcing of temporary labor, such as partners or contractors, see the following section on peak-load workforce strategy and planning.

## *Automation Systems*

Surprisingly, some PS firms today manage their resource pool either without the help of automation or with simple tools generally not up to the task of today's business needs. Considering the impact of just a few points of utilization of a typical labor pool, justification of investment to automate this important task is usually easy. Are you trying to manage a large and growing workforce with a spreadsheet? Resource management software (also commonly part of or referred to as PSA software) exists to create a database of resource pool information, enter and track project needs and progress, and produce reports and queries capable of reducing determination of project staffing needs by up to 90 percent. A human element is still needed to finalize resource selections.

## Peak-Load Workforce Strategy and Planning

The peaks and valleys of resource demands can make the process of maintaining a consistent level of "permanent" resources difficult. Hiring and firing people with every change in your resource demand profile is not workable, particularly from an employee morale point of view. Therefore establishment of a temporary pool of resources will help smooth the peak-load demands of your business. Determination of the size of the temporary pool should be made using historical and forecasted data. Typically, modeling a particular level as a starting point is helpful. Agreements for resources from contracting firms should include clauses that allow the right to hire contracted employees on a permanent basis.

## The Resource Management Office (RMO)

For medium to large enterprises, development and management of the processes necessary to effectively manage the resource pool is a necessary and beneficial investment. Particularly where the resource pool is shared across organizational boundaries, the RMO can play a neutral role and help break down the fiefdoms that sometimes exist in the enterprise. Typical functions of the RMO are:

- Establish overall GRM policies and process for the enterprise. This can be a difficult role early on as this is where the breaking down of the fiefdoms often begins.

- Provide governance for the process. It is important that the neutral nature of the RMO be exercised with clarity and sensitivity.

- Manage or provide direction to the IT function providing application support. The RMO should collaborate with corporate IT and the PS function on application needs.

- Provide resource planning support for supported organizations (e.g., planning assistance, reporting, alerts, query handling).

- Provide resource recommendations for projects. A very important aspect of this area is focus on the match of needs with available skills. There will be continuous pressure to "put my favorite person" on every project. Effective GRM focuses on the need, not the person.

- Continuous analysis of labor markets and labor pool distribution, and providing recommendations for expansions, reductions, and rebalancing of the labor pool.

- Management of the peak-load contractor pool and internal coordination with corporate partner/alliance functions. The peak-load pool would typically range from 5 to 20 percent of current needs but will vary depending on the type and nature of the business need.

## EFFECTIVE RESOURCE POOL MANAGEMENT

Resource pool management constitutes the next focus area. While many aspects of managing the PS resource pool efficiently and effectively exist, this dialogue focuses specifically on those key issues necessary for effective GRM. Key areas are:

- Management of centralized resources while providing the needed level of specialization in each region globally requires a different approach to resource deployment and planning. Because maintaining deep levels of specialization by region creates utilization challenges, a recommended approach is to create *centers of excellence* in certain skills or service offerings where depth of resource and thought leadership is needed. The centers should be dispersed across your geographic regions. Ambassadors of each center are geographically located and act as a virtual member of their particular center of excellence to maintain proficiency and provide regional input on marketplace activities and needs. Regional skills needs should be calibrated to forecasted needs, and ongoing rebalancing of specific skills should be performed to optimize resource location and utilization. Where peak-load depth is needed, people travel or are temporarily relocated as virtual teams form to service a particular project.

- Find the best balance of cost and skills. Every customer wants the "A" players on their project. The art to staffing a project is to find the right balance of cost, skills, and project management. Sometimes resource availability will dictate use of a labor from higher cost pools than desired, or vice versa. Re-balancing the base of skills is a constant exercise requiring continuous discipline and process improvement. Making these choices requires that the PS organization look at its gross margin performance over a range of projects to accommodate these inevitable resource imbalances. Simply put, no two identical projects will produce the same profit, but on the average, achievement of a target gross margin should/can be the desired outcome.

- Consider organizational issues. Establishing the "resource pool," or breaking down the fiefdoms, is probably the toughest issue most enterprises will tackle. Failure to do this well will mean the difference between success and failure. Corporations, long built on command and control structures, need to adopt shared resource pools for services, much in the same way companies have done for other more commonly shared services such as finance, human resources, and legal services. There are three important rules to establishment of a shared PS resource pool:

  1. **No particular department "owns" the resource**. The resources are recommended for a particular project by the RMO. The team responsible for execution of the project makes the final choices of the team, considering tradeoffs of other client and company needs.

  2. **A suitable personnel management system must be in place.** A plan must be in place to make clear to each employee who is managing their career, setting goals, doing evaluations, recommending merit pay and promotions, and so on. Technology companies can learn a lot from the traditional SI firms who have for years mastered the art of the "career counselor" model, which provides a manager to perform the above duties; however the daily manager of the employee is the project leader responsible for a particular project.

  3. **Senior management must proactively and visibly support the governance necessary for this model to work**. Continuous invasion or circumvention of the governance for the model will rapidly undermine the effectiveness of the shared resource pool.

## DEFINITION OF CORE SOLUTION OFFERINGS

The importance of services management and packaged services to GRM—the whole topic of services management and its potential impact on resource management—is more than can be covered adequately in this white paper. Key points to be made are: (a) packaged services improve the predictability of resource skill needs because a forecast exists/should exist for sale of these services, (b) improves the accuracy of resource forecasts because the base skills needs for a particular packaged service is known in advance.

Figure B-2  Resource Pool Management

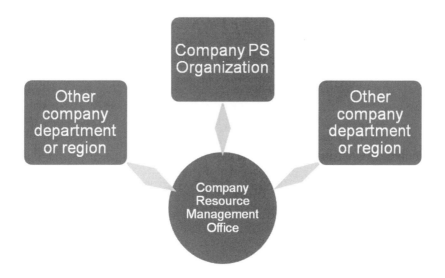

## MEASURING AND MONITORING

Measuring and monitoring is the next critical success factor. Inspect what we expect – effective measurement and monitoring systems are essential. Some key measures are:

- **Utilization:** There are three important elements to measuring utilization. (1) How will I measure utilization to include giving proper consideration to training requirements, vacation/illness time, internal meetings and staff work? (2) How will I record utilization? Time reporting will require some form of simple and convenient method to capture project work, preferably daily, to drive accurate utilization data and timely client billing. (3) What utilization targets will I set, and will my targets vary by job type and skill? Utilization targets should be set with an educated view into the marketplace and what competitive means by way of some industry benchmark. A good PS business plan will include utilization targets aligned with expectations of labor costs and revenues.

- **Overtime:** Measuring overtime is critical in two important ways. (1) It ensures a balance of workload, critical to maintaining employee morale and preventing burnout, particularly for highest performing employees who are typically most in demand. (2) It helps manage yield/gross margin on projects. Planning for some level of overtime is common as a way to improve profitability where exempt employees are doing the work. Overtime often is used as an effective recovery tool for projects slipping behind schedule.

- **Cost/Time to Hire/Train:** Tracking on-boarding time and costs, particularly for rapidly growing enterprises are important. This critical measure helps drive resource planning (How far in advance do I need to hire to ensure just in time project delivery?) and financial performance. It can also provide leading indicators on capacity and process related to support of hiring and training needs.

- **Cost per Full-Time Employee (FTE):** Just as a manufacturer would strive each year to reduce unit costs, well-run PS firms will view labor cost management in the same way. With cost of living driving wages higher each year, and benefits costs accelerating, a constant effort to find and build lower-cost labor pools is critical.

- **Training Time:** Key to maintaining high morale (and consequently lower employee turnover making your GRM job easier) is an effective training program for employees. Training effectiveness is a whole subject of its own, but important for GRM is for the enterprise to create a means to offer, promote, and measure investments in training. These investments should be tied to ongoing PS forecasts.

Proactive management of the PS data is facilitated by use of a management dashboard, readily available in some form for review and appropriate action. The dashboard would provide graphical updates on metrics such as utilization, FTE cost, overtime expense and distribution, time to staff, and so on.

# Appendix C

# Critical Success Factors in Selling Services

## By Kyle Andrews and Bill Hall, Pretium Partners

For over 20 years, Pretium Partners (www.pretiumpartners.com) has been helping product companies build the skills required to successfully sell services. They provide sales and marketing training and predictive assessments for talent selection, alignment and development. Principals and founders Bill Hall and Kyle Andrews have been involved in TPSA from the day it was founded, and have been great supporters in the effort to create an industry association dedicated to improving the success of technology service organizations. The previous appendix discusses the success factors to consider when sourcing technology services. I asked Pretium Partners to provide a perspective on the other side of the equation: demand generation. So many product companies are struggling with their ability to sell more complex services, and as this book points out, the need to sell services is only becoming greater. This appendix discusses why product companies struggle to sell services and what tactics companies should pursue to improve their service selling capabilities.

As covered in *Bridging the Services Chasm*, technology companies have been slowly but surely awakening to the fact that services are an essential part of their future. Service portfolios have expanded from basic remedial maintenance to a host of services that cover product application, consulting, multivendor support and more. The entire array of service types defined in this book. As these service "products" have been designed and companies have pushed to sell "solutions," sales forces have been asked to actually *sell* services instead of bargaining them away to earn the product business. Pretium would argue this transition from selling products to selling services has been in motion for over 20 years. Today, the technology industry is being forced to truly embrace and evolve its services business; yet, most companies still struggle to properly and successfully sell services.

To break the failure pattern described in Chapter 1 of this book, many product companies must become adept at selling an advanced services portfolio. While there has been progress and success in many areas of service sales, product companies must commit to three actions if they hope to succeed in this area. As obvious as they seem, these actions are historically poorly executed:

1. Select the right people for the sales role.

2. Develop sales skills and methods that make a difference.

3. Bridge the sales and marketing gap.

To understand why these three factors are so critical to success, it is helpful to take note of the history of selling products, services, and solutions. In the late 1980s, services sales efforts were challenged by then new circumstances. To name a few:

- Product sales people didn't understand the differences between selling products and services.

- Serious hypocrisy existed in management—deliberate or not—about services. Numerous problems unfolded from the fact that management did not really believe in the importance of services.

- Services were discounted or given away in order to ensure product orders.

- It was unclear who should sell services—a dedicated sales force; an overlay sales force, a product sales person (who would be a solution sales person), a sales specialist, etc.

- Product sales leadership did not accept sales practices required for solution sales success—longer sales cycle, being customer focused and consultative, holding back on product demonstrations and proposals until customer needs are well understood, etc.

- Services were often positioned at the end of the sales process where their value was dramatically diminished.

The degree of success in addressing these challenges varied among technology verticals and from company to company. Spotty progress was made, mostly by companies forced to become complete systems providers (IBM) or companies committed to provide niche industry solutions. However, broad-based breakthrough in services sales success has not occurred in the technology industry. Why?

**Ironically, the drivers for successfully selling services are virtually the same as the drivers for successfully selling complex enterprise products.** Pretium Partners and its principals have been working in or serving this industry for 25 years and have come to an important conclusion: Selling services just isn't that different from selling products. More specifically, it is not that much different from the way products *should* be sold. Over the years our experience tells us that the following are essential to service sales success:

- Build trust with the customer.

- Maintain a consultative behavior that focuses on problem identification.

- Be able to clearly understand and articulate the business impact of addressing (and not addressing) the customer's problems.

- Develop a balanced but not overstated explanation of value.

- Maintain a focus on the outcome of the service (business impact) instead of the features or service capabilities.

- Demonstrate effective governance/relationship management processes.

- Have the ability to assess and mitigate customer risks.

- Position services early as an integral piece of the solution.

- Sell at the right levels—the ones responsible for the business value to be generated.

To conclude the point, the elements of this list are also among the defining success criteria for solution selling; that is, selling high-end product, software, support services, professional services, outsourcing or combinations thereof. The "difference" that matters is this: product companies do not traditionally sell this way. Yet, product companies have managed enough success so as not to change their selling process (though success continues to get more difficult). Then, when a product company enters the service business, the services cannot be successfully sold the same way they traditionally sold their products. So within the company the difference is stark and services are the more difficult sale. As a company matures its product selling to a solution model, the same requirements then come back to the traditional product sales force, and selling behavior must change accordingly.

So, the success drivers for selling products and services are ultimately the same! However, broad success in selling services has not been achieved because of continued focus on factors that *are not* difference makers—services sales being so different than product sales, traditional sales process training—as well as factors that traditionally burden product sales success—product messaging that focuses on features not value, unrealistic belief in superior capabilities and the subsequent poor competitive differentiation, not understanding the difference in the sales roles, and more. To gain broader success in selling services, we would argue product companies must commit to the three action items we are outlining below.

## SELECTING THE RIGHT PEOPLE FOR THE ROLE

Service sales success begins with the right people. You must find the people with the highest likelihood for success. This is a different discussion from defining *who* sells services (dedicated sales, overlay sales, service sales specialist, product sales, and so on). This is about defining the success requirements for the role and then finding the right people that can execute on them. A depressingly common mistake is assuming that all sales roles are the same, or at least similar enough to be treated as such. Following this belief, it is common practice for product sales people to be moved into service sales roles, and for service delivery people to be placed in sales roles because they show sales aptitude. **Keep in mind, there are real differences between the service sales role and the product sales role.** Not so much because they are selling a different product but because of the role definition. **The success of a product sales rep will almost always be driven by their ability to acquire new customers. The ultimate success of the services sales rep is often driven by their ability to drive deeper relationships with existing customers.**

Success rates in hiring sales people are historically well below 50 percent and may creep into the mid-50s with refined talent-acquisition practices. This is a frightening statistic when one considers that these are the people responsible for company revenue.

One method companies have used in an attempt to improve their hiring percentage is competency modeling. This common practice creates a complete summary of competencies required for a sales role. They are created by modeling top performers with a goal of capturing the ideal success profile. This is valuable information but has a fundamental flaw when applied to hiring; that is, it is focused on finding the superstar and not on eliminating the bad hire. In most any sales force you will be able to find skills that are required for success, which are exhibited in both top *and bottom* performers. Therefore, these skills are false predictors of success, and hiring someone based on them means you are just as likely to hire a poor performer as a top performer.

The key to success is identifying the skills that will *predict* success. These are the skills present in top performers and absent in poor performers. Research conducted by the HR Chally Group has identified 14 unique sales roles, each defined by skills that *predict* success for that particular role. This unequivocally dispels the notion that all sales roles are the same. Assessing candidates (internal or external) against the right profile can improve selection by 25 to 35 percent, boosting hiring success into the mid-80 percent range.

## DEVELOP SALES SKILLS AND METHODS THAT MAKE A DIFFERENCE

HR Chally's World Class Sales Excellent Research, consisting of 80,000 buyer interviews and evaluation of over 210,000 sales people, cites *"While we would not dispute the value of basic selling skills such as questioning techniques, time management, and other traditional subjects, these have become foundational abilities that are now merely ante to enter the game of selling. In today's selling environment, generic sales training will produce generic results."*

The research also cites the top seven expectations that customers have of sales professionals. Among the seven are three that point directly to skill development that matters:

1. Understand Our Business.
2. Design the Right Applications.
3. Solve Our Problems.

All three of these point to the need for the sales person to focus on business-problem solving, designing solutions that are specific to those needs and identifying the business value created by the solution's implementation. In the conclusion of Chapter 1 of this book, Thomas Lah states, *"Customers are asking for more help realizing business value from their technology investments."*

Perhaps this sounds familiar. Focusing on the customers' business is not a recent revelation. Why does this remain a significant problem for service sales?

The ability to conduct comprehensive value assessment—business-based, value-focused selling to executive level buyers—differentiates sales teams because it addresses the customer's buying problems. The customer recognizes these skills and will give favor to the sales person who engages them in this way. This type of training seems commonly available, but in reality, it is not. In fact, virtually all sales process training includes a value theme; yet, that is part of the problem. It leaves the selling organization believing it has done the right thing.

Value assessment is much more than a value proposition, greater than emphasizing benefits, and substantially more comprehensive than a cost/benefit analysis. Traditional sales processes only insert this type of discussion into the greater process, not allowing the topic to be fully developed and diluting the little attention it is given.

Traditional sales process is still important but, as the research at HR Chally has found, it is ante. **The right value assessment skills and methods equip the sales person to earn confidence and credibility with executive-level buyers; to explore value created in the customers' business at the operational, management and strategic levels; to evaluate and mitigate customer risk, to sharply differentiate how value is created when compared to alternative solutions, and more.** When done in collaboration with the customer, it creates a balanced but not overstated explanation of value in customer terms.

## BRIDGE THE SALES AND MARKETING GAP

A few years ago in a training program lead by Pretium, a service sales team was developing a business case for a client. The proposed offer was an inventory management solution. In spite of the team's best efforts, they could not demonstrate a positive return on investment for the client. For the purposes of the classroom work, they discounted the service price significantly. (The irony is undeniable!) This illustrated one or more of the following three problems: The service was overpriced, the service created value but the sales people didn't understand it, or the service did not create as much value as the company believed. All three of these problems are marketing responsibilities. Incidentally, there have been industry studies that estimate sales people typically spend 30 to 50 hours per month searching for information and recreating customer-facing content. This is not how they should be spending their time.

Three months later, we had the privilege of working with the service marketing management team responsible for the inventory management offer so that we could help solve the problem.

This is just one example of the sales and marketing gap. Countless times we have heard marketing teams explain to us that sales doesn't know how to sell value. Just as often we've been told by sales that pricing is too high or that marketing does not equip them to properly sell the value of the solutions.

**The common goal of sales and marketing is to make sales more successful. Yet, even with the best sales talent, equipped with the training that matters, success is limited. It is limited by obstacles that lie not in sales, but in marketing or other business units with the responsibility for product/service management, pricing, message platform development, value definition, sales tool development, product training, and the like**. This gap exists either because a company is not addressing the connected elements of the sales model it espouses, or it is addressing them in an independent effort from the sales operations; thus, creating inconsistency.

The gap has many causes, symptoms and effects. Taking the following steps will help you leverage the efforts implemented in actions 1 and 2:

- Develop a *message platform* that has clear messaging for your solutions at four levels: market level, segment level, company level, customer executive level. This messaging becomes the basis for marketing and sales communications and helps prevent sales people from creating their own.

- Internal product sales training must include the answer to a simple question: What are the business reasons that the (market/customer) needs this product or service? Then elaborate while staying consistent with the message platform.

- Product management (of products, services, or solutions) must be able to build a business case for the implementation of their solution for a typical customer in the target market. The business case must: include the expected assumptions, identify alignment with the customer's strategic initiatives, summarize typical benefits at the operational and management levels including how to quantify common ones, outline common risks associated with the solution and how to help the customer mitigate them and points of competitive differentiation that matter to the business case.

- Develop sales tools, messaging and business case content that is consistent with the value assessment methodology the sales people are being taught to use.

## CLOSING THOUGHTS

In many respects the service sales challenges are not that different from 20 years ago. To date, efforts to overcome them have produced impressive results for a relatively elite group of product technology companies. In his conclusion to Chapter 1, Thomas Lah describes that the wave is coming, and "product companies will either be crushed by the weight or they will latch onto new business models that allow them to surf the surge." We would argue that to successfully surf this coming wave, product companies will need to take real initiative to create the skills and processes required to sell complex solutions. Without this initiative, product companies will find themselves in a "race to the bottom" as they offer more and more product features for the same or less profit. There are 20 years of past experiences at the disposal of product companies. The tactics to create service sales success is within the grasp of every product company if they are willing to reach. Surfs up!

# Bibliography

Christensen, Clayton M. *The Innovator's Dilemma.* New York: Harper Business, 1997.

Cusumano, Michael A. *The Business of Software.* New York: Free Press, 2004.

Gardner, Howard. *Changing Minds.* Boston: Harvard Business Press, 2006.

Gerstner, Louis V. Jr. *Who Says Elephants Can't Dance?* New York: Harper Business, 2002.

Howe, Jeff. *Crowdsourcing: Why the Power of the Crowd Is Driving the Future of Business.* New York: Crown Business, 2008.

Moore, Geoffrey A. *Crossing the Chasm.* New York: HarperCollins, 1991.

Pfeffer, Jeffrey and Robert Sutton. *Hard Facts, Dangerous Half-Truths and Total Nonsense: Profiting from Evidence-Based Management.* Princeton, NJ: Harvard Business School Press, 2006.

Rackham, Neil, Lawrence Friedman, and Richard Ruff. *Getting Partnering Right.* Boston: McGraw-Hill, 1996.

Ricketts, John Arthur. *Reaching the Goal.* New York: IBM Press, 2008.

Spath, D., and K.P. Fahnrich, eds. *Advances in Services Innovations.* New York: Springer, 2007.

# Index